FRESH

MORPHOSIS

1998-2004

First published in the United States of America
by Rizzoli International Publications, Inc.
300 Park Avenue South, New York, NY 10010
www.rizzoliusa.com

Copyright © 2006 Thom Mayne

2007 2008 2009 / 10 9 8 7 6 5 4 3 2

ISBN-13: 978-0-8478-2803-6

Library of Congress Control Number: 2005934997

Printed in Italy

CONTENTS

INTRODUCTION | *Thom Mayne* | THE PAST ISN'T DEAD. IT ISN'T EVEN PAST... WILLIAM FAULKNER |

Throughout the inhabited world, in all times and under every circumstance, the myths of man have flourished; and they have been the living inspiration of whatever else may have appeared out of the activities of the human body and mind. It would not be too much to say that myth is the secret opening through which the inexhaustible energies of the cosmos pour into human cultural manifestations...In the absence of effective general mythology, each of us has his private, unrecognized, rudimentary, yet secretly potent pantheon of dream. JOSEPH CAMPBELL

Much of substance has changed in the time since our last Rizzoli monograph was published. Much has changed, but much remains the same...strategies, instinct, process, commitment. Not a usual habit for me, looking back...yet the publication of a new volume of work is a logical point to stop, to assess, to check in with oneself to see if the trajectory as published represents in any way the trajectory as intended or as experienced in the making.

Peter Cook once described the early work as "gorged with language"—probably accurate. Our decisions have long focused on resisting reductionist impulses in favor of seeking working strategies that could bring resonance or authenticity to the work. We have long sought to bring more to bear on a problem, not less; to replay and rework problems that have long been solved, and to apply some intelligence from each previous piece of work to the method we'll adopt to address the work that is and will be. There have now been thirty years of layering and building an architectural methodology

and practice—it has the qualities of a culture by now—not moving forward via a singular authority, but by a group of tireless, optimistic professionals who comprehend one another's language and whose output I see now is working at its most agile and productive. The scale has reached a size that can comfortably accommodate the complexity of the methodology. I suppose we've been working toward this scale all along—the early work contains it all, much as the flavors of the ocean can be found in a single droplet.

Among the threads that I can trace from the beginning are those related to our process: it is a reiterative process whereby we question our initial assumptions and then continue to investigate and reinvestigate our initial responses. The operational strategy is not results-driven or inherently facile, not formally driven, but rather driven by process; they are operational procedures that have been honed and developed during the life of the practice. As part of the strategy, each element within a project is conceived not in terms of a

6

singular function, but as something multivalent, symbiotic, consistently engaged with the interstitial: with the spaces between architecture and landscape, between inside and out, private and public, old and new, awkward and lyrical. We remain attuned to the in-between conditions—whether in form or use—to explore an architecture that negotiates a territory for hybridization, for negotiating the contradictory realities that form the basis of our work. This strategy describes both a design process and an outcome that is understood in terms of relativity, serendipity, and relationship.

What's interesting for me to notice at this moment of reflection is the direct correlation between scale and discipline…the larger-scale work requires that we choose our trajectories early and remain disciplined in the face of multiple constituencies and interests that impact them. The agility that's been acquired over time has led us to develop an elasticity in spatial concepts that are capable of performing in an optimally responsive way. The architecture is not static, not of discrete categories, forms, or concepts, but is perceived as a continuous gesture that, when finished, describes a differentiated whole. Bernard Tschumi's description of architecture's resemblance to a "large contemporary city" resonates. It is messy and idiosyncratic and not subject to being organized

under one overriding system. It is, rather, capable of providing the generative material for new trajectories, methods, and outputs that add further to a coherent complexity that I so strive for.

The work in this volume represents a continuation of a methodology that we've followed from the beginning of the practice…an investigation of concepts as opposed to a method relying on a priori ideas or rules. We have remained process-driven and committed to the idea that architecture has the capability to speak—and to speak in broad political terms that have the potential to change the way we live and work. The projects now are more performance-driven in terms of their use of resources, their implications for the culture of the workplace, their relationships to the city. And finally, with the increased scale the projects have become more restrained—there may simply be more square footage over which to distribute the output of the method. Perhaps where the early, smaller projects seemed gorged there is now more room for the ideas to breathe.

Architecture is a discipline that takes time and patience. If one spends enough years writing complex novels one might be able, someday, to construct a respectable haiku.

A SERIOUS VOCABULARY: The recent work of Thom Mayne and Morphosis | *Peter Cook* |

Observe Thom Mayne through a morning in the studio, feel his intensity and total immersion in the action of architecture. Realize that, in several hours, you have heard none of those glib or easily digested phrases that even the best architects fall back upon (rolled out as explanations of the look or feel or process of the architecture). Nonetheless, the discussion has involved those looks, feelings, and processes—but as conditions that have wrestled with each other in a continuous and ever continuing search for the better architecture.

In choosing to base my observations around such a word as *vocabulary,* I wish to draw attention to the quality through which a number of characteristics compound toward the makeup of the architectural piece. Surely they include strategy, composition, countercomposition, attack, fragmentation, lucidity, fluidity, and—as the best always do—the search for the alternative.

From the first, the work of the Morphosis studio was thrusting, scratching, and picking. Picking away at the rational hut. Picking away first at the compound of huts. Then picking away at the shed. Picking away at the Modernist room. Picking away at the pavilion. Then, with some larger commissions, picking away through and into the ground. Then scraping and scraping it, slowly and with that same intensity and immersion, creating those marvelous scythelike sweeps across Asian hillsides, wetlands, or European brownfields. The scythes were, inevitably, riddled with folds and tucks and ragged toothlike pavilions.

During this "middle" period, Mayne and his people evolved a mannerism of rolling and tucking, dependent upon the power of the basic figure in order to evolve a composition. Over time, we could recognize that same set of instincts and maneuvers that characterizes the best interpretive procedures of the compositions emanating from the École des Beaux-Arts in the late nineteenth century or in some of the most sophisticated city plans of the twentieth century. A refined sense of hierarchy whereby the Vienna Expo '95 project could insinuate a set of armatures and articulated blocks swinging out from an audacious bridge over the Danube. Likewise, the nibbling of the river Seine in Paris by the restless matrices of the Paris Architecture et Utopie competition project.

Bypassing the simplistic hierarchies of architects who prefer to consolidate as much of the flotsam and jetsam of everyday life as possible into one or two major packages, or others who coerce out of the mundane a weary carnival of towers, domes, arcades, and set-piece situations.

How has Mayne avoided such a legacy of the "corporate neoclassic meets decorated barn" procedure that makes for much large-scale American architecture? Especially when the work ratchets up in scale toward that of the major urban landmark?

Surely by picking, picking...and then *honing.*

There is a telling parallel between the attention to profile or edge of fragmented pieces and the application of a palette-knife surface onto the early Morphosis models. A restlessness that turns imperceptibly into a coaxing action, as if stroking an angry cat, the energy of the parts being essential, but their temporary repose equally so.

To observe one mode of the play and emergence of the complex vocabulary we can track over the University of Cincinnati Student Recreation Center. A series of weaves are set up around the football stadium, and after a series of investigations we might come to realize that there is more to be wrought of the site and more to be added to the program than in the original, simple brief. So gyrations of line set up a dynamic with progressive twists of roof ribbons setting up a trajectory and resultant precipitations that encourage various chunks of building to descend from it and thus to augment the scheme. Through a combination of knowingness and delight, local conditions emerge that recall the intricacies of a medieval or Baroque town. Parts of the scheme swing or tumble in order to make them possible. Parts of it undulate or sneak into interstitial nooks. Ultimately, in what could become a crazy fallout, the sweeping ribbons and the powerful roofs maintain the focus of the scheme. Witty engineering and a related system of exposed and trussed nests complete the vocabulary.

Yet a delight in the exhilaration of swinging the figure, riding the walls like a biker—undoubtedly a part of the Morphosis vocabulary when appropriate—can be harnessed quite circumspectly. Not least when in the service of law and order. In a two-

9

hour description of the scheme to my students from London, Mayne became excited as he invoked the creative challenge of producing computer-generated maquettes that were exploring, modifying—in fact *honing*—the Wayne Morse courthouses. Yet compositional control is retained through that process. As the persnickety demands of justice have to be interpreted through the threads of separated circulation, the lyricism of the enveloping walls and the courtrooms themselves remains. By now—the early 2000s—Morphosis is increasingly fascinated by the possibility of lyrical line and surface in the evacuated space. Something of Sverre Fehn's Hamar museum ramp or Coderch's school of architecture in Barcelona strikes you from the plan—it has been a long time since anyone this good has enjoyed the deft insertion of curved space into a fundamentally rectilinear system and at the same time generated from it some pretty amazing clerestory stuff. Evacuation is made to happen in such a way that there is not simply ribboning void, but a constant reminder of spaces above and beyond, sweeping—or even lurching—upward.

Cooper Union's academic center takes this ambition even further, spinning round and erotically sweeping upward through eight floors of space. Was the strange oculus that spun up out of Kate Mantilini's restaurant in the mid-1980s.

Not the first manifestation of one nagging ambition: to create mystery from upward space, something preferred neither by the Modernists, the Rationalists, the American way of life, nor the Californian horizontals. At this point, one enters upon a speculation that cannot be proved or disproved: whether the quizzical attitude of Mayne toward architecture—questioning, questioning, and scratching forward, always beyond the obvious—was inevitably going to be attracted to the mysteries of the Gothic and the Baroque? Encountering gray skies and dark silhouettes in Baltic or Germanic surroundings, encountering the brooding criticality of new Austrian or Spanish friends, pulling something from the indulgence or wit of Soane's apertures or Mackintosh's hen-run, a component that could extend his language of exploded aperture. That would heroicize vertical space and vertical cuts but without the inevitability of external outcropping?

Yet in this architecture those Californian horizontals have not been left to rest. While riding a hillside at Pomona, the Diamond Ranch High School

spreads itself along two or three long ledges and is systematically made of strips. But there the expected repose is thwarted: not only do the roofs turn up, but so do the whole forms themselves. There are huge drifts of void-to-solid, there are jutting promontories, yet in a curious way the building still manages to be reassuring. Perhaps through the "sensible" quality of its components and lack of finickiness: the large slots are either of space itself or of straightforward glazing. The metal sheeting is ribbed—and again, very sensible. Even when the gymnasium becomes a bit structurally "show-off," it is at a big, sensible, barnlike scale. The value of this scheme to Morphosis was twofold: First it serves as a demonstration of scale, control, and competence with a serious mission that has led to very positive results in the sociology of the school. Then it is an inauguration of a series of gambits that can be applied to other large strips of building. At once shedlike and etched-out, but always direct. The cheeks, the corners, the slots are all riding high off the power of the basic geometry...and so they made the jump from *smaller scale with boldness* to *larger scale with character.*

From now on, further challenges can be met, challenges of both a social and programmatic nature as well as those rising out of the studio's wish to push the conventional boundaries. So in San Francisco, the Federal Building exists as a proposition of good government, good environment, of demonstrable—even rhetorical—sustainability and then, as if that weren't enough, a virtuoso engagement with the ground itself. The essential drawing of wind through the building is celebrated by a skirt of atrium that drapes and billows like the train of a bridal dress. This time there is no need to gyrate the surfaces; the folds reveal that mysterious upward trail of space. This time there is no need to be coy about the structuring of the barns (the day-care center and the plaza pavilion): it can flex and straddle to its heart's content, unashamedly part of the sail that flows over both eighteen-story wall and ground.

Perhaps only in the Madrid-Carabanchel housing project is there another development of the idea of descent from vertical stacking onto and *across* the ground. In this case the elements are housing and they are necessarily repetitious, but the urban implication is exciting and original: the apartments trickle down and then scatter off from the descent. The tyranny of "vertical" to "horizontal"—and their time-serving predictabilities—is finally broken.

Our dependence upon figure is questioned by such buildings, for the basics are so straightforward: in San Francisco, a slab and a skirt. Yet the interpretation is so evocative and so sophisticatedly developed that its composition becomes a stream of nudges and evocations, the one prompting the next and a typology arrived at that surely reopens the question of *figure* in the making of a large building. It suggests that the vocabulary arrived at reinvigorates urban boxes, and so the urban condition as we know it can be rethought.

Not that figuration can be totally abandoned by Morphosis. There are projects in which the figure is so enticing, so provocative, the city that contains it will never be the same again. So a triangular site on the edge of Klagenfurt becomes a model for city structuring. Far beyond the quiet balancing-out of elemental typologies (although there are enough of them to make a rich mixture—offices, housing, shopping, banking, and a kindergarten), it becomes a jostling confrontation with roots in the topology of the existing city here, "reconfigured earth" there, cultural heroicism elsewhere. The architecture is strong, metallic, slivered, jagged; it encourages the interaction of one directional entity to not only threaten, but (from time to time) destroy the integrity of the other. The cuts of the high school have now become inhabited; they have become sources for the growth of new saplings of jagged architecture. These saplings have undoubted power—as well as more than their fair share of form.

As in the high school, as in the San Francisco building, directionality can be worked with: as a falling slab runs some seven degrees to the horizontal, it carries the metallic meshes and louvers (of bold measure) with it. As a major bridge of structure shoots forward, it carries determined fins of metal with it as well.

At this point, the *airiness* of the recent architecture should come into the conversation. One could discuss nearly all the characteristics mentioned so far apropos nearly all the work and one could assume that it was solid: even in San Francisco, the overlaying might, conceptually, be upon a solid. But no! The layers are *matrices, feathers, wafts, grated surfaces*—call them what you will. Scan the whole range from the massive to the spearlike, from the slab to the fin, and your eye will be moving past the directionality and line of the first

through to the (very likely countering) directionality and line of the one behind. *Then*—and only then—expect the judder thus created to be threatened by the impact of a countergeometry *in plan.*

The vocabulary is that of flesh as well as of skin, of plate as well as corner.

By now, the vocabulary, formal, organizational, directional, aggressive, responsive and—just occasionally—reposeful, is confident enough to be very tough indeed...when it wants to be.

As a figure in the sky, the Caltrans building takes no prisoners, and as a figure on the ground it is surprisingly deadpan.

But what a hunk!

Just a bit seductive at night, with its tweaks of horizontal colored lights.

Just a bit mysterious by day, space encompassed by a series of single-directional folds.

A selected few horizontal blades.

The surfaces a dictionary of the most refined Morphosis meshes, fins, and large photovoltaic panels. Creative with the management of energy. Expressive with the management of surface. Purposeful with the management of mass. Exotic with the sudden eruption of form...and then tough again after the occasional explosion outward.

Now, with Cooper Union, Morphosis takes on New York. Far from the naughty little pavilions in the Venice alleys, the firm promises that city a rare interior room. The procedure over the years has rarely faltered; with a seriousness of purpose, this architecture has accumulated the contents of its vocabulary through the piece-by-piece establishment of components. These components have been consistently sharp—through honing. Through reexamination. More honing.

Plus immense flair. Mayne might find the quality intellectually suspect, but it is undeniably there, along with the rest.

Peter Cook is Professor of Architecture at the Bartlett School, and was a founding member of the visionary group Archigram in the early 1960s.

OBSESSION TURNED INSIDE-OUT | *Steven Holl* |

"I truly believe that I have constructed myself." <small>PHAEDRUS CONFESSES TO SOCRATES</small>

OBSESSION I first met Thom Mayne in 1984 when we were together for a week-long conference, most of which took place in Banff, Alberta, Canada. The conference began in Toronto, and on a long train ride across Canada a philosophy student introduced me to the work of Maurice Merleau-Ponty. Critical of the Kantian, Bergsonian, and Sartrean methods, I immediately connected architecture to the writings of Merleau-Ponty. I began to read all of his work that I could find.

The train trip had a turning point: the spiral tunnel, a famous construction through Mount Ogden. Its spiral space echoed the change in my thinking from the typological to the topological. I had accumulated years of typological research and was anxious to move my work to another stage.

Later in the trip at Banff and then in Vancouver (where, if I recall correctly,

James Wines had built an asphalt covering over automobiles at the World's Fair), I remember long conversations with Thom. His lecture at Banff immediately attracted me not so much for the organization but for the obsession. Here was a passionate man, obsessed with making architecture. What a day it was to meet a fellow artist who was really driven! One of the projects Thom presented that day was the 2-4-6-8 House in Santa Monica. When presenting the house Venice III, he described how he came to the site to find a concrete stair poured incorrectly so he personally rented a jackhammer and removed it. Architecture as an obsession is what originally endeared me to Thom, and today, although he has changed scale considerably, he retains that aggressive spark. When I visited the exhibition of the project Thom is making for the Cooper Union School of Architecture, I was excited to see a model affixed to a moving hydraulic mechanism that would break it open and reveal the

sections. Forgetting the building, this strange contraption expressed characteristic obsession.

INSIDE-OUT When I first visited the 1947 house of Luis Barragán in Mexico City, I was amazed at the complete absence of any exterior architecture on the street. The outside was simply crumbly stucco walls and typical windows along a nondescript urban alleylike street. Barragán's masterful work was all interior spaces, roof spaces, and hidden garden spaces. When Barragán was asked by clients of the Prieto House for a renovation to produce more light in their cramped kitchen he would develop this into an entire overhaul and have the Prieto's sign an agreement that all of their furniture would go; new pieces would be made for his architecture. Barragán was obsessed. All of his passion could be inwardly held in secretly unfolding sequences of space, light, and color.

Exteriors were always secondary to Barragán; interiority held the fascination. One of my first professors of architecture raised this to an axiom: Architecture should always be more once you enter it and experience the interior.

At the Pritzker Prize presentation of 1980, Barragán said, "I had been chosen as the recipient of this prize for having devoted myself to architecture as a 'sublime act of the poetic imagination.'" The qualities of the poetic imagination Barragán described—"Enchantment… Serenity, Silence, Intimacy, and Amazement"—are those of an inside-out architecture.

When the Thom Mayne and Michael Rotondi group Morphosis produced its first Rizzoli monograph in 1989, an interior view of the orrery at Kate Mantilini Restaurant, from 1987, was on the cover. I remember the experience of 72 Market Street as one of an incredible interior; the details a world in themselves.

ISOTROPIC SPACE The promise of a large government office building with no air-conditioning—a daringly green building with amazing spatial power—is rising in San Francisco. In Oregon, a large courthouse structure will soon be topped out. Regardless of the direction of measurement, these new works of urbanism seem to have similar physical properties. Isotropic space is homogenous; it implies the infinite. As Mayne's new urban compositions unfold in all directions, they seem to have an energy that stems from a classic cubic core and branches outward in relation to a warping language of detail to mass. The same cubic core that is central to his 1985 Sixth Street House can also be read in his latest completed work, the Caltrans District 7 Headquarters in Los Angeles. Buried in the huge Caltrans building there are two cubes; two ten-story blocks that have a very tall void within, separating and emphasizing them. On an urban scale, the folded planar elements developed after this core move are equivalent to the machinelike fragments that pepper and penetrate the cube of the Sixth Street House. However, now that the cube is inside, obsessive interior details have given way to a broad brush. Isotropic space, extant and independent of orientation, first emerged as a clear conception in the fifteenth century with the invention of linear perspective. Mayne's free and experimental development as an architect has allowed him the rare opportunity to jump scales, from the intensities of the Sixth Street House details to the urban space-making of Caltrans.

When I think of his work I must jump scales in my mind and imagine a new horizon of things held together at a different measure. If the machine fragments were thought of as microorganisms inhabiting the Sixth Street House, the new distension yields macroorganisms inhabiting the city, impetuously suspended in isotropic space. The minute obsessions developed in early interiors have taken on the heroic urban scale of exterior compositions. Mayne has jumped scales and turned himself inside-out.

Steven Holl is Professor at Columbia University's Graduate School of Architecture and Planning, and principal of Steven Holl Architects in New York City.

CINCINNATI IMPRESSIONS | *Jeffrey Kipnis* |

On a recent visit to the University of Cincinnati to see Morphosis's new student recreation center, I became interested in the conversation between it and Eisenman's nearby DAAP, the building that houses the school of art and architecture. I went to see the UC recreation center curious to explore what I felt to be significant differences in it, Diamond Ranch High School, Hypo Bank, and certain other recent projects from the work that first established the firm's standing as a speculative practice. For almost two decades, from the seminal 6th Street House and Kate Mantilini and to Cedars-Sinai, and the Crawford and Blades houses, Morphosis's schemes have been aggregates of discrete, articulated components arranged in machinelike contrivances, an attitude that remains evident today in Caltrans. Over the years, I have found it useful to approach the development of that body of work through the lens of inverted part-whole relations. The UC rec center and its relatives, on the other hand, use fewer, more inflected constituents in looser compositions. Though the air of ad hoc accumulation persists, the new ilk evokes more the scape than the machine, and I wondered how it would relate to the issues broached by its predecessors.

On the drive home, though, the conversation preoccupies me. The more I think about it, the more I race with impressions. It brings to mind two others whose comportment I have elsewhere called into question. It neither pits good against evil, as Frampton reported the Farnsworth/Glass House tête-à-tête, nor smart against dumb, as Rowe glossed Villa Stein against the Bauhaus. To the extent that the exchange at UC provokes

judgment, it does so in terms of inclinations rather than verdicts.

Because of their blatant difference from the other buildings on the campus, it will seem to most that the rec center and DAAP merely join to proclaim the virtue of idiosyncrasy against the banalities of the norm. Some will find that exciting, others annoying, but few will give any more thought to it than that. But for me, the poignancy of the conversation obtains from the discerning intensity it brings to bear on architectural ideas, not its defiances. Its topics may be familiar—construction, form, context, program—but its subject matter was something else again.

It is routine to associate Eisenman's architecture with ideas rather than building qualities, even if his intellectual aims are little understood and less regarded. On the other hand, while the originality of Thom Mayne's architecture is well celebrated, that appreciation usually takes the form of broad accolades for his maverick style and building craft; it is difficult to find a compelling exegesis of the work. But then, such caricatures pit content against style, and I have already noted that this conversation does not succumb to so simplistic a dualism.

In the parlance of the moment, both buildings are difficult, yet distinctly so. The DAAP's difficulties emanate from its considerably disheveled form, though it conveys an unmistakable if awkward coherence. The enormous rec center is not really a building at all, but an incongruous agglomeration of three or four dissimilar partial buildings quilted

together by a roof surface. But it is the fabrication that makes clear the disparity of ambitions.

The rec center's painted metals, aluminum, steel, various glasses, exposed concrete, and black and gray veneers make it as palpable as the pastel-tinted Dryvit and painted drywall interiors that cast the DAAP in insubstantial abstraction. Yet the construction of each is as unburdened by an ethic of materiality or tectonic candor as by the campus dress code. My sense is that in each, materials and construction operate at two levels, as overture, drawing attention to the main themes, but, more subtly, they call forth divergent affections—not moods, initially, but the harbingers of mood—much as instrumentation does for music. After all, before a single note plays, the choice of trumpet or harp or electric guitar shades all that follows, whatever mood or message the music pursues. Thus, while the use of materials in the two buildings seems to lend itself easily to a literal/phenomenal discussion, that would be a trap. The Rowe/Slutzky argument presumes that architecture (and painting) operates in and for one mode of awareness—that is, the close, scrutinizing attention of intellection and connoisseurship. It seemed to me that above all the UC discussion contests that presumption.

Attitude toward the campus completes the study in contrasts. The gregarious rec center lands smack at the epicenter of the campus, gloms onto the football stadium, and crowds several buildings. In a manner reminiscent of *le cadaver exquis*, it draws on its immediate surrounds piecemeal for raw material, here continuing a line or surface, there echoing one or another nearby shape. Though the rec center participates in the campus master plan, defining one side of its

"Main Street," for example, one would hardly call it compliant.

The DAAP, meanwhile, sits aloof, with its back to the campus, a sentinel posted at a gateway corner of the university grounds. Not asked to contribute much to the master plan, neither does it offer much, and what it did once offer was refused, it turns out. Aloofness, though, is a kind of participation, and the DAAP is by no means apathetic toward the campus. Commissioned as a major expansion of an already-existing building, the architecture of the DAAP fixates on the form of the original. In its fanatical elaboration on that form, Eisenman's building seeks to rethink the campus context as such.

Riegl comes to mind. In *Late Roman Art Industry* he speculates in Hegelian fashion that architectural space arises through a series of historical moments in the culturally determined apprehension of objects, or, in his vocabulary, in kinds of "sight." He begins his account with the surface preoccupations of Egyptian pyramids (*Nahsicht*—near sight), which develop into the relational interests of Greek temples (*Normalsicht*—normal sight). Space as such emerges in a first wholism of enclosed objects exemplified in the Roman Pantheon (*Fernsicht*—far sight).

Riegl had a thing for touch, so as far as he was concerned, vision's capacity to grasp reached its limit in Rome. From then on, spatial development continues through nonvisual, haptic phenomena. But I wonder whether or not more extreme, more contemporary modes of space—if that is even the right word anymore—might be achieved with the admixtures of his three "sights" made possible by modern construction? What happens when one

building indulges two or three of the "sights" simultaneously? In a strange way, that's what seemed to be going on at UC.

In any case, from the moment I approached the rec center and continued through its vast interior, wherever I scanned, my eye could not find a stable view line or a surface to rest upon. Not only does an unfathomable mix of voids and vistas permeate the building, but these are interrupted at any and every distance by modeled and inflected shapes, construction components, shadowy gray walls and part walls surfaced with various textures and reflectivities. Many of the surfaces themselves are unsettled. For example, a sliver left between each panel of the cement fiber board that surfaces much of the interior reveals more depth behind. I must not give the wrong impression, however, for the effect is neither dazzling nor vertiginous but something else: encompassing, as in a forest. Though still part-oriented, by muting the exaggerated interest that each and every element tries to demand in its signature work, Morphosis had advanced its architecture into the realm of the scape and pointed toward a new approach to the design of an all-space building.

An all-space building has been the holy grail of many lines of architectural inquiry, such as the research emanating from Wright that strove literally to construct an undifferentiated continuity between inside and outside. Houses by Neutra and Lautner come immediately to mind. It failed because the inside-outside metaphysic installed by building membrane and entry could not be overcome by simple optical or material methods—that is, by glass, minimized interiors, and/or unified landscape or floor surfacing. Recent projects exploring surface architecture, such as Foreign

Office Architect's Yokohama, have taken advantage of the scale and porosity of an infrastructural program to revive the question. Morphosis's rec center belongs to that body of work and contributes to it on several fronts, from its tactics for synthesizing part-based and surface-based design, to its suggestion for inducing a state of distracted attention with a fluctuating gradient field, not just of forms, but of material surfaces. The inside-outside membrane still presents a considerable hurdle, but the gradient field suggests possible solutions, such as the staggered tattering of the membrane employed at the rec center. In any case, buildings like Yokohama and the rec center make it clear that an all-space building can arise only in an urban situation, where both artificial surfaces and the rudiments of a constructed density gradient are native, rather than in the landscape, where the early efforts were concentrated.

The DAAP suggests an alternative extrapolation of Riegl. The idea of *Nahsicht* suggests that, however complicated the voids and vistas of a building may be, a judicious use of construction to proliferate surfaces may eradicate the space, perhaps a more radically contemporary achievement than all-space. Long aware of the abstraction wrought by the DAAP's Dryvit/drywall construction, I had never given much thought to the fact that inside or out, wherever the eye lands it dead-ends on a screen plane. The construction uses relief in conjunction with color as notation, but relief is so shallow that it only exaggerates the superficiality of the surfaces. Inside, the building boasts long, exotic vistas as one looks up from the main floor of the triple-height central hall through layers of flattened box columns chiseled into key forms by the design process.

Nevertheless, so pervasive is the flatness, so obstinately does it arrest sight's desire to inch forward, so ruthlessly do the cloying pastels wick away any spill of shadow, that it may be accurate to say that the DAAP had achieved an unmitigated erasure of space, leaving behind nothing but diagram.

George Hargreaves's UC master plan mixes a curious cocktail—one part pastoral, three parts formalist earth art, two parts townscape—to renovate a once dreadful campus into an ambulatory network swathed in pleasant enough surrounds. On the other hand, self-referential to a fault, it is at best indifferent to architecture and all but deaf to architectural experiments. In an early confrontation between the master plan and the signature architecture program, Hargreaves vetoed the realization of a decisive landscape component of Eisenman's original design concept. Ten years later, though, the master plan proves useful to the Morphosis project, albeit not as the pattern book intended. Interestingly, this relative vulnerability to exigent forces traces less to stylistic issues than to respective design processes. Process, of course, is the sine qua non of late-twentieth-century speculative architecture. Substituting an indexical record of the architect's thought and action for a prescribed product, process loosened architecture from rationalized method and its numbing catalogue of solutions.

Thus Mayne and Eisenman maintain steadfast allegiance to the idea of process. Yet that commonality belies a major difference: for any given project, Morphosis's process is always an improvisation, while Eisenman's is always a scripted affair. The difference amounts to much more than just a question of approach, because each derives from a distinct view of architecture's cultural instrumentality.

Eisenman views the building as an instance in a rhetoric of formal relations, and he pursues his speculation by exploiting instabilities inherent in architecture's time-honored catalogue of rhetorical forms, such as its typologies. Eisenman's process subjects the givens of a problem, its context and program, to an analysis of the established formal relations presented by the problem. The results of that analysis are then closely scrutinized to identify latent deviations and instabilities in those established formal types. Eschewing standard methods to correct or compensate for such defects, he rather invents generative formal processes to exploit them. For example, in the case of the DAAP expansion, the original building assumed a "Z"-form, almost, but not quite. For the DAAP, much of the generative process sprang from the small deviation in that "Z"-form. Thus derives Eisenman's claim to critique the cultural assumptions that underwrite the status of a so-called deviation and the impulse to correct it.

Once the generative process of a project is scripted, the die is cast. Whatever sensitivity the process has to the circumstance is front-loaded in the original analysis, which seeks to take advantage as far as possible of exigencies as sources of formal instability. The process is executed to its conclusion and recorded in the project materials—models and drawings. The project materials are then translated into the building, with material and construction decisions guided toward rendering the building itself as a faithful and legible publication of the rhetorical operations. The spaceless, ethereal abstraction of the DAAP's construction causes the tangible presence of the building to recede, to give way to another presence, the record of the generative process, much like the physicality of page and type recede to make way for the rhetorical presence manifest by reading. One cannot read words and see words at the same time.

Eisenman's analysis discovered another deviation in the contours of the surrounding landscape. The generative process exploited the two, relating the crooked "Z" to a distorted "S," with a common argument that sought to critique standard assumptions about the relationship of building to ground. The process concluded with a design for the project in three registers, two for the building, one for the landscape. The building components consisted of a back, the product of the "Z"-form operations facing the main campus zippered to a front, the massing of the "S"-form operations facing the road as the main public aspect of the building. A reverberation of the "S"-form operations into the landscaping completed the public front of the project. When conflict with the Hargreaves master plan prevented the realization of the landscape component, a significant dimension of the architecture was lost.

While Mayne may not publish his views of architecture and his theories of design process in polemic tracts to the extent that Eisenman does, that is not to say that his architecture does not submit an elaborated stance on both. In my view, it always has. Morphosis approaches a building as an assemblage of part relations, and it pursues its speculation by systematically disquieting architecture's accrued part-to-whole prejudices and clichés, always emphasizing part over whole. Its process is to sew arbitrary and intrinsically inadequate seed elements onto a given site, then to cultivate those into more complex ensembles through a series of improvised responses to the many and conflicting shaping forces that operate over the real time of the project. Though the seed elements have forms or, more precisely, shapes, in the main these have little rhetorical status— that is, they do not reference other historical or intellectual sources. Neither are they abstractions processed into a project later to be rendered as the building, since the particulars of component construction is fertile material for the architect's improvisation. As with any improvisation, process and performance are the same thing. To consider the process that led to the rec center is to consider the building itself.

The more I think about them, the more the two architectural processes correspond fairly to classical musical composition and jazz improvisation. The classical composer works in the space of rhetorical forethought, drawing on theories of harmony, form, orchestration and the catalogue of prior work that constitute the discipline as a discipline. The composition process scripts the score as a fait accompli, later to be rendered by performance. The sensual effect on the audience is at the very least enhanced by a familiarity with the work's rhetorical structure; for example, with the sonata's form and history. And it could be ventured that without that familiarity a listener might never be transported to the limits of the composition as it strives for bliss, ecstasy, rage, or revolution.

Jazz musicians sketch and notate improvisations before a gig, even publish note-by-note transcriptions. But the ultimate goal of improvisation is not the composition, but the performance, one that thrives on the moment, opening the music anew

to any and every influence, not just to the timbres of instrumentation, but to the unique voice of a performer's ax (the actual instrument), the passing invention of a fellow performer, and the feel of the audience. As the saying goes, in jazz it's the singing, not the song. Though a familiar tune may be the subject of the improvisation, the creative work is done on its parts, as the lick, riff, scat, cut session, and jam suggest. The moment of improvisation is "the outburst that turns life and music over to a witch, to the secret mystical agony that art offers," says jazz pianist and composer Gonzalo Rubalcalba.

More important, classical music and jazz constitute genres. They have aficionados, not partisans, they serve audiences, not constituencies, nor special interests nor user groups. Each is lived differently by its audience, calls forth and depends on different moods, different decorums, different body postures and sways, different ways to listen and pay attention. It would be as pointless to approach the intricacies of Elliot Carter's piano concerto two shots to the wind in a club thick with smoke, perfume, and sex as it would to ponder a concert by the Rubalcalba trio taut with thoughtful rectitude, mind readied for alert, probing concentration. But the two do not oppose passion to intellect; each, with its audience, lives thoughts and passions one way and then another. If Mayne's improvisation emphasizes a palpable immediacy and Eisenman's generative script the still remove of erudition, nevertheless the buildings in Cincinnati, too, cultivate audiences in the manner of genres. Come to think about it, why has architecture not evolved a discourse of genres? Genres and audiences organize us into a very different politics than what architecture likes to call politics.

But perhaps, after all, Riegl is the wrong place to start; maybe Wolfflin is better. In *Renaissance and Baroque*, Wolfflin places part-to-whole effects at the center of the distinction between the two architectural styles, the former calling attention to the parts as they harmonize into wholes, the latter dissolving part into whole. Then, calling upon the power of *part-whole* to resonate with other discourses, he elaborates the historical-stylistic distinction into what he sees as its deeper cultural consequence: two simultaneous but incompatible understandings of the human body. Renaissance architecture produces the body as an ensemble of parts in orderly relation to one another, the Baroque as an indivisible, fluid whole.

But it is another aspect of Wolfflin's argument that at the moment seems all-important to me. He ventures that the two styles work their respective wiles by conjuring in the viewer diverse modes of attention. Where Renaissance architecture evoked a close, scrutinizing attention that Wolfflin terms *perception*, the Baroque aroused a more dreamlike state he terms *atmosphere*. Though one cannot be in both states at the same time, neither are they categorically distinct. Nor do they constitute a dualism; they infer, rather, the possibility of a wide spectrum of attentions.

Now, at the limit, rhetorical relations have no parts in the sense of part to whole. As a rhetorical form, a "Z" may be broken, sheared, distorted, doubled, transformed into an "S," or left incomplete, but it cannot be decomposed into lines as parts, since the line carries no legible legacy of the "Z," any more than a meaningful word can be decomposed into letters as parts. (Etymological processes that devolve a word into its ancestry are themselves already rhetorical.) On the other hand, letters-to-word or lines-to-"Z" are part-whole relations, with correct spelling serving as an obvious example of an accrued part/whole prejudice open to critique (for example, Amerika). Thus, the two spawn distinct epistemological lives—that is, distinct ways of knowing and ways of living that knowledge. Yet, clearly, the situation is far more sophisticated than simple categorical division. As every artist knows part-whole and rhetoric can and do inhabit one another sotto voce. The DAAP has no parts, but obviously induces an advanced species of analytic attention in the family of Wolfflin's perception, one that has come to be called reading. The rec center has nothing but parts, yet evokes a kind of buzzy absent-mindedness more akin to Wolfflin's ambience. But, where Wolfflin's ambience requires a threshold entry, the effect of a curtain rising on a mise en scène, the engrossment of the rec center depends on suppressing the awareness of entry, so that one finds oneself in the scene without a sense of having gotten there.

For the rec center, Morphosis's design process began with but a few pieces: a set of parallel bars, like black piano keys, excerpted more or less from the firm's Crawford House (excerpted, not quoted, since a quote acts rhetorically), and a roof. As best as I can tell, the team started with virtually the same elements for the contemporaneous Diamond Ranch High School, where the roof eventually took on a topographical character, extending the surrounding landscape over the bars that became the main volumes of the school. The same design process began similarly at Cincinnati, where the roof extends the surface of the playing field of the horseshoe-shaped UC football stadium, which the rec center abuts, capping the stadium's open end. If I am correct about the

kinship between the design processes of Diamond Ranch and the rec center, the two constitute a case study in the minutiae of Morphosis's improvisational techniques: same lick, two renditions, one a stunning figure in the landscape, the other a crumpled sheet of urban tissue.

The inscrutable roof spreads down from the stadium to cover the site like a slick. Its rumpled edges do little to convey a separate identity upon it, yet, strictly speaking, the rec center itself is nothing but the roof. All the visually distinct parts of the scheme belong to other programs. That single fact is for me the pinnacle conceptual achievement of the project. Not just that it is all roof, though that in itself is not without some interest, given my inclination to approach Morphosis's work as a study in part-whole inversions, but that the nominal motivation for the entire undertaking, the student recreation center itself, is lodged in a space that does not exist as a building. As if to say, it is not the billet that kills you, it is the whole.

Unlike Diamond Ranch, when the rec center roof flows over the piano keys they pupate into a set of figural trusses that provide the long spans required by the basketball courts and pools. But their contribution to the architecture has nothing to do with expressed structure. To the contrary, skinned and sculpted as they grow, they become something else entirely. An inflected echelon syncopating through the space, they are rhythm. Whence, where to, and why? Does not matter; rhythms never need answer such questions.

Other parts join the figure trusses. A counter-rhythm of voids seems to traverse them, casual groupings of lightwells swiss-cheese the roof,

incongruously large cone shapes appear without rhyme or reason. But then, rhyme and reason belong to rhetoric; these things clearly got here from a process, but I do not hope to read it and nothing about it asks me to. Rather, as the parts accumulate, they braid into transient knots and unravel just as quickly.[1] Though I try, sort of, I cannot really pay attention; actually, I feel like I cannot stand still, that I have to keep moving or I'll block traffic. Reminds me how much I hate tourists on the sidewalks of Fifth Avenue. I walk past pools, basketball courts, a suspended running track, but also through a reef of fleeting episodes, brief encounters with improbable spaces, vistas, mirages of shape, and aggregates of matter. Once infused with the busy din of play, the space will be thicker, more distracting. Later, lost, starting to chafe at the sheer size and complexity of the place, I look through a splash of transparency in a wall and realize that I am looking out on a pedestrian passage through the rec center, one of several from the master plan that the space engulfed, against its will.

The first brief for the rec center only contained the sports facilities and support areas, but as the project developed the program mushroomed, much at the behest of Morphosis. The student housing, a classroom wing, and substantial food service facilities each entered the design process midstream, a vicissitude that I imagine might have stressed Eisenman's script beyond its limits, but merely provided more material for Morphosis's ad lib.

The rec center's iffiest but most interesting dare is its student housing, its biggest "part," an entire building. And it is a building, a light blue-gray, metal-paneled, six-story rectangular bar that all too obviously calls to mind sleek-modern corporate office parks. Setting itself apart from the rest of the project (not to mention everything else on campus) in color, material, and form, the building—and it is a building—deliberately flirts with banality to do some sly work as the scheme's foil. It affronts the cozy campus brick, which reaches hysterical proportions in Michael Graves's nearby mega-confection for the campus Engineering Research Center. One end of the housing bar juts out over the "Main Street" corridor, formally engaging the ERC, for which it provides a hedge wall to Graves's (desire for) a great lawn, with tongue in cheek. The other end of the bar doglegs into an angle. The angle's interior produces a formal terminus to a large swath of campus green, gathering the many paved walks that traverse it. On the side opposite, the vertex of the angle almost kisses the side of an existing field house. The resulting fissure between the two buildings brackets a pinched entry to an interstitial path through the rec center, one of several ad hoc entries and through-passages. Beneath these familiar formal maneuvers, the block has an ulterior motive with regard to the site. It inflates the diversity of the buildings in the immediate surrounds, pushing it beyond its sense of campus into generic metropolitan fabric, a cunning transformation that sets the stage for the particularly urban reverie the project seeks to induce.

Morphosis staves off the corporate image's threat of lapsing into mere irony by imbuing the housing block with an impression of great weight, difficult to achieve with Centria metal panels, a skin system designed to appear weightless. They jack the block off the ground, setting it on angled concrete wall piers like so many sawhorses. A few strategically located punch windows are inset deep, and

incongruously thin slot windows and louvers are staggered intermittently on the facades. Finally, the vast roof surface washes through the block at its first floor, excising a sizable chunk to leave a gaping glazed void just behind the bar's protruding tip, now dangling from the damage in dramatic cantilever. Drafting one floor of displacement, the massive bar floats flotsam on the roof surface, which in return acquires a tincture of viscosity for its own lake of space.

To accommodate the classrooms, Morphosis adds yet another part building, a bowed bar that extends the leg of the horseshoe and completes the frontage on one side of Main Street. Its curvature mirrors that of Buzz Yudell's student center across Main Street and echoes the "S" curve of the DAAP in the distance. A scarf of dark gray, semitransparent glass wraps and weaves from one part building to another as the center's basic membrane glazes the arc of classrooms, and a coronal brise-soleil of thin aluminum extrusions crowns its entire length. From the street, the bow form and brise-soleil pose as a segment of a stadium, a marquee that provides the only architectural suggestion of a main entry, and a weak one at that. To the extent that it acts as image, the arc's brief masquerade as stadium is rhetorical. But the mesh and glass strike an ethereal chord, a mute vibraphone to the housing block's trumpet, that modulates the shape-play from reference to allusion, a riff on the site as moment.

Where Wolfflin believed that architecture's cultural raison d'être derived from its various constructions of the body, I am more inclined to think of it as contributing to the construction of new collectivities of new selves. Obviously, both buildings have little faith in either the classical model

of campus as a sequestered retreat for the contemplation of truth or the current vogue for staging campuses as small towns. Eisenman's DAAP gives presence on the campus as only architecture can to critical thought, that insatiable, restless, skeptical reflection that demands much knowledge and even more concentration but is still unable to make up its mind, all the while casting doubt on everything and anyone else that can. In that sense, it is a deeply conservative academic building. Mayne's recreation center steamrolls over nicety to install the uncertainties, the erotics, the distractions, the fears, even the banalities of the city; it is OK with thinking, it is OK with not thinking, but it believes fervently in the ferment of the contemporary city—as campuses go, certainly the more radical departure. As I think more about the issue of audience, the two buildings make me wonder if perhaps the affirmative role of speculative architecture is less to offer critique than to spawn architectural genres for budding but as yet inchoate audiences who know their architecture must somehow be there, but are still waiting for it to arrive.

1. A set of graphic prints by Rebecca Mendez that will eventually paper the large cones that pierce the building at various locations may undermine the overall effect. The pictorial brilliance of the graphics may provide so strong a focus of interest that the remainder of the visual field will collapse from ambience into mere background, though the graphics themselves have a forest-and-field motif that might, on the other hand, amplify the ambience as camouflage. It will be interesting to see.

Jeffrey Kipnis is Professor of Architecture at the Knowlton School of Architecture, The Ohio State University.

MA(YN)E WEST | *Sylvia Lavin* |

A commonly stated if only secretly whispered fact about the Pritzker Prize is that award watchers believe they already know who will (and who will not) win for at least the next ten years. The only suspense for them is in what order the prizes will be given. So for these folks, surely it was no surprise that Thom Mayne, whose work has grown dramatically in scale, complexity, and prestige in recent years, has now received the honor, even if 2005 is a bit earlier than anticipated. Indeed, for some bookmakers there is a certain tragic inevitability about the Pritzker Prize, which made the press's response to Mayne-as-Pritzker-laureate all the more comic. Headline after headline announced with great astonishment that the bad boy of architecture had made good.

The funny thing about this staging of surprise is that while there have been some very well behaved Pritzker Prize winners, like I.M. Pei, an equal number of laureates have been quite ill behaved at various moments in their careers. Renzo Piano's Pompidou Center, Frank Gehry's own house, Rem Koolhaas's film scripts for Russ Meyer, and Zaha Hadid, generally speaking, epitomize deliberately disobedient architectural acts. Indeed, from the moment that Leon Battista Alberti mischievously passed off something he had written as an authentic classical text, the image of the modern architect and that of the naughty boy have gone hand in hand. Makes me wonder what is so especially bad about Mayne anyway and why he has been singled out from his confraternity of naughty boys.

Of course there is a long history of thinking that being bad is good and in fact of thinking that being bad is the only and best way of being good. All modern architectural personas have been made with at least a pinch of badness, be it the delirium of Piranesi, the politics of Marinetti, the buzzsaw of Gordon Matta-Clark, or the critical alienation of Peter Eisenman. Put most poignantly, badness is the condition of possibility for the avant-garde in its many and always transforming guises. So, in linking Mayne to all those good ole bad boys through the Pritzker Prize, it would seem that the center of the architectural profession is ready to integrate the outsider, not because it actually likes badness but because it now recognizes that bad makes good.

But I'd like to think that Mayne is bad in different ways, ways that are not so easy to make good, and that his badness might have some cultural and intellectual work to do that it does best while only masquerading as simple badness. All those good ole bad boys, beginning with Alberti and his fake text, were in fact less bad than they were good actors, trying on cultural roles and opening possibilities of action that were permissible only if they were pretend. Pretense, rather than authenticity, another word generally attached to Mayne, is that which allows one to try out new options. *Metamorphosis* is a play by Kafka, after all, and in Mayne's version, however implausibly, as he often presents himself as lacking in words, Mayne wrote the script, designed the sets, and played the lead. It reminds me of Bernini, about one of whose operas it was said that, "he painted the seanes, cut the Statues, invented die Engines, composed the Musique, writ the Comedy & built the Theater all himselfe." But rather than Bernini's Baroque Rome (where, in comparing himself to Borromini, he claimed he'd rather be a bad Catholic than a good heretic) or Kafka's cockroach-in-a-room, this time the stage is set out west, in L.A. Perhaps, in fact, Thom Mayne has morphed into Ma(yn)e West, after the actress who uttered the famous line "When I'm good I'm very good, but when I'm bad I'm better."

Mayne's good badness continues the work initiated by Mae West of upsetting the simple polarity of moralizing equations by acting against type. First, and despite the blond bombshell/gold-digger appearance, West was good with money and went from uneducated child of poor vaudeville parents to CEO and Hollywood executive. Second, while best known as an actress, West was more important as a playwright and authored many plays, and starred in the film versions of many of them. Her first play, *Sex,* landed her in jail, and she was able to write many of her more risqué early film lines, including "When I'm good I'm very good, but when I'm bad I'm better," only because they were performed before censorship codes went into effect in 1933. In fact, it is said, perhaps apocryphally, that the codes were written to control West's language in particular. But rather than silence her, the codes prompted her to develop her cunning manner full of innuendo rather than direct speech. ("Goodness! What lovely diamonds!" "Goodness had nothing to do with it.") Until West spoke out, there was no such thing as bad talk, as there were no rules to distinguish bad from good; once the rules were set, she started to play a different game. Hers, then, is not a morality tale of good and bad but a story of constant and strategic reinvention: she is an archetypal self-made American man.

So what does it mean to claim that the virtues embodied by Mae West now belong to an architect like Thom Mayne? Architects, too, suffer from the blond bombshell/gold-digger image problem, as the public often considers them, on the one hand, to offer nothing but good looks, and on the other, to be too implicated in capital and professional development for their interest in social issues to be taken at face value. And it must be admitted that architecture sometimes willingly serves itself up as this kind of bad—if beautiful—object. The net result, meanwhile, is that the behind-the-scenes role of the architect as author, not only literally as producer of texts like Mae West but as scenario planner, public intellectual, and link between culture and power, gets overlooked. Mayne's particular authority increasingly comes from exactly the same kinds of code-play that made West such a riveting figure. His most important recent projects are government buildings, a type long abandoned by architects as too overdetermined by code restrictions, and buildings with once unimaginable energy and environmental demands. Responding to these codes with both invention and innuendo, projects like the Eugene Courthouse and the San Francisco Federal Building stage a new type of public performance for architecture. They dramatize the possibility that a civic building might acquire collective weight not because of a sentimental iconography of sustainability or traditional forms of power but because they reinvent the very workings of public bureaucracy. Making available the idea that the machinery of government need not be a Kafkaesque nightmare of rigid authoritarianism but could become an adaptable and responsive organization is an increasingly urgent and useful thing to do today.

Of course, Mayne and machinery go way back, to the earliest Morphosis projects, yet Mayne has long since gone from being interested in gadgetry to being on the lookout for new forms of machinic behavior. The move away from a fascination with machines as

such is also related to the model offered by Mae West, because much of what was "bad" about West was that she spoke like a man and expressed desires antithetical to those of a good girl. Being intoxicated by machines is an equally clichéd symbol of masculinity, and it has been suggested by more than one writer that modern architecture's unbridled lust for technology was a kind of machismo compensating for the discipline's lack of power in other arenas. Architects like Mayne have never been more powerful than they are today: they no longer need the bravado of big machines for bigness' sake and have keenly caught on to the power embedded in new forms of intelligent masculinity. If Mae West, like all twentieth-century avant-garde heroes, was an outsider, a bad girl and a self-made man, perhaps Thom Mayne is an insider and a double agent who makes what I'll call, in contemporary parlance, metrosexual rather than macho buildings. The Caltrans headquarters in Los Angeles perfectly exemplifies this concept of the metrosexual building, which, with its sleek skin and discreet though prominent downtown presence, moves through the city like James Bond, shaken not stirred by a heightened sense of the urban and of the aesthetic and that takes pleasure in cracking codes and keeping very little secret. This, in my view, is not a bad thing but a good thing, and after all, as Mae West said, too much of a good thing can be wonderful.

POSTSCRIPT: After reading this essay, Thom told me that as a child he once lived in a house previously owned by Mae West. Seems like something rubbed off.

Sylvia Lavin is Chair of the Department and Professor of Architecture and Urban Design at the University of California Los Angeles.

Wrath Against the Cynical Machine | *Lars Lerup* |

ON WRATH Sampling Thom Mayne's proposal for the Olympic Village in Queens as part of the now-failed bid for the 2012 Olympic Games in New York I am struck by the *will to a world*—mind you, a complete *inclusive* world. This will is expressed in the total cooperation among all elements of the design. Here every aspect of the project (the housing, the gardens, the athletic venues, the landscape, the city, and so on) works together, *one bending for the other*. The view corridors hook up and look into the corresponding streets on nearby Manhattan island, the building bodies bend to meet the water, to shape harbors and beaches. Here there is no separation, no inside and its other—the isolated outside. Here there is no way to separate the athlete from the athletics.

We could explain this will to a world—to a total ensemble—as the side effect of the unique high-profile project, or, if we were less kind, as the ultimate opportunity for an architect to create the *gesamtkunstwerk*—once again—and thus dismiss the whole effort as circumstantial or willful. Mayne's will to comprehensive form could be confused with Eisenman's search for autonomous form, but the will to an inclusive world could not be further from the autonomous; in the Athletic City everything is included—the good, the bad, and the necessary.

The City, with its commitment to walking, is by its very nature athletic, while its other, Suburbia, is by its alphabetic car-driven separations only athletic once you hit the golf ball, or throw out the first pitch, and the car remains the ultimate locker room. Mayne's work on the City is motivated by the *vigor of the body*, far from the isolated formalism of the autonomous and closer to Corbu's architectural promenade. This commitment to the vigor of the body is in Mayne's case closely associated with *wrath against the somnolent drudgery of the suburban city*. A wrath that has with time matured radically into an *intellectual vigor* now in the dogged pursuit of what I will recognize as the cynical—dominating all modern culture. In its early *bodily* form Mayne would personally jackhammer an errant stair (while the clients and contractors were sleeping), while today, in its more mature and clearly more effective form, *sublime wrath* is embedded in and permeating the practice. Mayne's mature wrath is no longer motivated by anger, but by conviction, now directed squarely at the suburban city—the very center of what Rem Koolhaas calls Junk Space. The tattered matrix, with its alphabetic isolations, consumerism, and alienation from everything real, is the cynical machine. Thom Mayne has found the focus for his wrath.

THE CYNICAL CITY AND ITS ENEMIES The cynical suburban city (Mayne's own habitat since he moved to Los Angeles) is an apparent amusement for the cynics, while being totally corrupt for Mike Davis, charmingly exotic for the late Reyner Banham, and utterly detestable for Peter Plagens. And for those who commute collectively some thirty-five years a day, as we do in Houston, the cynical city is simply drudgery and will remain so until a barrel of oil hits $150, when the commuting life will all change to road

wars. As architects committed to action, Mayne and Morphosis could never settle for a negative project but had to find the formal means to combat the cynicism. Inadvertently, they were to take up an ancient struggle against the cynical—as old as our memory of the City. Peter Sloterdijk, the German philosopher, writes:

If we look today at [the] nurturing and living spaces in which deviation and critique, satire and cheekiness, cynicism and willfulness thrive, it becomes immediately clear why we must fear the worst for embodied cheeky enlightenment. Before our very eyes, cities have been transformed into amorphous clumps where alienated streams of traffic transport people to the various scenes of their attempts and failures at life. For a long time now carnival has meant not "inverted world" but flight into a safe world, of anesthesia from a permanently inverted world of daily absurdities.[1]

Living spaces, willfulness, enlightenment, amorphous clumps, streams of traffic. We know instinctively that we are in the realm of the City and therefore, at least historically, also in the realm of Architecture. But we also know that we are in the head of a philosopher living in southern Germany surrounded by the *mittellandschaft* that stretches from Basel to the Ruhr. The issue of the cynical city is now everywhere; what is architecture's role in this disastrous trajectory? Sloterdijk's *Critique of Cynical Reason* of 1983 can help us to elucidate such an inquiry. If we start at the bottom in the "safe world," we can work ourselves up to the top of the complex quotation above, and if you bear with me, we will eventually return and find Architecture and Thom Mayne at this peak—next to "kynicism."

We can now find safe worlds in every suburban city, from Mexico City to Salt Lake City, in the form of gated communities, replete with walls, guards, weaponry, and canine protection. These human safe zones all innocently referred to as subdivisions are escape vehicles from the "amorphous clumps"—from the vast, drifting horizontal city, spread by the developer's pastry knife, that now covers every flatness in the developed world and then some. Market-driven forces, motivated by the bottom line and shaped by the most common of denominators, have rudely replaced the romance of the City (and its carnivals) with the easiest, the most bankable, the most generic, the flattest, and the most simple-minded expression of habitation, land value, and entrepreneurship. The result is an alphabetic city consisting of coherent letters (subdivision, shopping center, school, church, post office, and so on) set in a striation of freeways—the "alienated streams"—the chaos of leap-frogged space.[2]

Moving closer in from this satellite view, we see that the horizontal city is not only physically striated and chaotic, but also highly variegated socially and economically. The vast archipelago of more or less guarded subdivisions is a truly postindustrial (or, more aptly, *sans*-industrial) landscape. As monocultures, the tracts of single-family houses, town homes, or apartments, gathered in more or less sequestered enclaves, would be eerily one-dimensional con-finements if it weren't for our ability to Google out of them. Here in look-Mom-no-hands land, production is invisible, but products are only a few clicks away: veggies from California, steaks from Chicago, barbecue equipment from China, oil from Nigeria, water from Colorado. A couple of additional clicks, and delivery is immi-nent, via fiber optics, faucets, pumps, supermarket shelves, cans, and (a bit more demonstratively) on trucks. This systematic denial of a world—Mayne's will to a world—is the center of all wrath against Suburbia, since it allows its denizens to forget about all the world's troubles and opportunities for renewal. If it weren't for the 50 percent divorce rate, the subdivision would be the eternal summer camp, where no one works, and all is fun and games—and TV. This apparently calm tidiness barely hides the fact that the social and economic underpinnings of these little paradises are totally dependent on the "alienated" outside, with its build-ing technology, zoning regulations, local and federal regulations, resource allocation, mortgages, industry, and politics, politics, politics. The modern gated subdivision has become replacement therapy, taking us away from our "daily absurdities."

Viewed from above, the thousands of quaint subdivisions are not alone in their extreme rationality. What Sloterdijk calls "the enlight-ened false consciousness" is present everywhere in this Alphaville of isolated rationalities, from shopping centers to churches, each with its own generic expression. In contrast, the "alienated streams of traffic" snaking their way through this archipelago of order are part of a chaotic infrastructure, much like the inside of a wall in one of those neoclassical suburban houses, filled with a mess of insulation, wiring, and ducts of various kinds. But unlike in the suburban house, in the city everybody knows and everybody sees this shadow world—what it takes to hold up the rationality—and sprawl is not pretty. Inescapably, it seems, the modern city is not only the locus of cynicism but also the apparatus that produces it. Thus the City, whether the European *Grossstadt* or the vast hori-zontal city of the New World, is the fundament for this new cynical enlightenment. Sloterdijk traces the emergence of the purveyor of this cynical enlightenment as the "mass figure…well-off and miserable at the same time."[3] This in turn is a radical transfigura-tion of the original Greek *kynic*, whose *enfant terrible*, the agora philosopher Diogenes, laughed, masturbated, and urinated in full view of the Athenian *zoon politikon* (whose political shenanigans and private misdeeds may have been the origins of the Cynical City). Sloterdijk writes:

[Diogenes'] "cynical" turn against the arrogance and the moral trade secrets of higher civilization presupposes the city, together with its successes and shadows. Only in the city, as its negative profile, can the figure of the cynic crystallize in its full sharpness, under the pressure of public gossip and universal love-hate. And only the city can assimilate the cynic; who ostensibly turns his back on it, into the group of its outstanding individuals, on whom its liking for unique, urbane personalities depends.[4]

MORPHOSIS Keeping Diogenes in mind, while tumbling out of Athens and the history of the City—with its heroics and its

cynicisms—we are back at the offices of Morphosis in the City of the Angles. Rummaging through the drafting hall while scanning a mass of projects, it is clear that there is no sign of Diogenes' dawdling. This is a place of intense work. Yet there is a sense of Diogenesian otherness in this space of difference that stands out against the surrounding city. A space where the pure form of architectural econometrics has been replaced by pleasure, delight, laughter, innovation, productive working conditions, and old-fashioned enlightenment motivated by a sense of authentic urgency—Mayne's wrath. Sloterdijk writes: "What is 'authentic' will always be something else. You must know who you are. You must consciously experience being-unto-death as the highest instance of your potentiality: it attacks you when you are afraid, and your moment has come when you are courageous enough to hold your ground in the face of great fear."[5]

I have a suspicion that Mayne has lived this quote. Yet Mayne's courage and tenacity has taken him beyond the acceptable play-ground of authentic architecture (such as the museum, the home of the autonomous, where most of his equally famous colleagues have found a secure haven for their practices) to city schools, courthouses, banks, and administrative buildings—the seats of bureaucracy, the centers of the information society. Here in the bosom of conservativeness and legendary cynicism, Mayne has broken ground both literally and conceptually. By acting at the core of everyday working life, Mayne has joined ranks with Dio-genes and what Sloterdijk somewhat cryptically describes as the "kynical impulse," the impulse of the not yet corrupted cynic.

Tracing this impulse in a photograph by Brian Finke of a lunch period at Diamond Ranch High School, which Morphosis com-pleted in 2000, we can see that the students are in *their* world (laughing), although they have clearly never seen anything like it. When asked about it, one student said, "Most people think it's pretty awesome."[6] The building springs out of a sordid ground by rejecting all the formal cynicism embedded in thousands of schools across the land. Yet contrary to some observations, Dia-mond Ranch is not "far out" but very "close by," just out of the architectonic ground that Los Angeles has always mysteriously supplied. And from further back, in the historical ground, springs the ancient agora—now the central spine in the school. Although Diogenes may be gone, his *barrel* is still here, far beyond the established and conventional, the dull and defeatist. *This is physi-ognomic enlightenment.*

It is against this horizon that we can see how Thom Mayne's originally quixotic struggle against the cynical has become a for-midable force unsettling the premise of the cynical machinery—in our schools, offices, banks, and government buildings—giving us architectural form commensurate with the cultural aspirations of democracy.

1. Peter Sloterdijk, *Critique of Cynical Reason*, trans. Michael Eldred (Minneapo-lis and London: University of Minnesota Press, 1983), 118.
2. "Leapfrogging" refers to the practice of jumping across land that has been recently developed, and so raised prices around it, to cheaper land just beyond.
3. Sloterdijk, 4–5.
4. Ibid., 4.
5. Ibid., 205.
6. Zev Borow, "One Big Geometry Exam," *New York Times Magazine*, sec. 6, May 18, 2003.

Lars Lerup is Dean and William Ward Watkin Professor at Rice University's School of Architecture.

Exclusively Mutual | *Eric Owen Moss* |

MEANWHILE AT S.O.M. I remember walking the campus at U.C. Berkeley in 1968, long-haired students on the march, announcing each cause célèbre with kaleidoscopic signage...Two years later, on a sojourn at Skidmore, Owings & Merrill in San Francisco, I noticed the same long hair, now on the heads of the S.O.M. partners, and around the corner at Macy's the heretofore raucous graphics metamorphosed on Macy's bags and wrapping paper.

I'm fascinated by the infinitely dexterous and adaptive capacity of American commerce to quickly absorb the appearance of innovation, and by so doing, (perhaps) emasculate the innovator's underlying subversive prospect.

SINBAD THE SAILOR A similar cultural metamorphosizing is detectable in the recent evolution of the language itself, which fractures when the predictable amalgamation of capital letters, nouns, verbs, and periods is insufficient to communicate (for some poet or other). Tentative, new language forms—structure, phrase, vocabulary—emerge: "sinbad the sailor, tinbad the tailor, jinbad the jailer," and so on...

...and as quickly (and surprisingly?), the new is absorbed and becomes, almost seamlessly, a part of the lexicon, with an immediate place in the latest Webster's.

KAFKAESQUE This interrogatory speculates on the nature of this now predictable cultural journey, from the precarious acceptance of an original instinct to its broad public acknowledgment. Example: What does the now common usage of the term "Kafkaesque" have to do with *The Trial* or tabloid journalism's adoption of the "surreal" label to do with the art of Breton, Rothko, or de Chirico?

And a corollary: Does a public ratifying of a poetic insight compromise or abet the poignancy, idiosyncrasy, and contentiousness of the original discovery?

Or: How does the dissemination of an idea affect its depth, as it assumes a more "comfortable" place in the cultural lexicon?

THE "HATE YOU/LOVE YOU" CASE The architecture rejection/acceptance, instinct/method, "hate you/love you" case adds this essential irony:

...ipso facto, an architecture initiative requires at least a modicum of public acknowledgment in order to emerge as architecture.

THE METAMORPHOSIS OF MORPHOSIS Let's use the architect Thom Mayne as the protocultural remodeler, and the current metamorphosis of Morphosis from relative anonymity to public plausibility as the prototype private-to-public journey.

IN THE REAL FORBIDDEN CITY Thom's story starts in the world's real forbidden city, contemporary Los Angeles.

Why is the city significant? It's a relatively young city, and perhaps only relatively a city, so its persona is formative and preliminary... (a perfect venue, in retrospect, for Mayne). Los Angeles' reputation as something of an urban experiment is manifest in the city's collective propensity to endlessly but incompletely reimagine itself...(again, in retrospect, a perfect venue for Mayne). And this never quite determined city is forever under investigation by a changing cast of civic heroes and villains, including a few who are sometimes both. Thom Mayne is one of the both.

THE EQUIVOCAL CITY So the Mayne investigation is synonymous with the advent of an architect whose experimental form language uniquely characterizes the equivocal urban experiment that is Los Angeles.

The Mayne experiment resonates publicly because the architecture forecasts the emergence of a particular city at a particular time, makes genuinely palpable, spatial, and tactile a physiology, a persona, an architecture, that signifies the conscious arrival of the city. And all the while the work retains its subversive, sometimes antagonistic, in the process of, piece by piece character...a puzzle in which the pieces are invented during assembly.

MAYNE THE TWO-TIMER, EXCLUSIVELY MUTUAL
Two-timing here was crucial—the extroverted rise of the city; the introverted growth of the architect...not mutually exclusive; rather, exclusively mutual.

The architect had an instinct—it would have been different in a historic, pedigreed city, but Los Angeles is neither. As Thom interrogated the happenstance city, heretofore lacking any iconic speculation on how its evolving definition might translate as architecture, he began, tentatively at first, to introduce a lexicon, an image, a spatial strategy, an iconic sensibility, that the city's conceptual tensions suggest.

RINGSTRASSE VETO Never a Champs-Élysées, or Ringstrasse, or Ramblas, or Fifth or Michigan Avenues, or Red Square...No pedigree-derived urbanisms or the architectural manifestations that inevitably accompany those histories.

POPULIST THOM Thom's initiative is intrinsically populist: it references implicitly the forbidden city of the 1992 Los Angeles riots: fire red, then black smoke and gray concrete...Architecture that is an unresolved tension: street corners, freeways, concrete riverbeds, power grids, abandoned railway tracks...and the apparently endless lateral extension as the city grows...

...but never symmetrically (not the architecture; not the city), which would indicate a Los Angeles affiliation with a traditional master plan, and an equilibrium or balance, and a mastery of history that, in Thom's rendition, would represent the anticipation of a conclusion Los Angeles should never claim.

GET OFF AT THE WRONG EXIT There's an old Los Angeles joke that you can get off the freeway at the right exit or you can get off at the wrong exit, and it doesn't make any difference. It's that L.A. sense of inconclusiveness and often banal homogeneity, sometimes dark and aggressive, sometimes nonchalant and indifferent, that is very much the sense of the city expressed so succinctly in Mayne architecture.

Simultaneously reticent and confrontational, forbidding, intriguing, welcoming...the architecture delivers an all-inclusive emotional gamut in space and surface. And it's absolutely genuine. No punches pulled. We who inhabit the place had an instinct for what the city was; we sensed the city's sense; and when Mayne designed it and built it, we saw it, and recognized ourselves and our city immediately.

Jacob Burckhardt defined and labeled the Italian Renaissance four hundred years after it took place. Ditto Mayne who didn't wait quite as long to configure the underlying asymmetrical tensions of a city in a perpetual state of becoming. He both founded and expropriated an architecture that belongs to the city and is the urban epiphany that explains and elucidates it.

L.A.'S STENOGRAPHER Mayne, perhaps inadvertently, became L.A.'s stenographer, decoding what the city dictated: "Nobody tells me anything new," said Friedrich N., "so I tell myself my own story."

L.A. is not a city for architecture, though it is a city for architects. You have to look hard and long to locate those special G.A. moments amidst the freeways, tracks, tracts, power grids, and momentary high-rises. But they're there...and Thom is contributing his share. And each particular inevitably affirms the forbidden city as source, a context learned from, which now learns from him.

HERE'S HOW THE ARCHITECTURE WORKS

A series of objective and subjective assaults,

but never convinced,

never a true believer.

He succeeds,

then deserts his success...

invents a move forward, then reverses direction...

uncovers a propitious vantage point, then wanders away from it...

discovers a way to see and understand,

but simultaneously suspects that way of seeing and understanding.

As it makes its paradigm it disowns that paradigm...

as it disowns its antecedents, it creates new precedents.

And shock,

enduring shock, is a fundamental tool.

Order/reorder,

shape/reshape,

space, yes/space, no,

texture/retexture,

pattern, yes, pattern no/pattern less,

surface/no surface,

technique, yes/technique, no...

a perpetual unbalancing and re-un-balancing.

MAYNE AS A SYNONYM Mayne is a double meaning. He's a synonym, a ditto. As he epiphanized and linguistified L.A.'s character, he invented an iconography of his own. It's not the iconography of the ascetic introvert, but the iconography of the populist extrovert. It's not an import from Prouvé or Lods or Le Corbusier or Stirling (although Thom must have looked at all those guys...and laughed). Mayne architecture is the architect's transmutation of the home-grown voice of Wilshire and Alvarado. And if L.A. urbanism is contagious, then the architecture portends a form language suggestive of what might soon be arriving in any number of other cities.

Perhaps this is Los Angeles at its self-confident best: not much interested in any collected or collective a priori allegiances.

The forbidden city, as Mayne delivers it, is a world intent on creating its own authority. No historic grafting, Thom's work, like the city he taught and learned from, is a race with a moving finish line.

THE CENTER AND THE EDGE In a sociopolitical sense, Mayne architecture won't make the world better or worse. But Thom gave a twenty-first-century city an unvarnished sense of itself, and by building pieces he built a Mayne lexicon. Thom didn't make the world better or worse; he made it different. He got on the magazine cover, but kept his office in the garage. The edge didn't come to the center, as did haircuts at Skidmore or graphics at Macy's.

In Thom Mayne's case the center went to the edge, where poignancy, idiosyncrasy, and subversion endure.

Call Him Thom Mayne | *Wolf D. Prix* |

STONER AVENUE, WEST LOS ANGELES

How could I not love the street name "Stoner Avenue," since it always reminds me of the Rolling Stones? And how could I not like the name "Morphosis," since it always makes me think of the Rolling Stones song "Sister Morphine"?

I was standing there in a little garage filled with models and drawings—Zaha had given me the address as an inside tip when I was still in London—and I was trying to figure out how the people on the team might look. A tall man came through the door—he had to duck a bit—carrying in hand a black book that I recognized as my *Architektur ist jetzt* (Architecture Is Now). "Nice book," he said, and I was proud, because he wasn't just well known as a young architect, but also as a magnificent draftsman.

CALL HIM THOM MAYNE

"Call me Ismael," begins one of the most beautiful books in world literature, which across endless pages describes Ahab's battle with the White Whale. And one of the best descriptions of architecture can be found in this book: "Would now the wind but had a body; but all the things that most exasperate and outrage mortal man, all these things are bodiless, but only bodiless as objects, not as agents." Thom Mayne's architecture can be described as the White Whale, if you will. And he is Ahab.

AHAB. JERUSALEM

The lecture from Thom Mayne begins, the stage is dark, and he alone is in the beam of the solitary spotlight. Standing there tall, bowed forward slightly, he begins by reaching for his glasses, thumb and middle finger span the designer frames, pressing them to the bridge of his nose, as though he could now see better. Slowly, without pictures, fully concentrated, he begins to wrestle with the theme of architecture. And Melville's description surfaces in the back of my mind, from the unconscious, like the White Whale from the sea.

ARCHITECTURE

Folded, crumpled buildings encompassed by a metallic skin. Not the light plumage that birds wear to fly. Instead, skin stretched between bones, like the wings of pterosaurians.

THE DRAWINGS

The structures and architectures that Mayne's drawings evoke on the retina of the eye resemble the networks and patterns of an elegant dress. And I recognize all of the graphic lines and surfaces in what is built.

THOM

Thom keeps his promises. What he can do effortlessly, drawing, makes him precious. What he must wrestle for, the words, makes him valuable. He is Ahab, who defeats the White Whale. We can see that in his buildings.

August 2005

Wolf Prix is Vice-Rector and Head of Institute of Architecture at the University of Applied Arts, and a founding principal of Coop Himmelb(l)au in Vienna, Austria.

THE BOUNDING MAYNE | *Michael Sorkin* |

For years the media, ever eager to narrow our understanding, have been describing Thom Mayne as rebellious, countercultural, a '60s hangover. This characterization sets up an ongoing story that seeks to explain how this insubordinate character winds up with a giant project list of courthouses, government agencies, banks, academic buildings, and other facilities that might otherwise arouse the suspicion of someone so steeped in the politics (and architecture) of opposition.

Two divergent accounts are offered. The first is that Mayne has sold out, surrendering his tortured soul for celebrity and big bucks. This is nonsensical. If one thing can be said about Morphosis, it is that its path has been both clear and uncompromised from the get-go. The firm has reached its present level of accomplishment by tenaciously keeping faith with its own investigation, three decades of dedication, research, and consistent ethical values. These principles—which have never sought to de-link desire from form—remain the basis for the singularity of the Morphosis project.

The second explanation for this straw-contradiction is that Mayne's values have triumphed, that his politics have infused the work. This is much closer to the truth and I would simply add that Mayne—at sixty—is now dealing with clients from his own cohort, that a lot of the hippies, yippies, friends, and fellow students who once wanted no future in the system are now judges, doctors, scientists, bankers, and bureaucrats. These clients, far from being recalcitrant philistines, have been exemplary in their curiosity, engagement, and support, ready for the adventure of authenticity.

It's also true that a "progressive" position within the field of architecture has moved its location: values that once produced pure resistance have now found forms of advocacy with which they can proceed with a clear conscience within the system. The most important of these is the defense of the environment: our reds have become green. The environmental movement has reread historic struggles against inequality in a new planetary frame and the project of sustainability has emerged as a crucial medium of social redress and amelioration. Although this has produced much green architecture as window-dressing and camouflage, it has also resulted in the growth of a dedicated cadre of architects with a truly global view of justice.

Morphosis arrived at its powerful environmental sensibility via a long and careful trajectory. Of course, Los Angeles helped, a climate benign enough and a culture body-focused enough to demand easy communication between inside and out—the aesthetic flow of nature though the house—as a fact of life. The transplanted European Modernism of Schindler and Neutra, the native styles of Greene and Greene, Gill, and Wright, and the elaborations of Ain, Soriano, Lautner, Elwood, and others of the "second generation," as well as the still flavorful impact of Gehry and those inspired by his formally liberating practice, were powerful antecedents. Their influence—so strongly articulated by Esther McCoy, John Entenza, Reyner Banham, and others— helped foreground the object *in place*, its interaction with surrounding visual, cultural, and natural ecologies.

From all of these, Morphosis received ideas about permeability, about the simplicity of the envelope, and about the endless expressive possibilities of detail. With these cues, the firm developed an ethos that productively located intensity downward. That is, the smaller the detail, the more susceptible to high elaboration. This acknowledged both the importance of the hand of the literal maker (something that grew out of a long-standing relationship with a series of local fabricators) and the nature of eccentricity in relation to the scales of public and private.

The ethical valence in the work of Morphosis is thus multiply sourced. From the first, the firm has been devoted to that old Modernist jones: honesty of materials. This has entailed the direct use of materials in their "raw" condition, their modification into a sympathetic tectonics (being what they want to be), their legible, frequently mechanical joinery and connection, and the visibility and celebration of their structural role. It has also—as with other practitioners of the Los Angeles schools—involved the reduced use of concealing finishes and a penchant for self-cooking patinas. Each element seems clearly motivated by its nature as a part, not functionalism exactly but an artistic version that expands its overly reflexive principles to a broader, but still highly controlled, horizon.

All this has also led to a clear attitude toward the key metric of embodied energy, a richer reading still of the particularity of the element. Although the sense of the integrity of materials has been lifelong with Morphosis, it has become clearer—as we all become greener — that renewable wood worked on site or that steel fabricated nearby is in a different class from aluminum, plastic, or long-traveling exotics. In this sense, Morphosis has used what is effectively a "native" palette at global scale, substituted embodied intellectual energy for thermal or kinetic varieties. The result is not the quasi-folkloric insistence on straw bales or adobe, but a much more nuanced understanding: Morphosis is flourishing in the "official" culture because they are creating conditions that are simply sensible and that extend the visual and conceptual resources these clients bring with them.

Morphosis grew into its leadership in sustainable architecture from this fundamental preference for "simple" materials and from a taste for minimum technology in their use. In such recent projects as the Caltrans Headquarters in L.A. or the Federal Building in San Francisco—enormous undertakings both—Morphosis has ingeniously understood and designed solutions to thermal performance that are predicated on a rigorous and learned application of the philosophy of less is more to the use of energy. This has yielded very sophisticated strategies for passive cooling and ventilation in climates that are, to say the least, challenging. The San Francisco project, in particular, is meant to run—on most days—with no air-conditioning whatsoever, and this is at the core of its importance. Within a formal envelope recognizably that of the "office building," Morphosis has produced work that advances the state of the urban workplace by miles.

This achievement lies in the ability to both scale up a set of passive strategies developed in smaller projects and to integrate these strategies into an artistic vision of building that has proven rarely compatible with them. Just as the practice's architecture has long been associated with the art of the screen, with the layering both of space and its defining elements, so treatment of energy systems smoothly enters this discourse of combination. Both literally and conceptually, this understanding of the "space of flows" in buildings has enriched the work—especially in section—at the scales of both the wall and the whole.

Morphosis was born with a love of the mechanical, not merely its representation. In the formative work with Michael Rotondi, this was expressed in a rich eccentricity of joinery and contrivance. Projects were filled with moments of constructed intensity, sometimes in the form of useful objects—chairs, tables, cabinets, doors, and so on—and sometimes in the form of mechanisms that simply exceeded any clear description of use, the machine for machine's sake, an abstracted representation of the formal quintessence of purposive construction, like the explosive object in the big dining room at Kate Mantilini's restaurant.

The addition of the idea of flow to this ubiquity of mechanism forms the basis for complex strategies of modulation. And, a clear identification between the social and the environmental has produced a merger of tectonic and mechanical means that marks the originality of Morphosis's synthesis. Dramatic spaces rising through buildings do not simply manage air and act as chimneys, they serve as visual connectors and describe a public grandeur, sited in the buildings' commons. By setting up powerful regions of intercommunication, this architecture serves as an agent of community, reinforcing the collective identity and social contact of those working within these buildings both by creating spaces of encounter and by associating those spaces with advanced environmental action.

This comes together very beautifully in San Francisco. The circulation armature is remarkable, making the right-angle turn from horizontal to vertical via careful spatial modulations that begin street-side with an entry plaza (holding a freestanding public cafeteria) and canopy, leading to an atrium and elevator lobby, and opening again in a three-story "sky garden" on the eleventh (of eighteen) floors, again public. This complex but legible social space is further activated by a skip-stop elevator system that obliges the interaction of the stair, attenuating the "unprogrammed" space of exchange in the vertical axis.

The San Francisco building is a slab, quite thin, which permits the deployment of most workspace along its perimeter and a resulting access to views, natural light, and fresh air from operable windows. The slab configuration is also crucial to the energy-saving strategy. By radically reducing reliance on mechanical air handling and artificial lighting, the firm estimates that 70 percent of the cooling load can be dealt with via natural ventilation and energy for light cut by one quarter. A series of passive systems is topped off by extensive computer management that will automatically turn lights off when natural levels reach a certain point or when spaces are determined to be unoccupied and that will open and shut vents in the building's "living skin" to keep temperatures comfortable.

Such "active passivity" is increasingly part of Morphosis's style of working and, in many ways, represents the essence of their project. It reflects and extends the attitude embodied in the earlier work with its strategy of intensified detail. Its recursive quality allows big systems to learn local sensitivity, to respond not simply to the particulars of use and occupation but to the uneven behavior of climatic effects over the course of a day, season, or year. Such a distributed, small-element system opens a strong dialectic with Morphosis's growing taste for bold envelopes. In both the San Francisco building and Caltrans, the interdependence of small and large elements does not simply reformulate the historic conceptual rift between envelope and systems, it brings the buildings alive, a genuinely organic strategy.

How well this works in practice will soon be seen. Certainly everything is technically as it should be, the result of research in collaboration with leading scientific experts. The huge multiplication of automated moving parts that enables the active passivity of the system—the hundreds of servos and pistons to open and close the windows and shades—will inevitably perform unevenly, testing the redundancy of the system and its maintenance protocols. As with the mechanical irises on the south facade of Jean Nouvel's Institut du Monde Arabe in Paris, victims of their own elegant delicacy, preserving the robustness of the simply conceived but complexly installed system is likely to be a challenge. And this begs a key question for the ongoing realization of truly green architecture, which must have, as its grail, ever simpler solutions and which must, as well, live with new, more relaxed styles of imperfection.

The wonderful headquarters for NOAA outside Washington, D.C., adds an additional element. Like much of Morphosis's work, this project studies the relationship of building and ground, an old concern most formatively expressed in the underground Cedars-Sinai cancer pavilion of 1988, where the insulating earth is used to protect human vulnerability by creating a calmly embedded space focused on the light. By reading the earth not simply as mass but as a series of laminations, the firm has arrived—along with other architects in its formal ambit—at the conceit of the earth as a folded plate, able to detach itself as necessary from the "ground" to form a building envelope or to enclose one. The masterful sections that characterize so many Morphosis projects often carve

into the earth to displace a too-dogmatic grade, blurring the line between the built and the found. Other projects deal with the earth/building seam by disengaging the elements, allowing topography its autonomy beneath lifted slabs and fragments.

Morphosis uses metaphors that logically grow from the nature of NOAA's activities, the use of satellites to study the earth and its atmosphere. Reflecting this, the building elevates a long bar, filled with control rooms and topped by the antennae by which NOAA communicates with its orbiting satellites, above a large, partially submerged element that houses the agency's office and service spaces. The disengaging void between bar and berm penetrates the wide lower element, carving out a large courtyard to introduce daylight into the earth's depth. The effective section of the structure thus extends from outer space into the earth, precisely parallel to the axis of observation of the agency itself and to the vision of the architects.

By joining the calming logic of Euclidian space to the invisible and immaterial flows that give architecture its reason for being and by closely identifying the prosody of detail and organization of building to clear social and environmental agendas, Morphosis has created a way of building that is both sui generis and rich with implications for architecture in general. This is an architecture of tremendous hope, planetary in its implications. Unlike architectures that fetishize the difference between the "natural" and our own intelligent design, the work of Morphosis is pioneering a new negotiation, a weave of form and behavior that neither slights architecture's long accumulation of original shapes and habits nor forgets for a moment its complete dependency and dramatic influence on the fate of the earth.

Michael Sorkin is Director of the Graduate Urban Design Program at the City College of New York, and principal of the Michael Sorkin Studio in New York City.

WORKING THE LANGUAGE | *Anthony Vidler* |

If there is a single unifying theme that runs through the work of Morphosis, from the first small domestic projects to the more recent large-scale public and institutional works, it is an avoidance of the conventions of what might be called modern "style." Eschewing the commonplaces of the late twentieth century, whether derived from the West Coast Schindler-Neutra tradition or the Expressionist experiments of Scharoun and Taut, Morphosis has consistently chosen what might be called a "third way" in the development of its unique architectural language. Founded on a process of investigation, rather than on the selection and distribution of already formed elements, it relies on a potentially endless iteration of alternatives, transformations, and experiments in an almost filmic sequence of models, drawings, material manipulations. Indeed a synoptic review of the process involved in producing a single "final" design would look much like a Marey sequence that, speeded up, would simulate three-dimensional movement toward a solution. In this sense, the firm has remained true to its name, elevating the metamorphosis of form to a fine art, as a means of production rather than a system of representation.

In the first decades of the twentieth century, when, in the confusion of architectural approaches that emerged with the avant-garde experiments after 1900, the word *style*, once the revered leitmotif of nineteenth-century historicism, was outlawed, to be replaced by an assortment of substitutes. For the modern "classicists," like Le Corbusier and Mies van der Rohe, "styles" were replaced by formal qualities—volume, surface, plan—or a simple refusal of "academic" categories altogether in favor of a revived idea of "building art." For the more transcen-

dentally minded, like the neo-Plasticists or the Suprematists, the solution was to develop a totally new manner built up out of abstract components assembled in a newly conceptualized spatial continuum. Others, Expressionist or Dadaist, preferred to experiment with so-called non-Euclidian geometry, developing a gestural architecture that seemed to translate emotion directly into form.

Mid-century attempts to tame and re-academicize this field of formal expression were divided between those, like Henry-Russell Hitchcock and Philip Johnson, who wanted to impose a new stylistic category—the International Style—and those who, like Colin Rowe and Reyner Banham, in different ways, felt that avant-garde experimentation had exhausted its potential and that the solution was to accept a certain codification (Rowe's "Modern Mannerism") or search for another way entirely (Banham's "autre architecture") based on the yet untapped technological potential of modernity.

Perhaps inevitably, these latter solutions were in their turn bound to repetition and stylistic exhaustion, a fate turned to good effect by those self-styled postmodernists who called for a retreat from abstraction and a return to the good old styles of a supposed humanistic past. This, in turn, once more reduced architectural discourse to a debate among rival styles, and even sparked a new interest in the word *style* itself, so long banned from the vocabulary of modernism.

For those interested in continuing a modern tradition, whether as "neo-avant-gardists" or counter-postmodernists, the solutions offered by the late twentieth century were

narrowly defined. Architects like Peter Eisenman, Richard Meier, and John Hedjuk, following Rowe, felt it imperative to return to the early modernist languages of Corbusian and Surrealist practice; others, like Richard Rogers and Norman Foster, influenced by Banham, explored the potential of technology and program, lauded by the modern movement, but as yet unfulfilled, developing a number of "high-tech" solutions; and, more recently, still others, like Greg Lynn and Karl Chu, exhibited a growing optimism around digital iteration and its ability to construe quasi-biological, apparently organic forms that seemed finally to realize the promise of much modernist functionalist ideology. While "high-tech" stressed a visual continuity with the Modernism of Fuller and Prouvé, the bio-formalists drew on a range of precedents, from Expressionism to DNA structures.

There was, however, one strand of Modernist experiment left untapped—that which understood architectural expression to be the result of a process that had no determinably finite beginning and no predictable end. Such experiments had been launched by the Dadaists as early as 1914 and taken up by artists like Kurt Schwitters in his Merzbau and Frederick Keisler in his Endless House. Both these examples were, as opposed to the almost classical procedures of Modernist design, apparently interminable in duration. The Merzbau was constructed over a long period of time, between 1923 and 1950, in a process of addition, subtraction, and transformation; the Endless House was developed over twenty-five years as a series of experiments in calculating space as a direct extension of the changing haptic forms of the body.

But such alternative languages were, in the last instance, pitched against the emerging norms of Modernism, and not especially concerned with the renewal or continuation of a modern tradition. Morphosis, by contrast, has always sought to remain modern, while at the same time reformulating its codes of expression by means of a complex process of iteration and reiteration, a process that has less to do with the assembly of preformed parts, or the transformation of already known typologies, than with the reinvention of language itself.

But in this evident refusal of the classical rules of composition in favor of the less secure path of formal and material exploration there lies a number of problems, not the least of which, comparable to the nature of psychoanalysis ("Terminable or Interminable," in Freud's terms), is the determination of an endpoint. Where, in the generic design procedures of Modernism, such a point is, so to speak, indicated from the outset, within the boundaries of a predetermined type, a set of preformulated linguistic elements, or the ruling conception of functional adequacy, for Morphosis there is no such security within the formal structures of an already existing style.

Secondly, Morphosis's iterative method, without the guarantee of a known language, immediately opens the door to the danger of an unbridled, if not incomprehensible, expressionism, one that simply refuses intelligibility as an ideological, countermodern position. Morphosis, however, sustains two basic principles of continuity with Modernism—or rather with that classical modern movement represented by the twin poles of Le Corbusier and Mies van der Rohe. The first is a commitment to the spatio-functional determinant, one that while largely separate during the early period of the avant-gardes, leading to an uneasy treaty between formal and functional demands, is renewed with

special force in Morphosis. The second is an equally strong commitment to the material of the work itself, both physical, in the sense of materials, and intellectual, in the sense of programmatic concerns. Tying these two nonnegotiable principles together is the work itself, a work that consists of treating each as if it were a kind of material, working with space as if it were as plastic and solid as steel, and with steel as if it were as transparent and plastic as a thought.

Iteration for Morphosis, in these terms, represents at once research and a method of totalization. "Program," no longer separated out from form or material, is here inseparable from the generic materials of thought and construction, to be worked into shape and form conceptually and physically at the same time as every other determinant; "form," no longer conceived of as an abstract language in itself, is bonded to the molding and cutting of materials; "materials," finally, find their role extended as form-givers as well as form-receivers.

A recent example would be the projected new academic building for the Cooper Union, planned for a single-block site in the East Village of Manhattan. Here the design process, which, in the summer of 2005, was still under way in development and evaluation stages, began with the severe restrictions of the site and its tightly controlled zoning envelope, within which there was little freedom of movement given the projected program. The exercise, then, was to explore a series of possible combinations of interior organization in order to test the proportional allotment of public to programmed space. Early on, it had been decided to find the public realm of the building in the vertical dimension, continuous with the vertical circulation and providing visual access through

the seven stories of laboratory, office, and classroom space. Iteration after iteration tested the limits and potential forms of this vertical movement path, as it twisted obliquely through the structure, capturing both interior and exterior views, and marking the front surface of the building in such a way as to provide some three-dimensional relief from the strict enclosure of what was, for all intents and purposes, a seven-story loft building. The result was a sequence of small models, computer-plotted in three dimensions, that allowed the client and architect to select those most promising to develop at the next scale. The process, as it emerged prior to design development, resulted in a work that in an earlier phase of Modernism might well have seemed based on a typological selection drawn from precedents such as Le Corbusier's Swiss Pavilion in the Cité Universitaire: raised on *pilotis* and constructed in reinforced concrete with steel cladding. The difference, however, resided in the process, and ultimately in the uniqueness of the product, as it explored simultaneously the spatial dimensions of the program, the urban responsibilities of the freestanding form, the technological demands of the flexible laboratory and teaching functions, and the material and energy-saving potential of a suspended "second skin" facade.

The architectural language of Morphosis thus emerges as both "Modernist" in its continuity with the ideals of the early-twentieth-century modern movement, and contemporary in its application of digital and material techniques to a unique design process that refuses convention and platitude in favor of aesthetic exploration and invention.

Anthony Vidler is Dean and Professor at the Irwin S. Chanin School of Architecture of The Cooper Union.

ALL WE NEED TO KNOW | *Lebbeus Woods* |

I am as dazzled as anyone by the inventiveness and dynamism of the buildings, by the complex but still readable arrangements of spaces, and the sharp, angular geometries that never repeat themselves but seem part of a single, coherent family. I am equally taken with the innovative use of industrial materials, dominated by metals and glass, that have been given a lyricism transcending not only their mundane origins, but their use by any other architect since Mies. While I am not a follower of the idea of "sustainability" (why settle for merely sustaining?), I deeply respect the effort to integrate new, more energy-wise technologies in what used to be called a "systems approach," when it was practiced by SOM-Chicago back in the 1940s and '50s and while it seemed possible to build architecture with a sense of social responsibility and aesthetic originality.

Morphosis has done these things and more. They have risen to prominence, if not dominance, through a kind of guildlike work ethic combined with a canny grasp of the forces impacting the field of architecture today, the ones broadly setting its priorities and delineating its goals. Yet what concerns me here is what these buildings, and their underlying motifs, contribute to the field of human knowledge.

Louis Sullivan once said, "They will tear down your building in twenty-five years. What will remain is the *idea*." He understood that it is the building that is transient, whatever its cost and however solid its construction. Even though a few of Sullivan's best buildings have been recognized as historically important and saved from demolition, he would have been the first to dismiss this postponement as missing the point. He was no Platonist, and was less interested in the eternal aspect of any idea than in its service to human ends, poetic as well as practical. This may seem a contradiction, in that human

ends themselves are transient, but transience itself is relative. The longevity of ideas—if they are innovative enough—exceeds that of the buildings they inspire. The central ideas of his breakthrough Guaranty Building in Buffalo lived on in Chicago's Hancock Building, the World Trade Center towers in New York, and the Bank of China in Hong Kong. They will live in any future tall building with vertically stacked, rationally modulated floor plates supported by a structural frame that is also the exterior enclosure wall. Other compelling tall buildings have been designed, such as Bertrand Goldberg's "corn-cob" towers in Chicago and Gordon Bunshaft's Lever House, but the organizing architectural ideas of Guaranty transcend the experience of the building itself and enter, philosophically speaking, into the wider field of human knowledge. There, they are available to serve, in ways never anticipated, continually evolving human needs.

In Sullivan's day, innovative ideas had to do with making buildings simpler by removing excessive ornamentation and historical references that usually cloaked a formulaic conventionality of design. Today, very nearly the opposite is the case: innovative ideas have to do with making buildings more complex. Not more complicated, which is exactly what Victorian tastes had done with objects of design and which Modernism fought successfully against, but more complex in the expression of what a building is expected to be. This involves not only changing technical demands—complex lighting, security, heating and air-conditioning systems—or new methods and materials of construction, but also what we might call cognitive and affective demands of people to experience in a tangible way the brave new world of changes we are living in. Very often these changes have little physical presence, or none at all. The computer, which has radically affected nearly every aspect of our lives, is a little box that sits on a table, and keeps getting smaller even as it becomes more powerful and pervasive. Talk as we will about cyberspace, it exists more as an effect than as an experience. Television receivers started out as little boxes and are now growing larger, and will eventually become walls; their ubiquity will make them all but invisible. And how do we experience the radical restructuring of society affecting the ways we work, live, play, hope, dream, and believe? Economics and politics create everyday crises and upheavals that we can experience only personally, but still must somehow integrate in a social sense as we walk the same old streets and go through the motions of being normal. Our lives are increasingly complex, yet we hardly experience their reality in an outward, communal way. The visual arts picked up on this disparity long ago, but their immediate audience still amounts to a cultural elite. Architecture, on the other hand, can be met on the same old streets and has the chance to engage all who traverse them. Considering that, its place in the field of knowledge becomes clear: architecture is central to our contemporary understanding of change.

The work of Morphosis has been for some time at the forefront of exploring complexity as both an architectural strategy and a social reality. The building types Morphosis has been commissioned to design are not those of the cultural elite—museums, concert halls, and high-profile corporate office buildings—but schools, housing, and public buildings such as courthouses and government offices and laboratories, with notoriously low budgets and high demands for utility and efficiency. Governments are held accountable to the taxpaying public in ways wealthy private institutions and individuals are not. This repertoire of projects already sets Morphosis apart from other architectural firms gaining worldwide recognition. No doubt there will one day be a Morphosis-designed art museum, and a concert hall, and a skyscraper, but these will convey not only the Morphosis style—hard-edged and deeply

layered—but also a sense of its ethics, which are eloquently working-class and do not aim to please, placate, or entertain. I cannot think of another architect or firm of the present era that has based its practice so much on hard-won principles of design that come from confrontation with everyday realities in the pursuit of high art.

It seems to me that there are four keywords that allude to these principles, set the tone and agenda of the Morphosis practice, and constitute the basis of its contribution to the field of human knowledge. The first is *collision*. The second is *distortion*. The third is *interrogation*. The fourth is *incompletion*. Each is, in its own way, far afield from the optimistic buzzwords eagerly used by architects who hope to have clients and, therefore, to build. Separately, they are disquieting. Taken together, they constitute the basis of a truly *critical* practice.

Morphosis clearly understands that the changes overtaking our society and each of us, not simply as citizens but as individuals, cannot be entirely harmonious. There is not enough time to find common denominators, or create a leveling consensus, or resolve in a congenial way the old and the new, the already understood and the unexpected, even the alienating. So its designs allow different spaces to be different and, in their interaction, to simply collide. The Hypo Bank in Klagenfurt is an excellent example. The spatial effect is unsettling and exhilarating. Its inhabitants and observers are allowed not only to witness a new "world in painful birth," but to be part of it. Indeed, it is their presence, their inhabitation, that gives it meaning, as they, too, in some aspects of their emotional and thoughtful selves, are also just now struggling to be born. That this bank is intended to be a financial vehicle for a rapidly changing, new/old region of the world—Austria in relation to Croatia and Slovenia, two former states of Yugoslavia that only recently have gained independence—underscores the point. The effect of the building is not only symbolic, but actively instrumental. The experience of the architectural collisions is heuristic: it enables us to understand and more fully integrate ourselves with the dramatic and rapid social changes underway.

Sudden changes also have another effect on the familiar, which for many is extremely difficult to cope with, and that is distortion. Here we might make an analogy with physics, and the distortions of time and space brought by Einstein into the predictably homogeneous universe of Newton and Descartes. The first effect that change is likely to have before bringing an entirely new configuration into existence is to distort what is already known and accepted. "Space is warped!" declared the headlines of the *New York Times* in 1919, after Einstein's theory of gravitation had been proved. From Einstein's viewpoint, space was curved due to the force of gravity. But to the wider public, space had been warped. The familiar and the already known had been distorted. So with the Diamond Ranch High School in California. The usual four-square rooms for learning and gathering and moving are stretched and pulled by new sets of forces, as yet little understood or explained. But everyone knows, instinctively, that they are the forces of change, shifting the equilibrium of space, and also of knowledge. Their final form remains for the future to determine, but for the present, the strangely familiar new forms prepare us for the eventual by insisting on our ability to adapt, to find new horizons, to regain our balance, and to learn.

A major feature of Thom Mayne's creative trajectory is his skepticism, his incessant questioning of everything, including himself. Anyone who has heard him speak in public knows that he is filled with doubts and uncertainties. This, once again, sets him and Morphosis apart from other "star" firms and their principals, who usually give self-congratulating sales pitches instead of candid, questioning lectures. But Mayne and his firm know that, in this era of unpredictable events, constant interrogation of the situation is, at the least, a survival tactic. Just as the Internet has swept aside, in a decade or so, comfortable assumptions of what constitutes a human community, and grassroots pressures have dramatically altered our perceptions of race, gender, and sexual orientation, so the projects of Morphosis have cast new light on design's dependence on stereotypes. The old formulas of functionalism, which assigned one space to one use, are brought into question by distortions of the familiar and collisions of different systems and elements that once were not apparent or resolved in advance. Innovation is a direct result of asking questions about what is normally assumed. Doubt, as it were, is the sponsor of invention, and—lest we lose sight of the fact—invention, especially in the form of rethinking the already known, is what is demanded of new works in any advancing field of knowledge.

We need to look at the field of architecture today, and to the knowledge it creates, not in terms of products, but in terms of processes. Architecture, which embraces so many other fields and speaks more than any practice to the specifics of our contemporary condition, must not pretend to be aesthetically complete. Classical architecture, in the form of a Parthenon or a Notre Dame, could claim to offer a kind of summary of a society's aspirations and its knowledge. Today's buildings must be more modest, even as they seek to valorize the high aims of human strivings. The buildings of Morphosis, with their questionings, their distortions of the known, with their unresolved, frankly exposed collisions of differences, are self-consciously incomplete. Their aesthetic is the opposite of what Alberti required of "beauty, which is that to which nothing can be added; and that from which nothing can be taken away." Beauty, as a reflection of divine perfection, was complete, eternal. In contrast, the buildings of Morphosis seem to crystallize, with sharpness and unflinching candor, precise, unique moments in time. These happen to be moments in our own time. Their beauty cannot console us with prospects of the eternal, but can appear suddenly in the glint of sunlight on metal and glass. Or when standing in a space where we don't know how to behave, but realize we can learn. Or in seeing strange new silhouettes against the sky. "Beauty," Keats once wrote, "is truth, and truth is beauty; that is all ye know on earth, and all ye need to know." The buildings of Morphosis tap into the devilishly complex truths of our time, and that is all we need to know.

Lebbeus Woods is Professor at the Irwin S. Chanin School of Architecture of The Cooper Union, and co-Founder and Scientific Director of RIEAeuropa, an institute devoted to the advancement of experimental architectural thought and practice.

SHR PERCEPTUAL MANAGEMENT

...place of tomorrow.... more competitors....more products...more brands........more words....more messages....more claims....

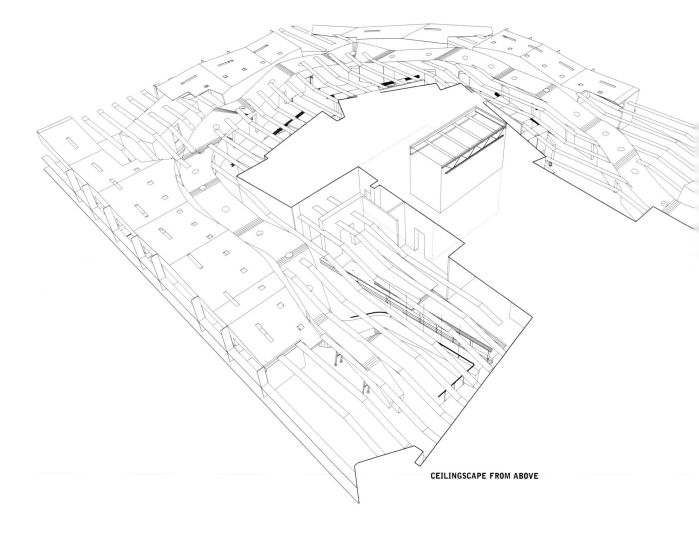

CEILINGSCAPE FROM ABOVE

This egalitarian scheme for a sixty-person advertising, design, and marketing firm reinterprets conventions of status, corporate culture, and productivity. The architecture supports and expresses the collective nature of creative intellectual capital—SHR's product. A team-based organizational strategy replaces the traditional workplace hierarchy; concurrently, a shift occurs from cellular, individual spaces to hybrid space at the service of the increasingly collective product.

Based on the need for both privacy and team interaction, distinct architectural gestures define functional zones within the existing "U" of raw, nondescript office space. The primary, serpentine gesture of demarcation—a thick, inhabited wall of office partitions—curves from one end of the space to the other. The creative teams occupy the flow of the serpent, with workspaces opening to the shared

central design studio. The management and support offices, which require complete privacy, occupy the glazed perimeter of the space. Linear, folded screens of perforated metal float above the interstitial work areas; attached to the bottoms of the existing trusses, they reveal the architecture of the generic shell. Floors of polished concrete, exposed steel beams, natural wood, and ephemeral walls of theatrical scrim complete the material vocabulary.

This project affirms the potential of architecture's role to affect human activity, especially with respect to the culture of an office. As such it marks the beginning of an ongoing preoccupation that continues to inform our more recent large-scale office projects.

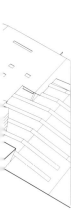

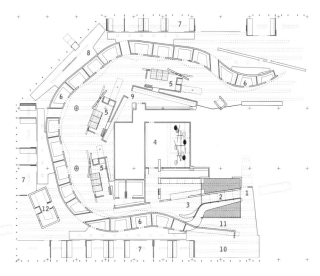

FLOOR PLAN

1 entry 2 bridge 3 reception 4 conference room 5 client team conference rooms 6 creative offices
7 management offices 8 executive offices 9 art dept. 10 lounge 11 gallery 12 computer room

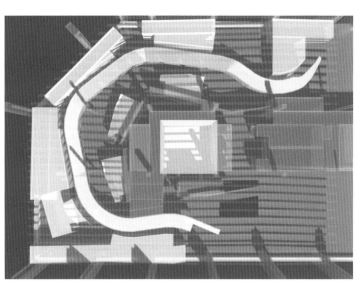

CEILING PLAN

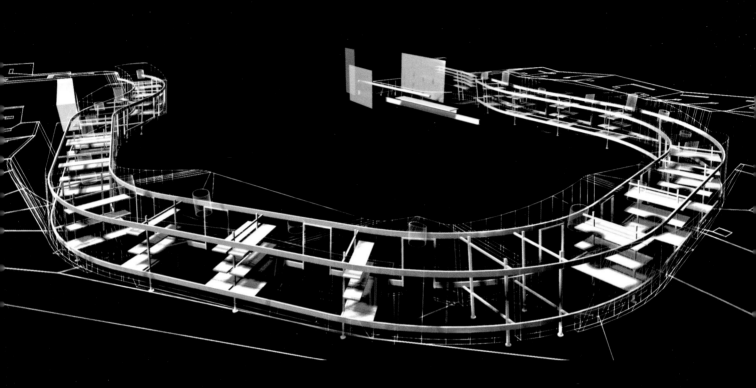

NORTH FRAMING PERSPECTIVE

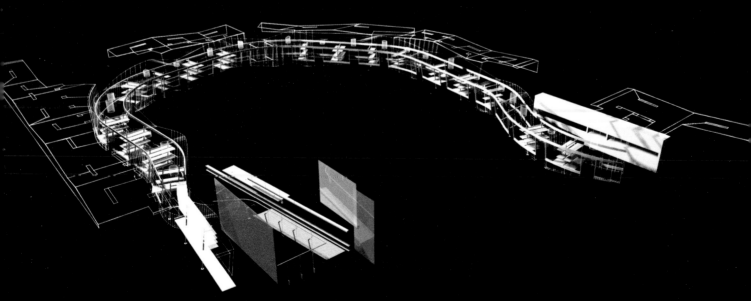

SOUTH FRAMING PERSPECTIVE

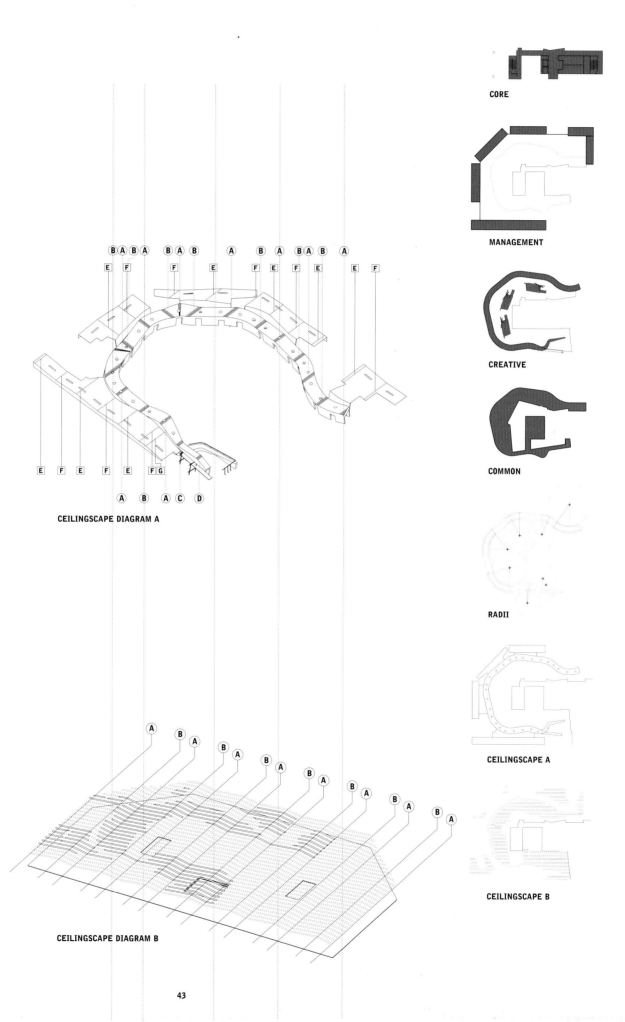

CEILINGSCAPE DIAGRAM A

CEILINGSCAPE DIAGRAM B

CORE

MANAGEMENT

CREATIVE

COMMON

RADII

CEILINGSCAPE A

CEILINGSCAPE B

45

SHR PERCEPTUAL MANAGEMENT

DATE: 1997-1998 LOCATION: Scottsdale, Arizona STATUS: Built SITE AREA: 15,000 sf/1,394 m² tenant improvement PROJECT SIZE: 15,000 sf/1,394 m² PROGRAM: Interior office space in a three-story generic office building.

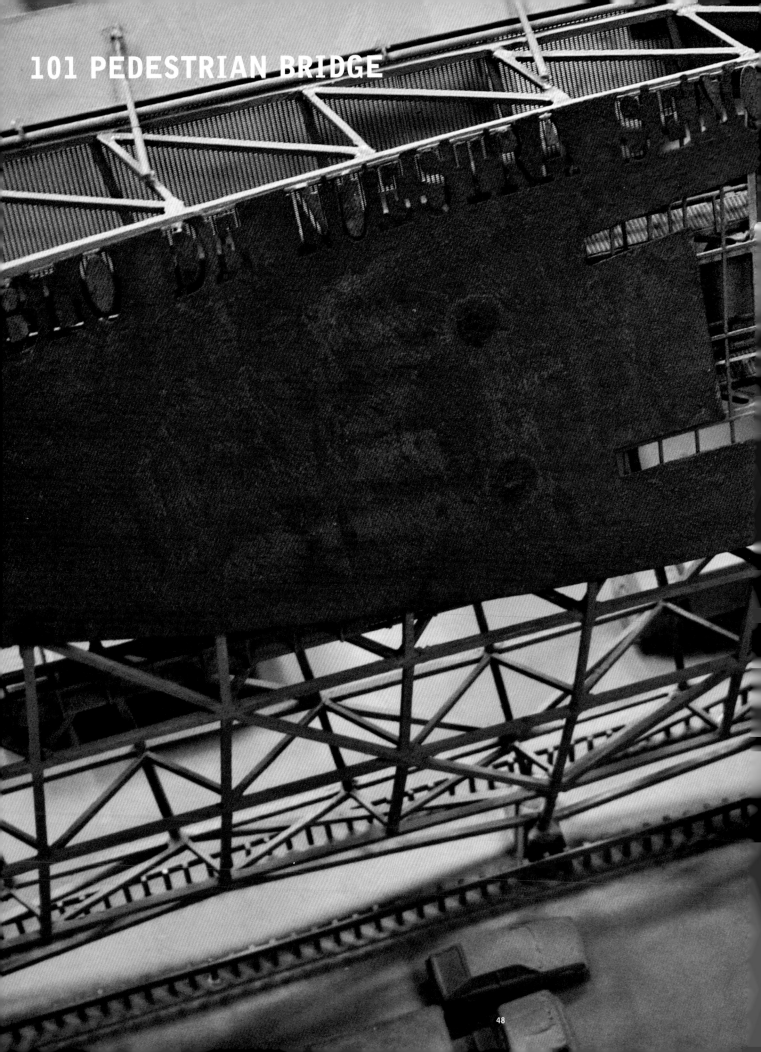

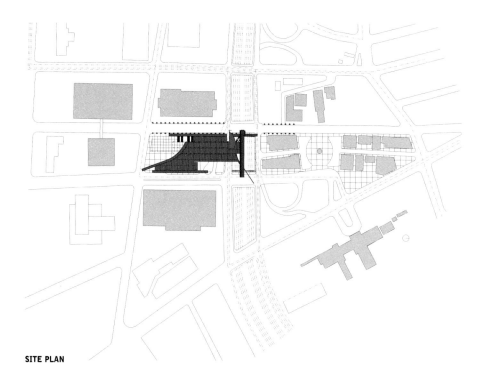

SITE PLAN

This new pedestrian passageway bridges the civic fissure created in Los Angeles' downtown by the construction of the 101 freeway some fifty years ago by filling it with an iconic civic space. And yet, the design for this icon grew out of a nonsite—the very void in the urban fabric carved by the freeway.

The *parti* responds to both the future potential and the deep-rooted history of the area. The straight edge, with its ephemeral media display, symbolically faces new Los Angeles to the south. The curved edge, with its permanent steel text, is a fragment, a reflection of the circular *zócalo* to the south—the original civic space of the pueblo of Los Angeles. On the north side, the frame supports an electronic display apparatus—a forum for the work of artist Jenny Holzer and a programmable catalogue of events that reflect the expansiveness of Angelino culture. The south side of the frame bears a curved panel of weathered Cor-Ten steel, incised with the fixed words "El Pueblo de Nuestra Señora la Reina de Los Angeles," the original name of the city.

The semitransparent, porous structure frames a space that is simultaneously public and private—a Situationist "living room" in the middle of the city. Within the frame of the bridge, an urban-scaled staircase at mid–Main Street provides access to a restaurant and an observation deck overlooking the freeway. Ascending one story, the pedestrian arrives at an elevated platform, the equivalent of a traditional *piano nobile*—the public living room—of a European palazzo. A landmark for both L.A. native and tourist, the bridge orients the pedestrian to the historic Main Street axis. The porous structure lifts over the freeway, so the motorist remains visually connected to the city's skyline at precisely the point where downtown's most vital memories are stitched together.

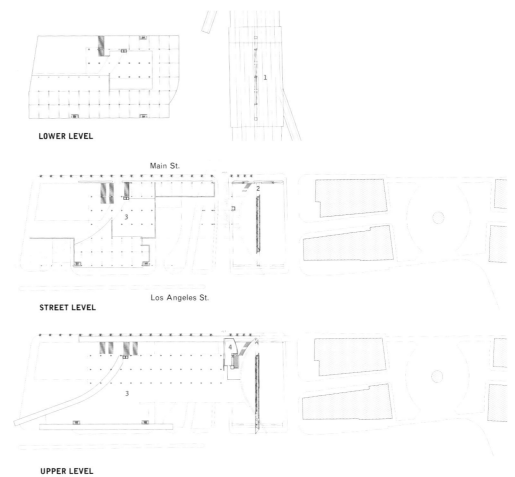

LOWER LEVEL

Main St.

STREET LEVEL

Los Angeles St.

UPPER LEVEL

1 101 Hollywood Freeway 2 exhibition arcade 3 new L.A. Mall 4 "GO" cafe

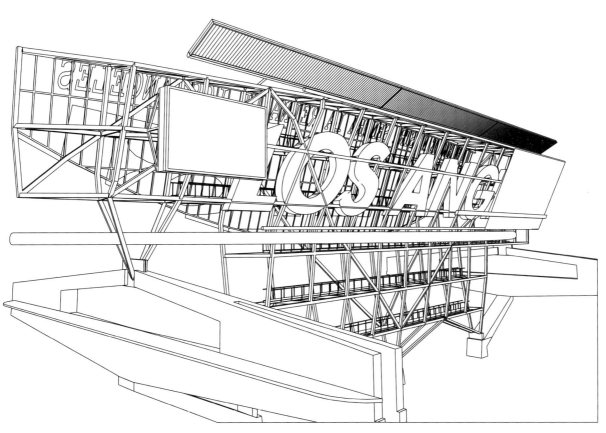

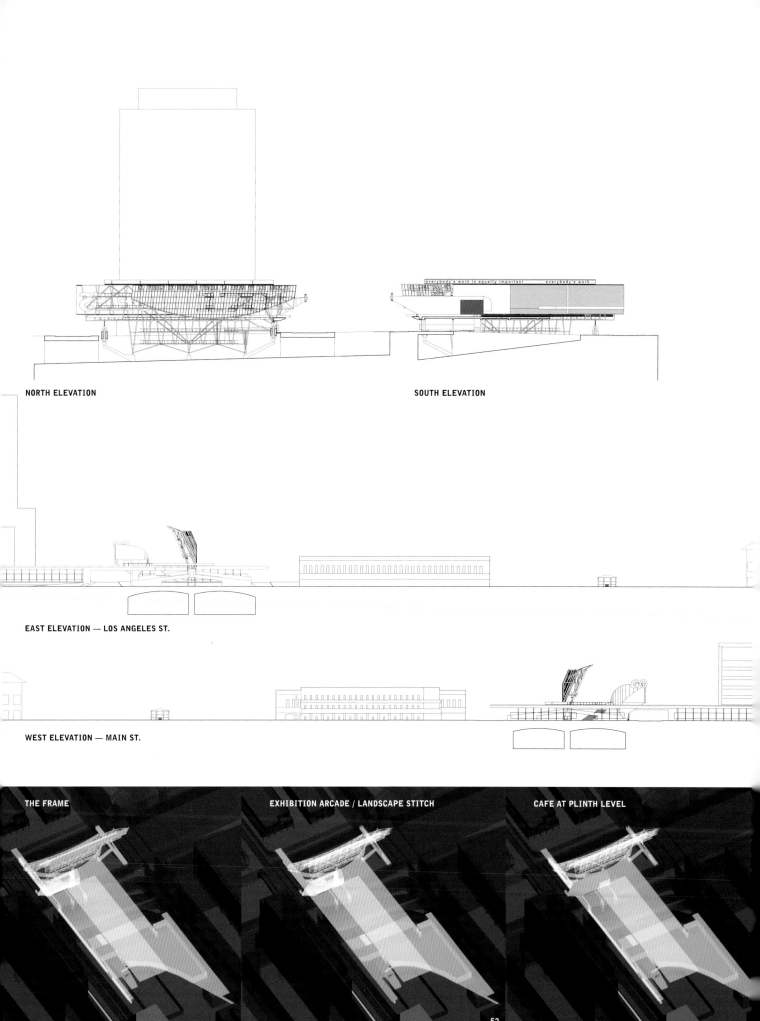

NORTH ELEVATION

SOUTH ELEVATION

EAST ELEVATION — LOS ANGELES ST.

WEST ELEVATION — MAIN ST.

THE FRAME

EXHIBITION ARCADE / LANDSCAPE STITCH

CAFE AT PLINTH LEVEL

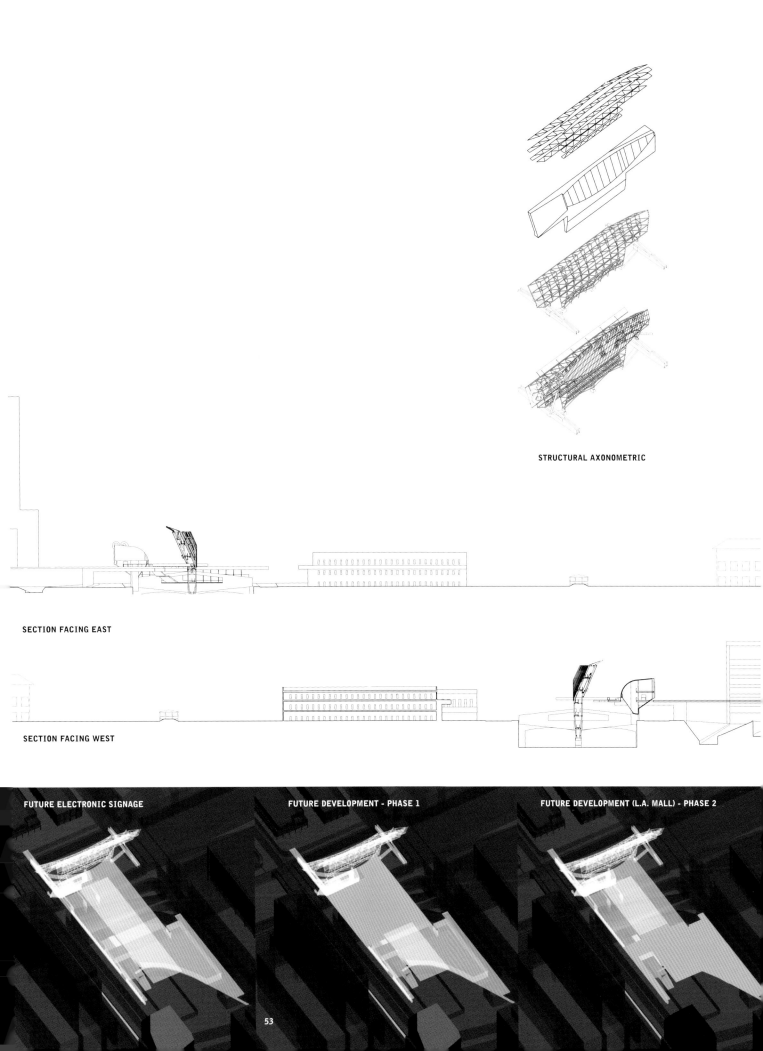

STRUCTURAL AXONOMETRIC

SECTION FACING EAST

SECTION FACING WEST

FUTURE ELECTRONIC SIGNAGE

FUTURE DEVELOPMENT - PHASE 1

FUTURE DEVELOPMENT (L.A. MALL) - PHASE 2

101 PEDESTRIAN BRIDGE

DATE: 1998 LOCATION: Los Angeles, California STATUS: Competition SITE: 101 freeway overpass, downtown Los Angeles PROGRAM: Downtown pedestrian bridge, with digital/electronic art display, across the 101 freeway; steel truss frame erected over steel and concrete buttresses.

PALENQUE AT CENTRO JVC

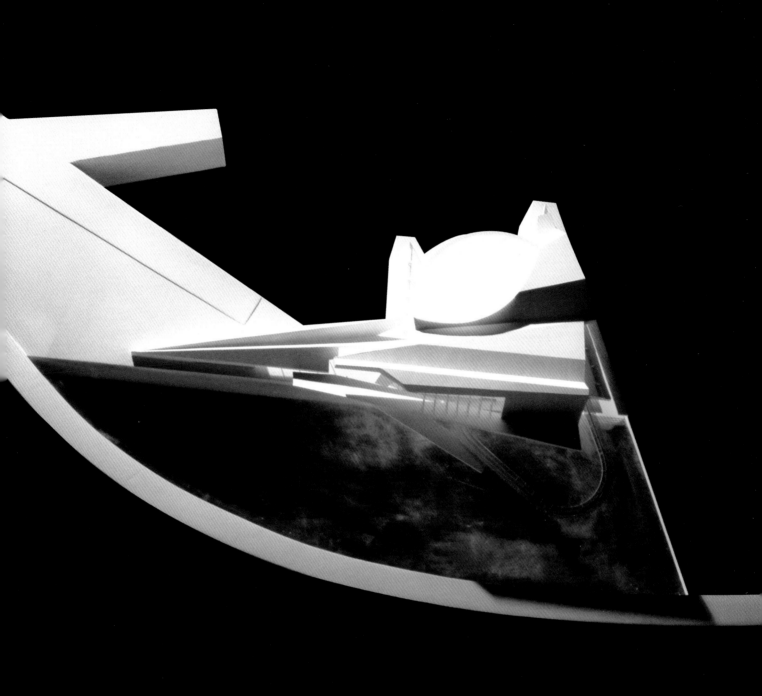

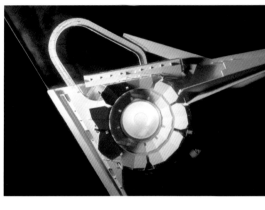

0 100M 200M   .5K

MASTER PLAN

1 water 2 roads 3 landscaping 4 pedestrian routes 5 parking 6 buildings 7 areas for future development 8 palenque

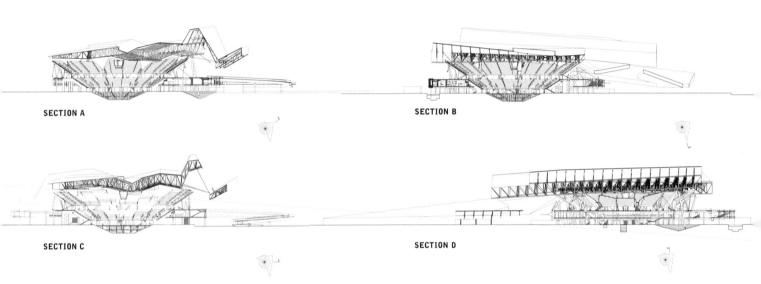

SECTION A

SECTION B

SECTION C

SECTION D

Since pre-Columbian times, *palenques* have traditionally accommodated the spectacle of *pelea de gallos*—cockfighting. Relatively recent changes in cultural attitudes have broadened the *palenque*'s role; it is now seen as a performance and entertainment venue that hosts events such as concerts of *musica ranchera* (folk music), boxing matches, and public assemblies.

The layered, adaptable, open-air arena makes three discrete transformations to accommodate a variety of event requirements. In the typical layout, reminiscent of ancient Mayan building structures, the lower seating of the arena is carved into the earth to form an intimate stage for the *gallos* ritual. In this version, temporary hydraulic or lightweight steel structures can be erected over the small lower arena when necessary to expand the arena by two further incremental steps, for sporting events and stage performances.

A disc and a folded plane intersect to form a hybrid roof that mimics the profile of the surrounding mountain range. The roof form peels away from the landscape, becoming perceptually detached from the earth, while the ellipsoid "fragment" hovers over the concert stage as a vestige of the order below.

The walkways, ramps, and stairs that orbit the arena link it with the other elements of the new cultural and commercial urban center at the edge of Guadalajara. The *palenque* integrates dynamically with the adjacent cluster of new buildings, the site, and the culture.

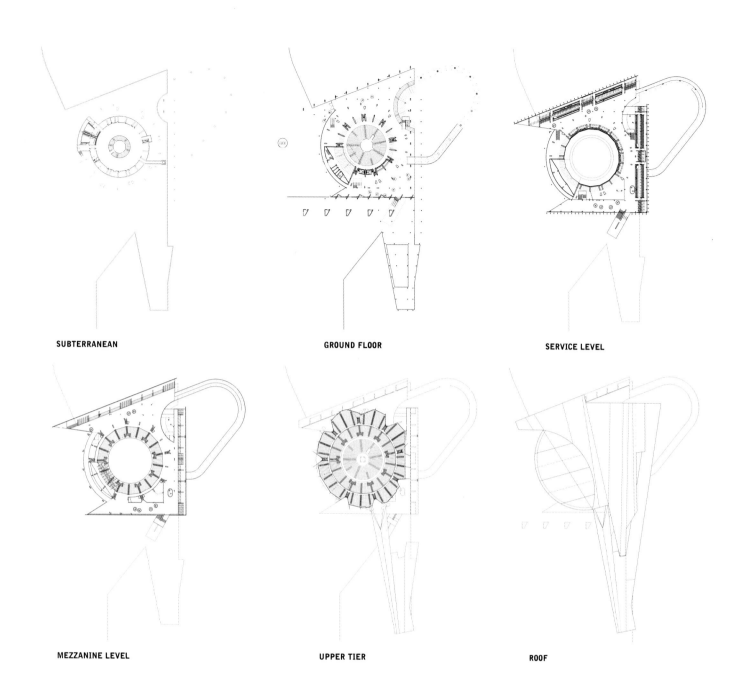

SUBTERRANEAN

GROUND FLOOR

SERVICE LEVEL

MEZZANINE LEVEL

UPPER TIER

ROOF

EAST ELEVATION

WEST ELEVATION

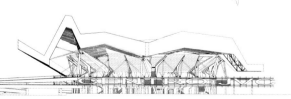

NORTH ELEVATION

SOUTH ELEVATION

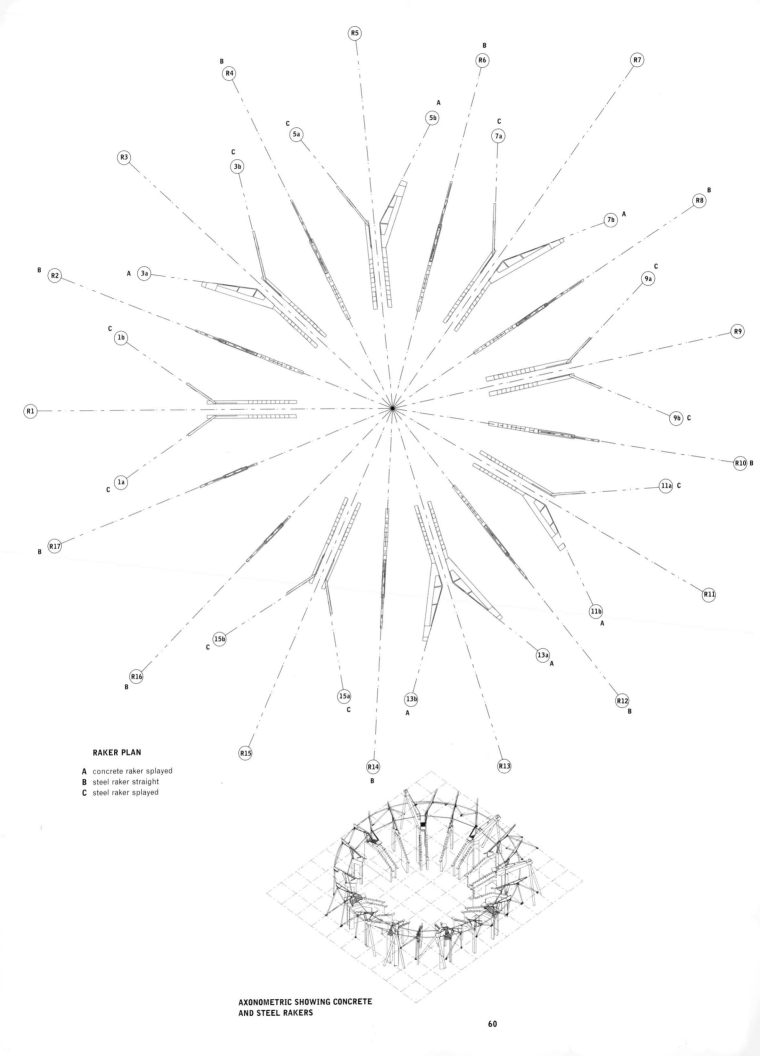

R5

B
R4

B
R6

R7

C
5a

A

5b

C
3b

C
7a

R3

7b   A

B

R8

A   3a

B
R2

C

9a

C
1b

R9

R1

9b   C

C
1a

R10   B

11a   C

B
R17

11b
A

15b
C

13a
A

R16
B

15a
C

13b
A

R12
B

R15

R14
B

R13

RAKER PLAN

A concrete raker splayed
B steel raker straight
C steel raker splayed

**AXONOMETRIC SHOWING CONCRETE
AND STEEL RAKERS**

60

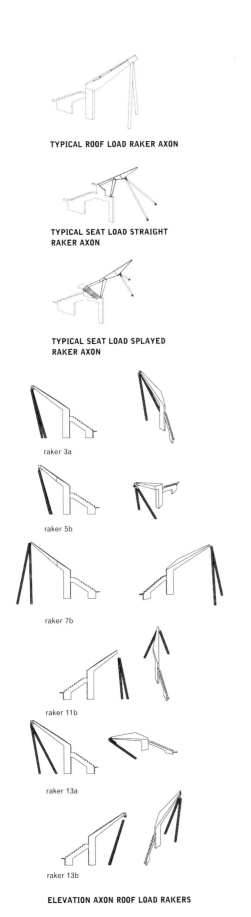

TYPICAL ROOF LOAD RAKER AXON

TYPICAL SEAT LOAD STRAIGHT
RAKER AXON

TYPICAL SEAT LOAD SPLAYED
RAKER AXON

raker 3a

raker 5b

raker 7b

raker 11b

raker 13a

raker 13b

ELEVATION AXON ROOF LOAD RAKERS

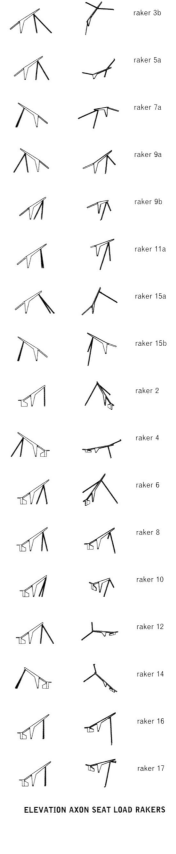

raker 1a

raker 1b

raker 3b

raker 5a

raker 7a

raker 9a

raker 9b

raker 11a

raker 15a

raker 15b

raker 2

raker 4

raker 6

raker 8

raker 10

raker 12

raker 14

raker 16

raker 17

ELEVATION AXON SEAT LOAD RAKERS

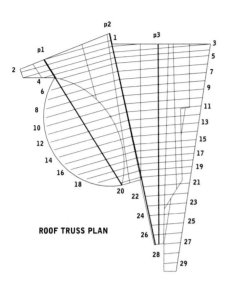

ROOF TRUSS PLAN

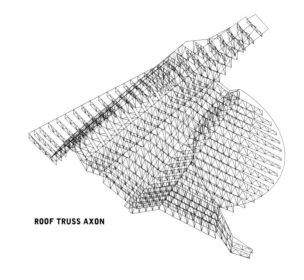

ROOF TRUSS AXON

p1

p2

p3

PRIMARY TRUSSES

1

2

3

4

5

6

7

8

9

10

11

12

13

14

15

16

17

18

19

20

21

22

23

24

25

26

27

28

29

SECONDARY TRUSSES

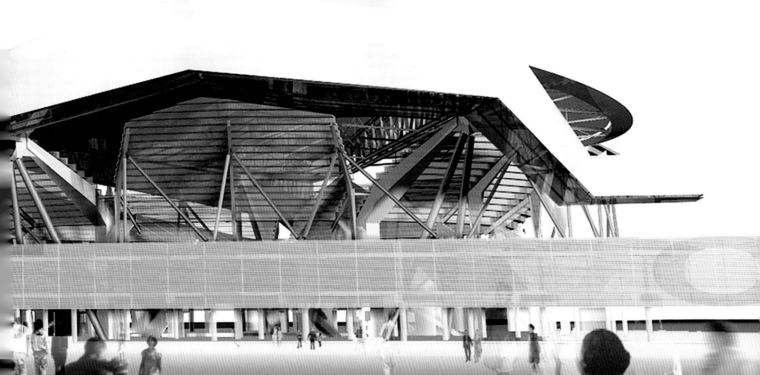

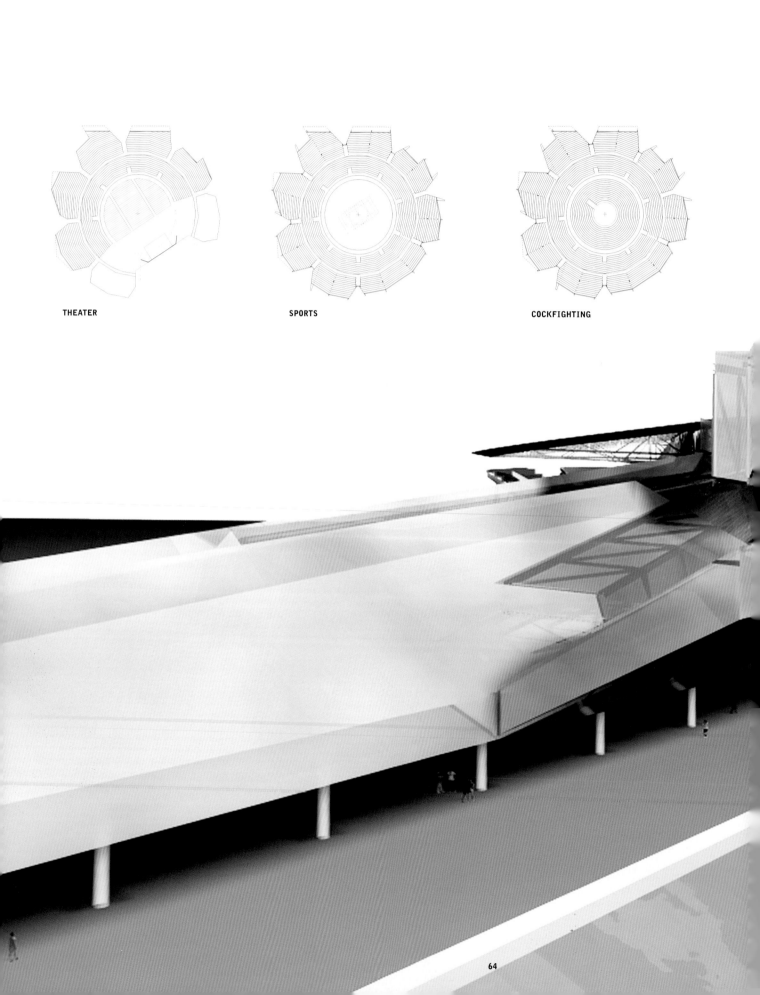

THEATER

SPORTS

COCKFIGHTING

PALENQUE AT CENTRO JVC

DATE: 1998-2007 LOCATION: Zapopan, Jalisco, Mexico STATUS: In Process SITE AREA: 140,000 sf/13,007 m² PROJECT SIZE: 240,000 sf/22,297 m² PROGRAM: 6,250 seat multipurpose stadium.

INTERNATIONAL ELEMENTARY SCHOOL

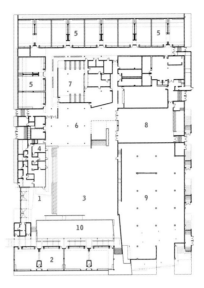

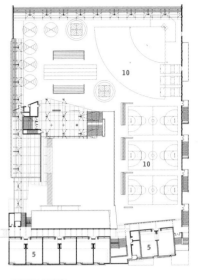

FIRST FLOOR

SECOND FLOOR

1 entry 2 kindergarten wing 3 courtyard 4 administrative offices 5 classrooms 6 covered lunch area 7 library
8 multipurpose room 9 parking 10 playground 11 courtyard 12 kitchen 13 teacher's support space 14 corridor

In post–World War II Los Angeles, schools were built on the suburban model, typified by single-story buildings on sprawling, grass-covered, five-acre sites. High urban real estate prices, combined with a dearth of large empty parcels of land, have rendered this model obsolete for most American cities today. Our stacking strategy, which locates the playground and other open areas of the program above the classroom spaces, cut the land requirements in half and allowed us to allocate resources to a higher quality building. Multifunctional playgrounds and outdoor athletic facilities are carved into the roof planes; children literally play on top of their world, safely above and out of sight of the school's urban context.

The perforated metal wall that embraces three of the four facades is essentially a boundary transformed into an architectural element— a skin without a body. The vertical screen develops into a horizontal surface, which in turn defines a space for classrooms, library, food service, and maintenance areas. Functionally freed from the task of enclosing volumes, the facades assume new forms: bleachers for seating, perforated screening for shade, and a folded play structure.

The bar of classrooms turns the street corner to embrace the gateway to the school, where a large mural provides a backdrop for the lower-level outdoor courtyard, the primary gathering place for the student body.

The students assemble daily alongside over-sized names, quotes, and faces of Leo Tolstoy, Maya Angelou, Octavio Paz, and hundreds of others—a timeline of geographically diverse figures in literature. The didactic surface communicates directly to the students in this typically multicultural urban school. Even if they are still too young to read the work of most of these authors, they will, after six years of exposure to the names and faces, begin to develop a consciousness of our common literary culture.

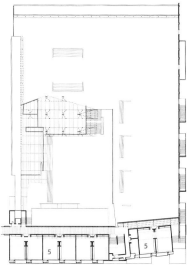

THIRD FLOOR

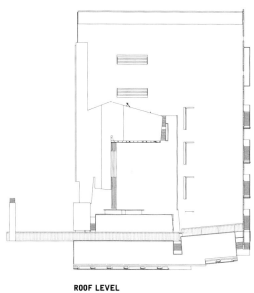

ROOF LEVEL

EAST-WEST SECTION

NORTH-SOUTH SECTION

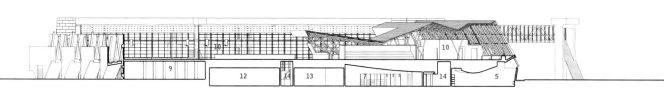

NORTH-SOUTH SECTION

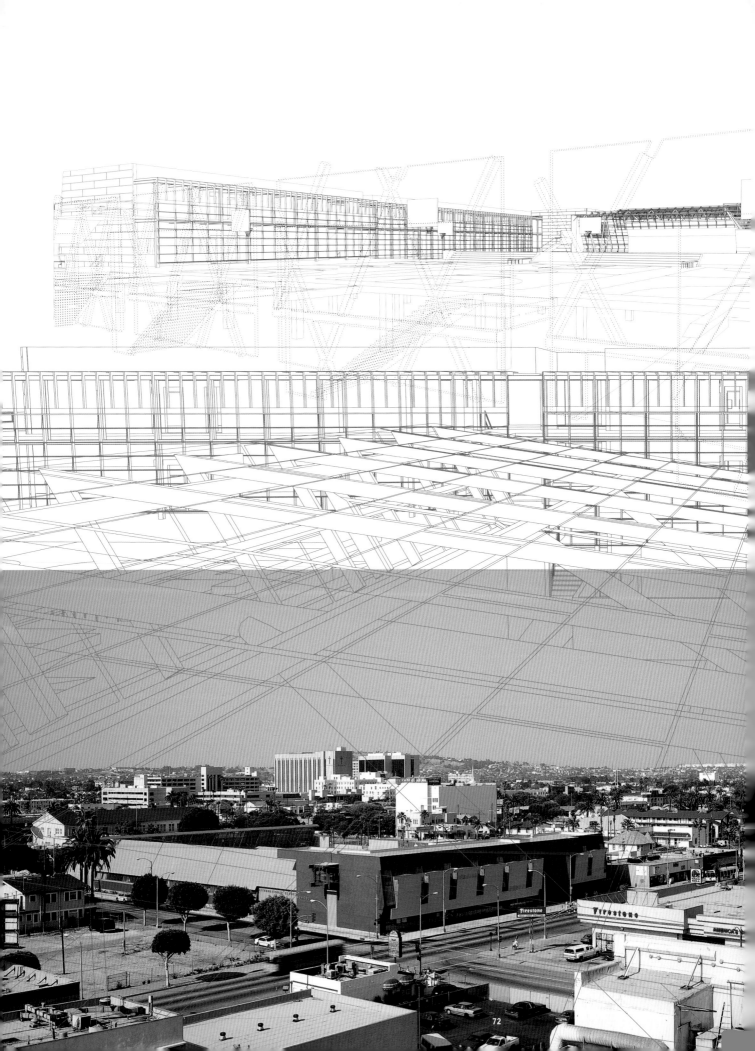

73

INTERNATIONAL ELEMENTARY SCHOOL

DATE: 1997-1999 LOCATION: Long Beach, California STATUS: Built SITE AREA: 2 acres/.81 ha PROJECT SIZE: 91,000 sf/8,454 m² PROGRAM: 33 classrooms, library, computer classroom, multipurpose room, lunch garden, administration, rooftop playground, and covered parking for 60 automobiles.

LUTÈCE

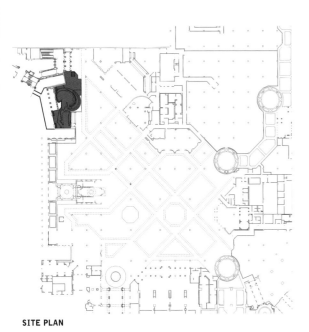

SITE PLAN

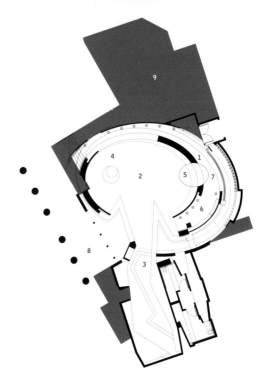

FLOOR PLAN

1 reception 2 main dining 3 private dining 4 chandelier
5 Suh sculpture 6 bar 7 wine cellar 8 patio 9 kitchen

"Nothing was real except chance. Everything had been reduced to chance, a nightmare of numbers and probabilities."

Paul Auster, *City of Glass*

Overlapping, connected spaces, generated by centripetal force, orbit the main dining room; an architecture of chance, with origins in the roulette wheel and ball, that most architectonic of Las Vegas's games. The curved wall segments seem to spin about their off-center axis as irregular cutouts perforate the drum form, revealing views of adjacent spaces. Encircling the main dining area is the reception area, bar, wine storage, patio, and a private dining room. A white, bronze-banded wall in the form of a conical ellipse wraps around the main dining room and functions as the key organizational gesture, creating a sense of movement between areas.

On entering the restaurant from the chaos of the Venetian Casino, one passes through a bronze portal etched with a conceptual plan of the restaurant—an inverse Alice's looking glass. Once inside, an army of tiny sculpted figures, with arms raised above their heads, supports the elliptical glass floor beneath the guest's feet. This sculptural installation, by artist Do-Ho Suh, contains nineteen thousand human figures, equivalent to the entire population of the resort at a given point in time. Lutèce is an oasis from the casino's strategically planned insular, disquieting environment, its design both a foil and a reference to the casino's frenetic air of chance and motion.

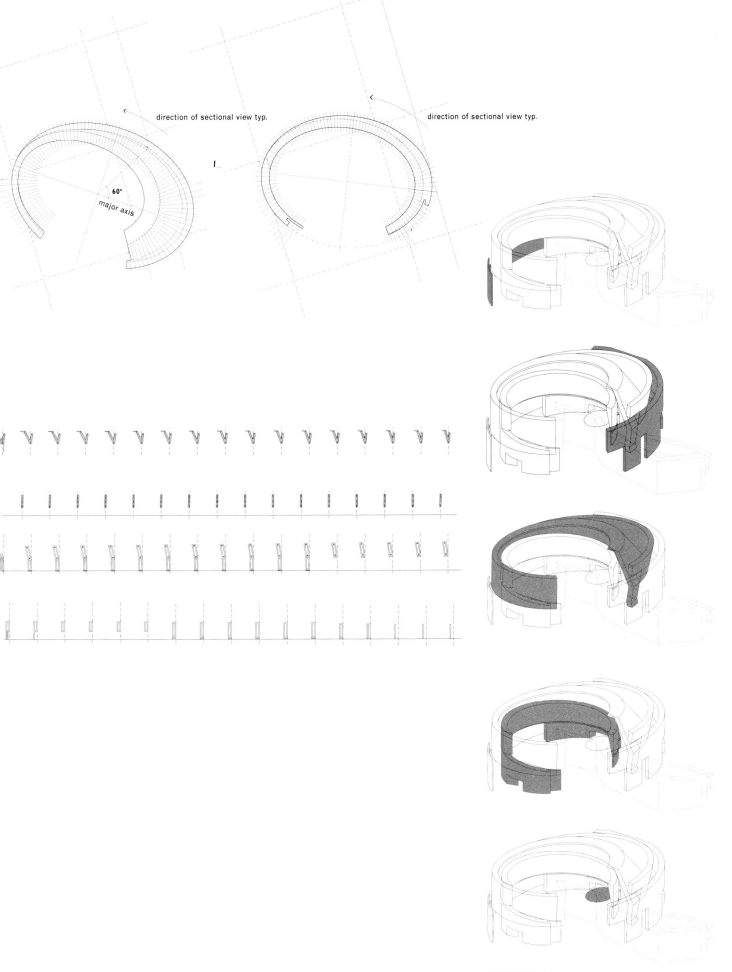

direction of sectional view typ.

direction of sectional view typ.

60°
major axis

ELEMENTS 1-5

LUTÈCE

DATE: 1998-1999 LOCATION: Las Vegas, Nevada STATUS: Built SITE AREA: 6,000 sf/557 m² within the Venetian Hotel and Casino PROJECT SIZE: 6,000 sf/557 m²
PROGRAM: 290-seat restaurant.

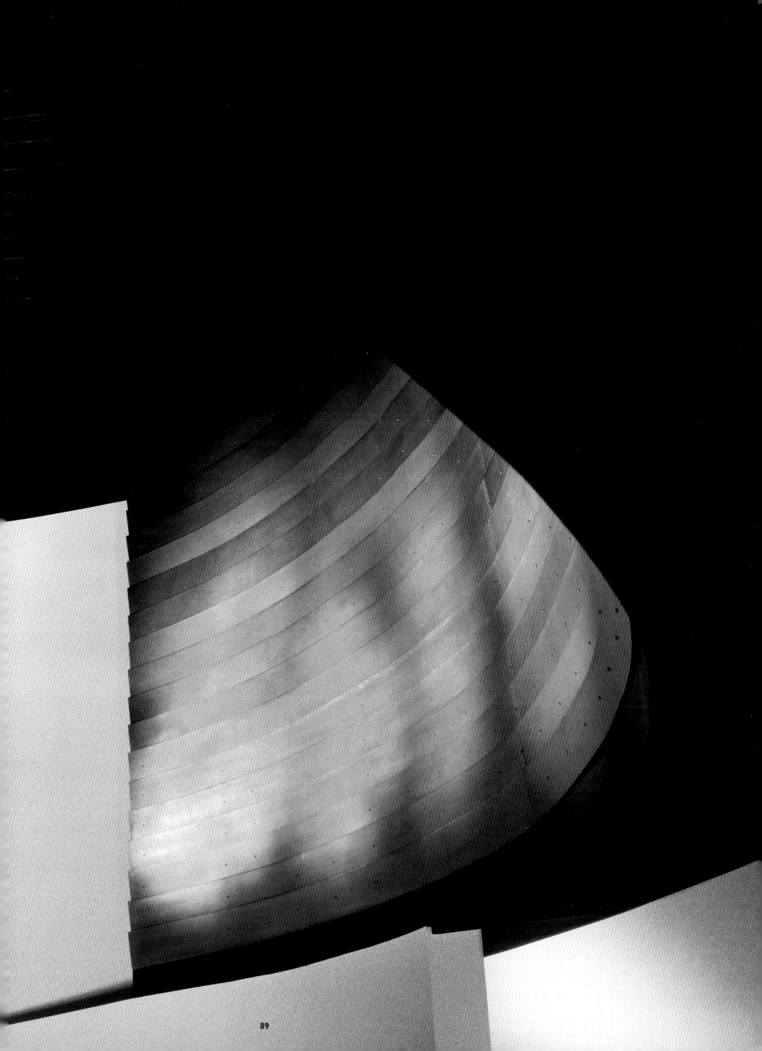

TSUNAMI

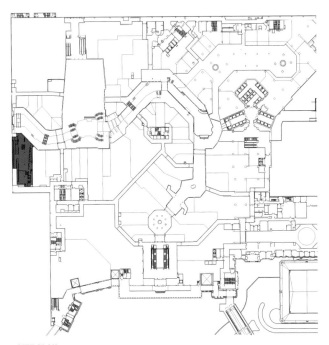

SITE PLAN

Rather than overtly simulating a visit to an Asian city, Tsunami presents an experience through a formal reinterpretation of the tropes that define Las Vegas; surfaces bend back and delaminate to expose *an idea* of architecture rather than a copy of architecture. The hybrid design mediates between the immateriality of a two-dimensional image and the presence of a three-dimensional volume. In the tension between these two systems—the graphic and the spatial—a coherent order emerges.

The geometrically manipulated plane defines and modifies the space. Artist Rebeca Méndez's densely collaged graphic elements of Asian culture suggest a sense of place through color, density, saturation, and imagery. The flat graphic surface morphs in three dimensions—an inner lining that bends, folds, and wraps—creating a dialogue between the figurative logic of drawing and the spatial logic of architecture.

We were interested in exposing the underside of Las Vegas architecture to question notions of reality in this famously ersatz place. The process began by rendering void the space for the restaurant to create a black box back-drop. Stripped of its coverings, Las Vegas is a desert filled with nearly identical concrete and steel infrastructures concealed by sur-faces meant to resemble something other than what they are. In Tsunami, we chose to par-ticipate in the game that is Las Vegas by accepting the terms and locating an authentic project within this radically synthetic place.

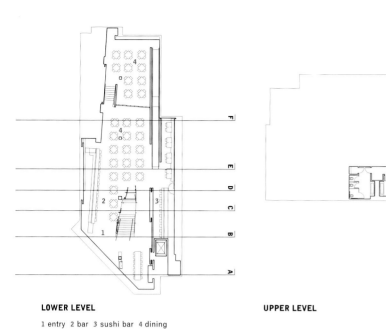

LOWER LEVEL

1 entry 2 bar 3 sushi bar 4 dining

UPPER LEVEL

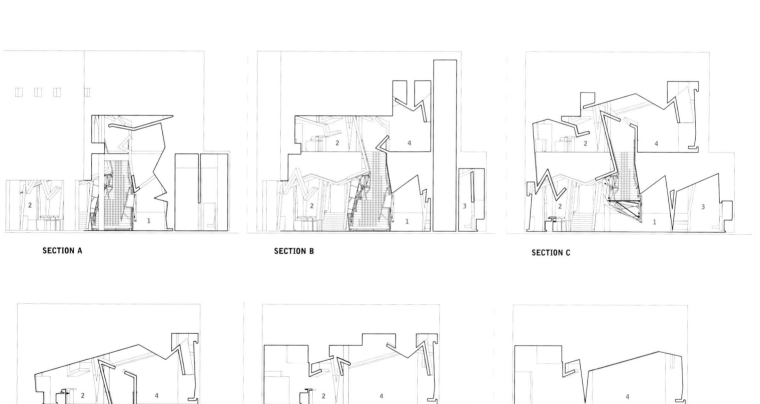

SECTION A

SECTION B

SECTION C

SECTION D

SECTION E

SECTION F

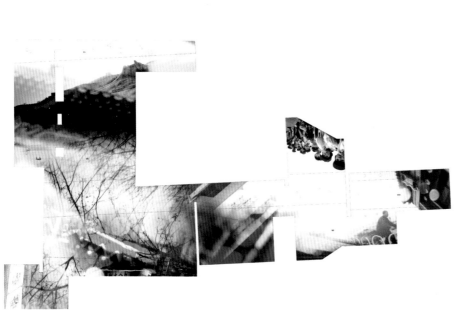

WALL ONE UNFOLDED

WALL TWO UNFOLDED

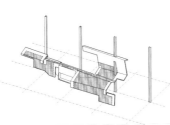
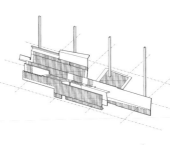
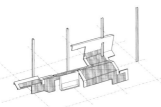
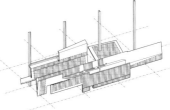
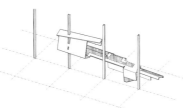
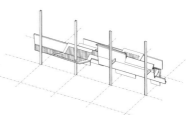
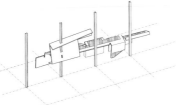
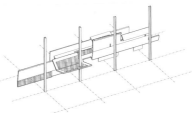

WALL THREE UNFOLDED

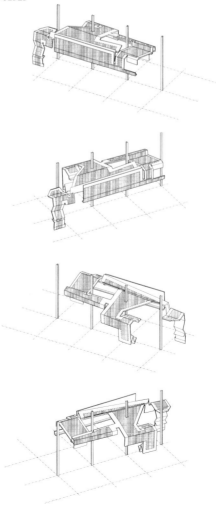

TSUNAMI

DATE: 1998-1999 LOCATION: Las Vegas, Nevada STATUS: Built SITE AREA: 10,000 sf/929 m² PROJECT SIZE: 6,000 sf/557 m² PROGRAM: 326-seat restaurant located in the Venetian Hotel and Casino.

SILENT COLLISIONS / NAI EXHIBIT

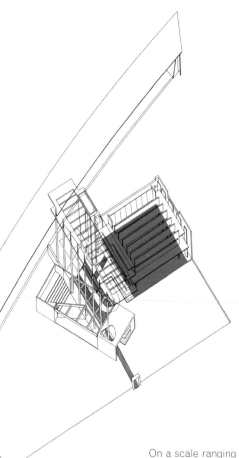

On a scale ranging from biological time to accelerated media time, architecture tends to operate at the slower end: our experience of the built form changes with light, temperature, and climate over the course of the day, while the physicality of a building itself changes over the course of seasons and years. Reflecting architecture's diurnal transformation, the exhibit structure moved at a nearly imperceptible rate, completing one full cycle in the span of one hour. The dynamic folds of the structure, wrapped in luminous fabric, were suspended within the volume of the static, permanent gallery, slowly extending and contracting, from horizontal to vertical, open to closed, public to private. The enclosure of the exhibition thus

transformed and evolved over the course of a visit: it became an abstract timepiece. A lone, stationary chair—a symbol of the necessity of sustained observation—beckoned the viewer to stop in order to perceive and contemplate the protracted movement.

At the lower level of the museum, a catacomb-like structure was erected to display two decades of architectural drawings and models. The two layers—one in a constant state of transformation and the other concrete and tectonic—interconnected to complete the exhibit, which was both a retrospective of our work and itself a transformation of space at a one-to-one scale.

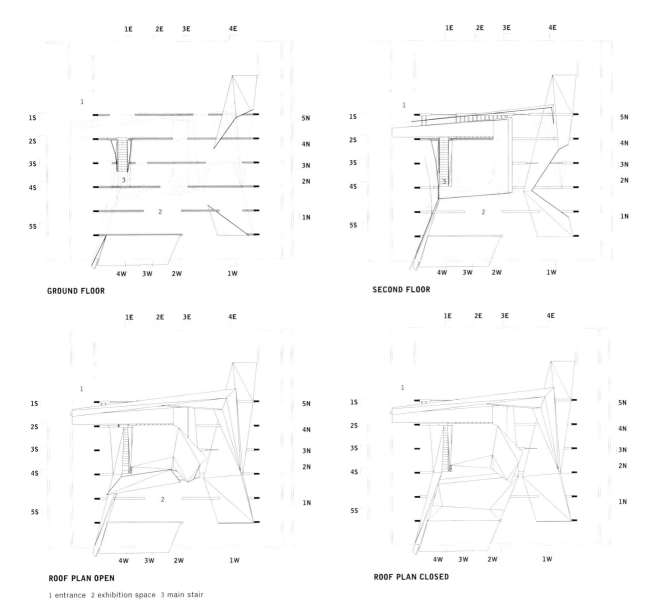

GROUND FLOOR

SECOND FLOOR

ROOF PLAN OPEN

ROOF PLAN CLOSED

1 entrance 2 exhibition space 3 main stair

One of our central concerns has been to develop strategies through which architecture can connect with the urban environment without dampening the richness of human experience. The exhibition construction enacted the processes of the modern city—the play of transitory forces within built space. The visitor entered into a *process* through which the body's relationship to space and time could be subtly and perceptually modulated. The human body and the architectural space engaged in a uniquely urban dialogue of chance encounters, perceptual gaps, fragmentation, unexpected collisions, and juxtapositions, unlikely to be experienced the same way twice.

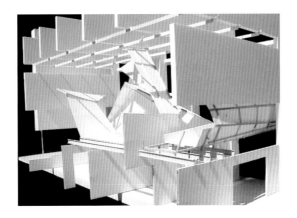

SILENT COLLISIONS / NAI EXHIBIT

DATE: **1999** LOCATION: **Rotterdam, Netherlands** STATUS: **Built** SITE: **Netherlands Institute of Architecture** PROJECT SIZE: **6,000 sf/557 m²** PROGRAM: **Exhibition design.**

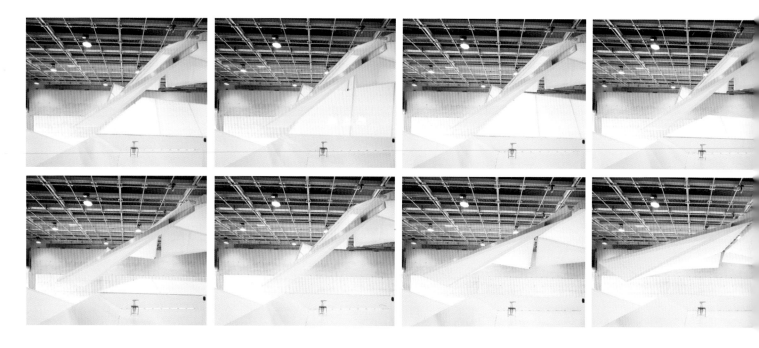

PHOTOGRAPHED AT FOUR-MINUTE INTERVALS

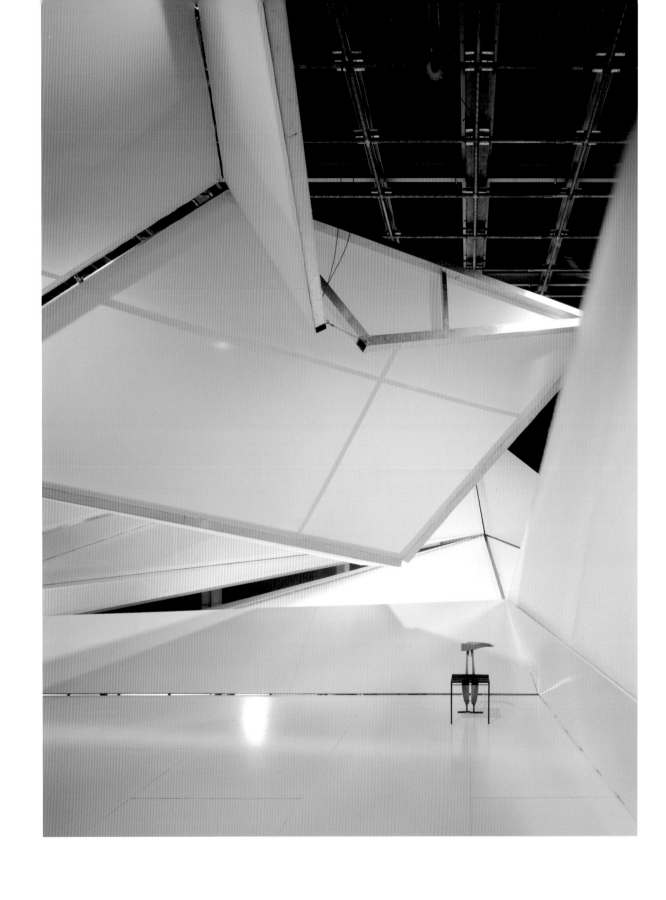

AZALEA SPRINGS WINERY

AZALEA SPRINGS WINERY

DATE: 1999 LOCATION: Napa Valley, California STATUS: Unbuilt SITE AREA: 16.4 acres/6.64 ha, vineyard 5.7 acres/2.31 ha BUILDING AREA: Total (including exterior workspaces): 31,208 sf/2,899m² ENCLOSED PROGRAM: Winery and tasting room: 8,591 sf/798 m² Barrel storage caves: 3,016 sf/280 m² PROGRAM: Winery and gallery.

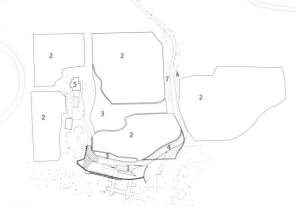

SITE PLAN

1 new winery and tasting room 2 existing vineyard to remain 3 new vineyard to be added 4 existing vineyard to be removed 5 existing house 6 staff parking 7 visitor parking 8 crusher pad 9 fermentation tanks 10 main entry 11 office 12 storage/office 13 storage 14 barrel storage caves 15 loading zone/bottling area 16 gallery/tasting room 17 outdoor viewing balcony 18 kitchen 19 outdoor patio

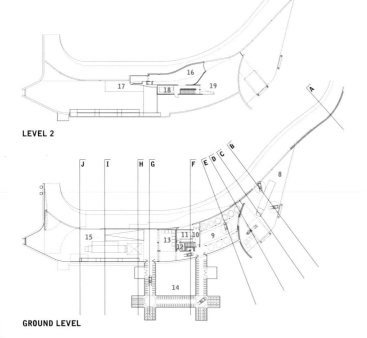

LEVEL 2

GROUND LEVEL

COR-TEN STEEL ENCLOSURE

FRONT ELEVATION

Azalea Springs Winery takes cues from the art of winemaking and inspiration from the landscape to develop a structure whose form and materials meld with the natural topography of the vineyard.

By embedding the winery in the hillside and integrating the grape delivery roadway into the roof of the building, maximum advantage is taken of the sloping site to facilitate the gravity feed method. This method, which gently moves wine from vine to crusher to fermentation tank to bottle, avoids the use of disruptive mechanical pumps and ensures the highest quality wine. The rear placement and integration of building and road reduces the incidence of aural and visual contamination from truck and car traffic while also allowing for unobstructed views to the fields of grapes. The linear continuity of movement across the landscape, from highway to winery to residence, is a literal expression of the simple, linear fluidity of the vinification process.

Cor-Ten, with its physical sensitivity to its climatic environment, is used as cladding material on the winery's facade in reference to the way in which a wine's qualities are shaped by its terroir—the elusive effect of the regional environment on the wine. The monochromatic application of this material serves as a transitional element between the low grape vines in the field and the tall firs on the hill behind the building.

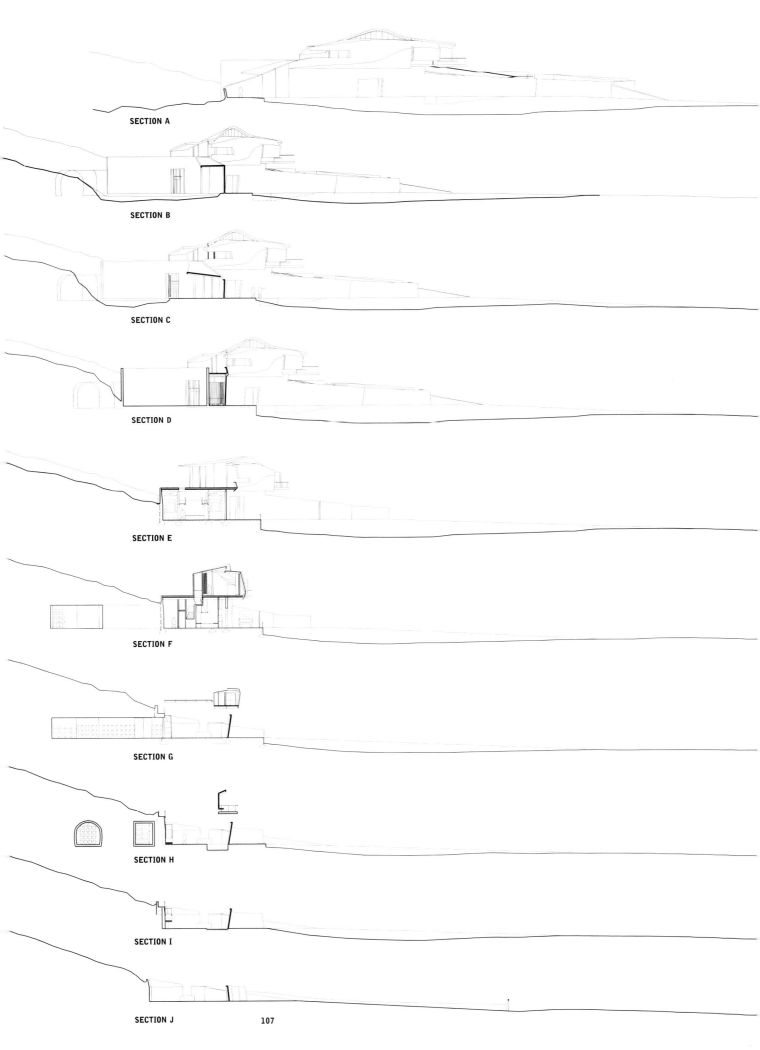

SECTION A

SECTION B

SECTION C

SECTION D

SECTION E

SECTION F

SECTION G

SECTION H

SECTION I

SECTION J

NEW CITY PARK

SITE PLAN

New City Park's multilayered surface moves and folds, integrating a high density of public and private commercial, recreational, cultural, educational, and community-oriented programs. The proposal examines a strategy for making a public urban space that relates to the complexities, diversity, indeterminacy, and ambiguities of contemporary experience.

The park functions as an organizational strategy for a polyvalent metropolis. The scheme is built around lines of connection and displacement; it organizes the program topologically, in three dimensions—in contrast to the city's typical planimetric organization. Superimposition, augmentation, and layering increase the utility of the site without sacrific-

ing open space. Advancing ideas that initiated in our Paris Utopie (1989) and Vienna Expo (1995) projects, the park redirects many of the programmatic functions to the lower strata, a series of ground planes, or shifting datums.

At over eighty acres, the armature of public open space connects Manhattan's interior with the river; it runs from Penn Station over the rail yards and down toward the Hudson River, where it terminates in a floating beach platform. In the areas flanking the park, zoning envelopes and restrictions, points of connection, and border conditions set design parameters for additional private office, commercial, and residential structures.

The diversion of Midtown's westward development across the project site protects the low-rise residential community of Clinton, currently in the path of development, and instead locates new density adjacent to the most intense multimodal transportation system in the region. The transportation plan maximizes the utility of the existing infrastructure, and makes strategic additions to the network: a new street-based light rail loop and automated People Mover connect with Penn Station trains, subways and buses, and the ferry.

SIMULATION DEVELOPMENT SCENARIO

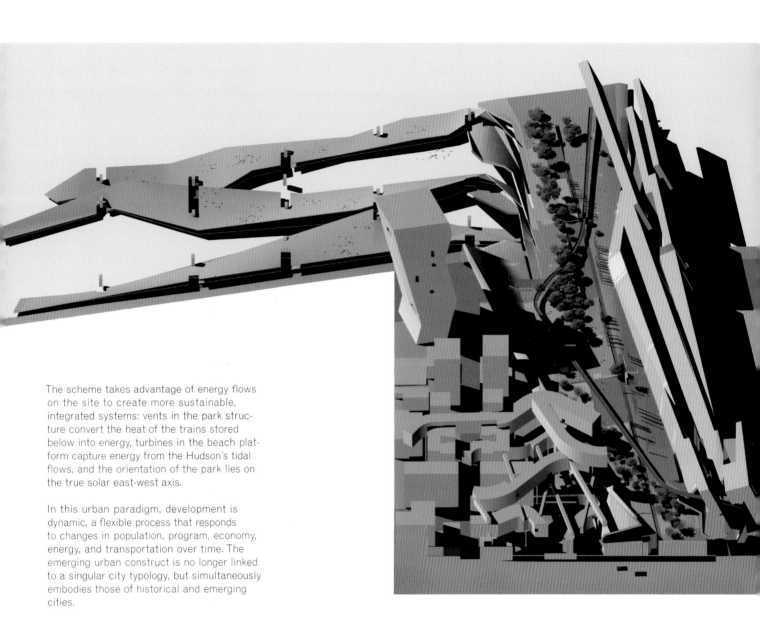

The scheme takes advantage of energy flows on the site to create more sustainable, integrated systems: vents in the park structure convert the heat of the trains stored below into energy, turbines in the beach platform capture energy from the Hudson's tidal flows, and the orientation of the park lies on the true solar east-west axis.

In this urban paradigm, development is dynamic, a flexible process that responds to changes in population, program, economy, energy, and transportation over time. The emerging urban construct is no longer linked to a singular city typology, but simultaneously embodies those of historical and emerging cities.

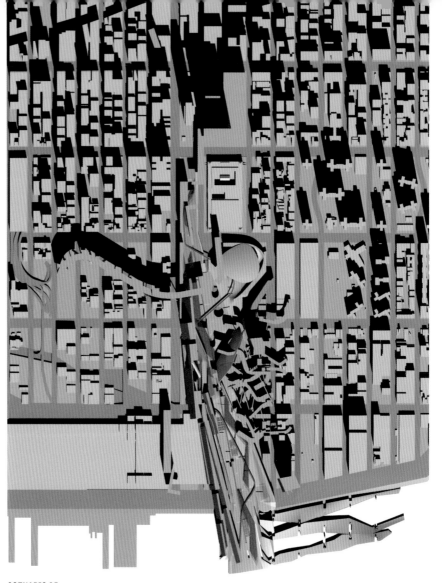

SCENARIO 15

SCENARIO 2

SECTIONAL MODELS OF PARK

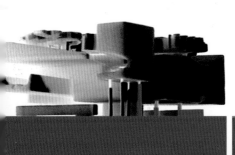

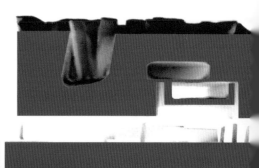

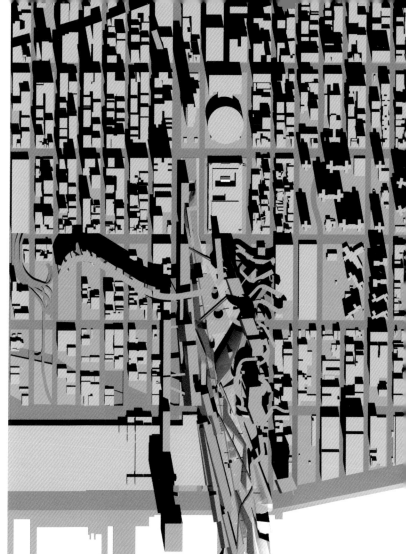

SCENARIO 33

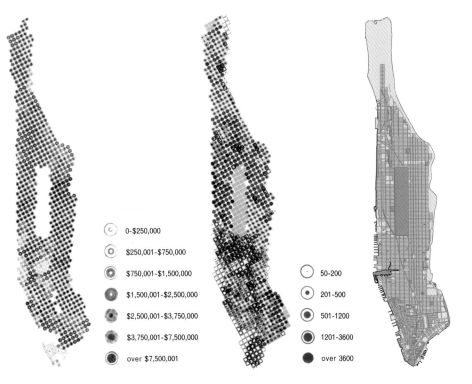

PERSONAL INCOME

- 0-$250,000
- $250,001-$750,000
- $750,001-$1,500,000
- $1,500,001-$2,500,000
- $2,500,001-$3,750,000
- $3,750,001-$7,500,000
- over $7,500,001

POPULATION DENSITY

- 50-200
- 201-500
- 501-1200
- 1201-3600
- over 3600

EXISTING PUBLIC PARKS IN MANHATTAN

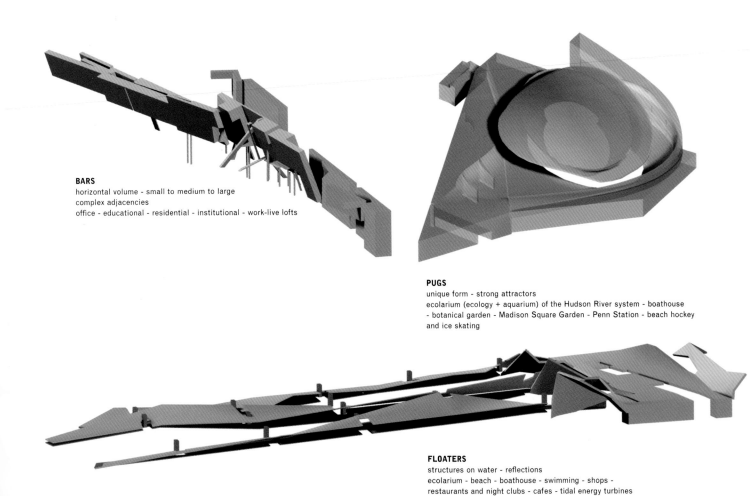

BARS
horizontal volume - small to medium to large
complex adjacencies
office - educational - residential - institutional - work-live lofts

PUGS
unique form - strong attractors
ecolarium (ecology + aquarium) of the Hudson River system - boathouse
- botanical garden - Madison Square Garden - Penn Station - beach hockey
and ice skating

FLOATERS
structures on water - reflections
ecolarium - beach - boathouse - swimming - shops -
restaurants and night clubs - cafes - tidal energy turbines

114

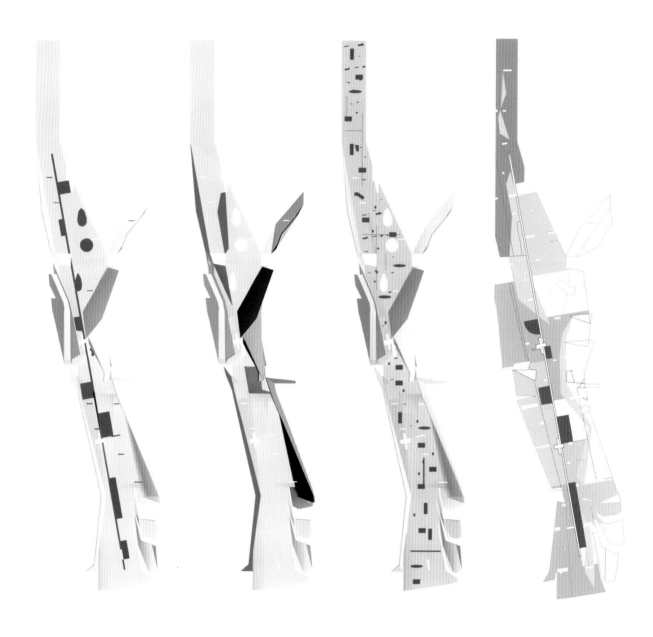

NEW CITY PARK

DATE: 1999 LOCATION: New York, New York STATUS: Competition SITE AREA: 80 acres/32 ha PROGRAM: 3.5 million sf/325,162 m² planning/urban design proposal for Manhattan's West Side.

GRAZ KUNSTHAUS

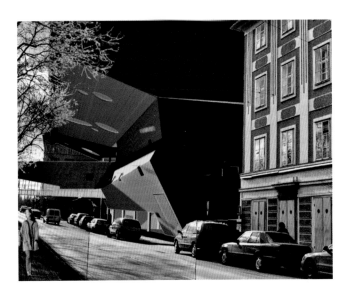

A metaphorical barge floating in the sky, this urban intervention connects the public to the art institution. Sight lines and project vectors along the banks of the Mur River set up axial relationships to historic places, frame the extended context for pedestrians on the approaching footbridges, and link the Kunsthaus to the city of Graz.

The scheme separates the public program into three primary components: a central circulation spine; a series of event, project, and meeting spaces; and a vast, partially cantilevered Kunsthalle—the largest single exhibition space in Graz. Since the entire site area was only two-thirds the footprint required for the Kunsthalle exhibit room, any solution would have to cantilever part of the space over the street. The Kunsthalle thus floats over an adjacent building's airspace and the sidewalk, and

brackets a civic plaza. The punctured underside of this two-thousand-square-meter open-plan volume gives the visitor the sense of being suspended in space, experiencing the building's lift over the street. Architecture is essentially removed from the principal curatorial space, providing a neutral palette and form, and a flexible plan for various lighting and load configurations.

Beyond its function as a service appendage to the galleries, the armature of circulation operates as a public event space. The dynamic circulation passages mediate between the controlled gallery space and the exterior urban spaces and inflect the adjacent edges of lower ancillary galleries.

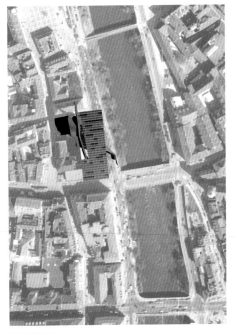

SITE PLAN

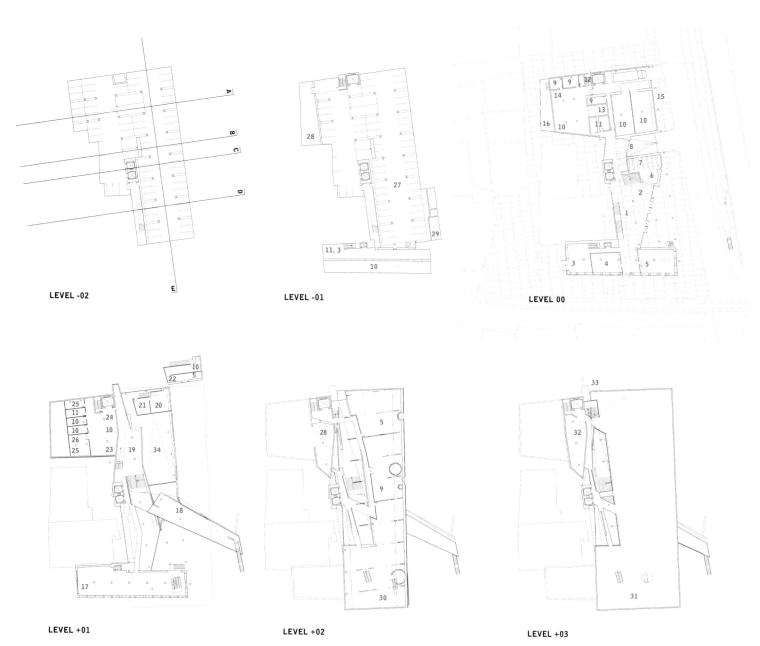

LEVEL -02

LEVEL -01

LEVEL 00

LEVEL +01

LEVEL +02

LEVEL +03

1 lobby 2 information zone 3 coffee shop 4 museum shop and office 5 project meeting space 6 ticket sales 7 coat room/cloak room 8 meeting area 9 office 10 storage
11 bathrooms 12 security 13 garbage room 14 packaging/storage 15 loading dock 16 commercial use 17 media center 18 restaurant 19 lobby for event space 20 seminar room
21 catering 22 translator booth 23 shop/restoration 24 shop 25 lounge 26 janitor 27 underground parking 28 mechanical 29 electrical power substation 30 forum for photography
31 exhibition hall 32 workspace 33 crane 34 event space

GRAZ KUNSTHAUS

DATE: 1999-2000 LOCATION: Graz, Austria STATUS: Competition SITE AREA: 58,029 sf/5391 m² BUILDING AREA: 87,813 sf/8158 m² PROGRAM: A multiuse facility to contain office, commercial, and café/restaurant spaces, as well as an exhibition space and studio gallery, an event area, and project space to encourage collaboration between educators, the museum, artists, and teenagers.

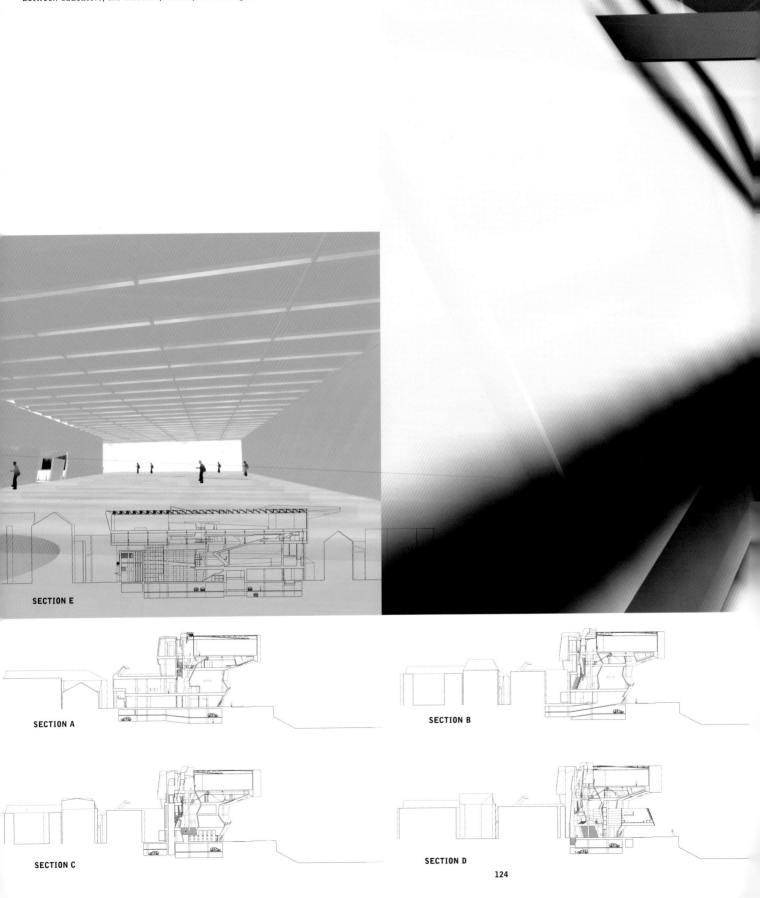

SECTION E

SECTION A

SECTION B

SECTION C

SECTION D

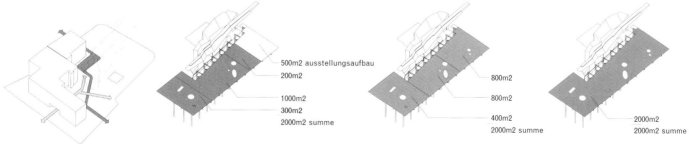

| 500m2 ausstellungsaufbau |
| 200m2 |

1000m2
300m2
2000m2 summe

800m2

800m2

400m2
2000m2 summe

2000m2
2000m2 summe

VISITOR CIRCULATION   **SEQUENCE DIAGRAM**   **VARIATION FOR SMALL**   **VARIATION FOR**
                                                               AND MEDIUM EXHIBITION   **LARGE EXHIBITION**

UNIVERSITY OF CINCINNATI
STUDENT RECREATION CENTER

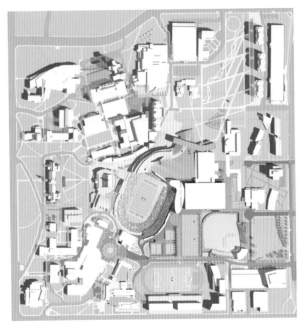

CAMPUS PLAN

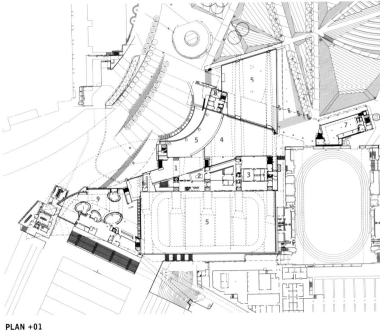

PLAN +01

Weaving as a means of establishing flow to resolve the site's disparate staccato of existing buildings and edges informs the principal strategy for the University of Cincinnati master plan. We were interested in developing a series of connective events to engage peripheral flows on the campus in order to generate or augment an urban density and to encourage, rather than dampen, the polyvalent nature of social experience on campus.

Forms reflect found conditions and contribute to a strategy for cohesively incorporating numerous existing structures with the additional 350,000 square feet of recreational facilities, classrooms, housing, campus store,

dining hall, and varsity aquatic center that are included in this new facility. Conceiving the main circulation corridor as a series of weaving strands, we placed "Main Street," the primary campus thoroughfare, in such a way as to concentrate and direct the movement of students. The contoured element of the new housing building funnels students onto the campus green, feeding the force-field of movement through a "pinch point." Secondary pedestrian paths penetrate, intertwine, and wrap buildings, further relaxing a reading of discrete objects on a homogenous field, and substituting a thick mat of cohesive trajectories in its place.

Augmented ground has been an evolving interest in our studio; here a thickened ground mat becomes a means of adding program to site. The new recreational facilities are tucked beneath a curvilinear plane of landscape—a field of undulating mats, punctured with light openings. The housing bar, lifted on *pilotis*, overlooks this "roofscape," which smoothes the transition between the sunken football field and the higher grade of north campus. The scheme resolves many of the site's awkward idiosyncrasies, and the new cohesive texture embraces the complexities of campus life.

SECTION NORTH-SOUTH THROUGH CLASSROOMS AND BLEACHERS

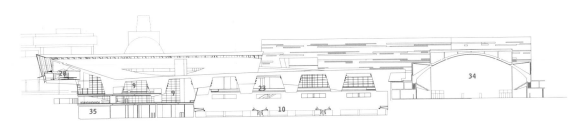

SECTION WEST-EAST THROUGH GYMNASIUM

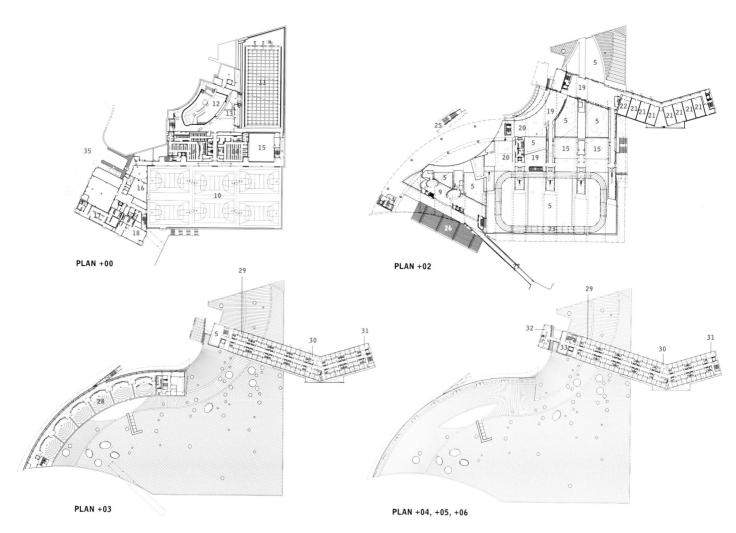

PLAN +00

PLAN +02

PLAN +03

PLAN +04, +05, +06

1 recreation center entrance lobby and public passage 2 recreation center entrance control 3 recreation center administration 4 exterior plaza 5 open to below 6 juice bar 7 convenience store 8 housing lobby and administration (on 2 levels) 9 "Marche" (food services) 10 gymnasium 11 50m recreation pool 12 leisure pool and spa 13 wet classroom 14 changing rooms and showers 15 multipurpose room 16 gymnasium storage 17 visiting football team area 18 home football team area and field storage 19 fitness area 20 weight training area 21 racquetball court 22 convertible squash court 23 suspended running track 24 entry lobby to classrooms 25 exterior stair up to classrooms 26 new stadium bleachers 27 new bridge to basketball arena 28 large classroom (6 total: 75 seats) 29 typical student housing unit (2 single bedrooms per unit) 30 residential assistant unit (1 on each floor) 31 study lounge 32 resident director's unit (1 of 2) 33 common room 34 armory field house (existing) 35 loading dock

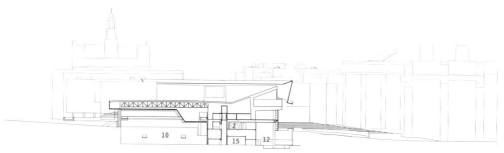

SECTION NORTH-SOUTH THROUGH LEISURE POOL

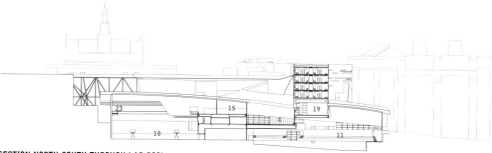

SECTION NORTH-SOUTH THROUGH LAP POOL

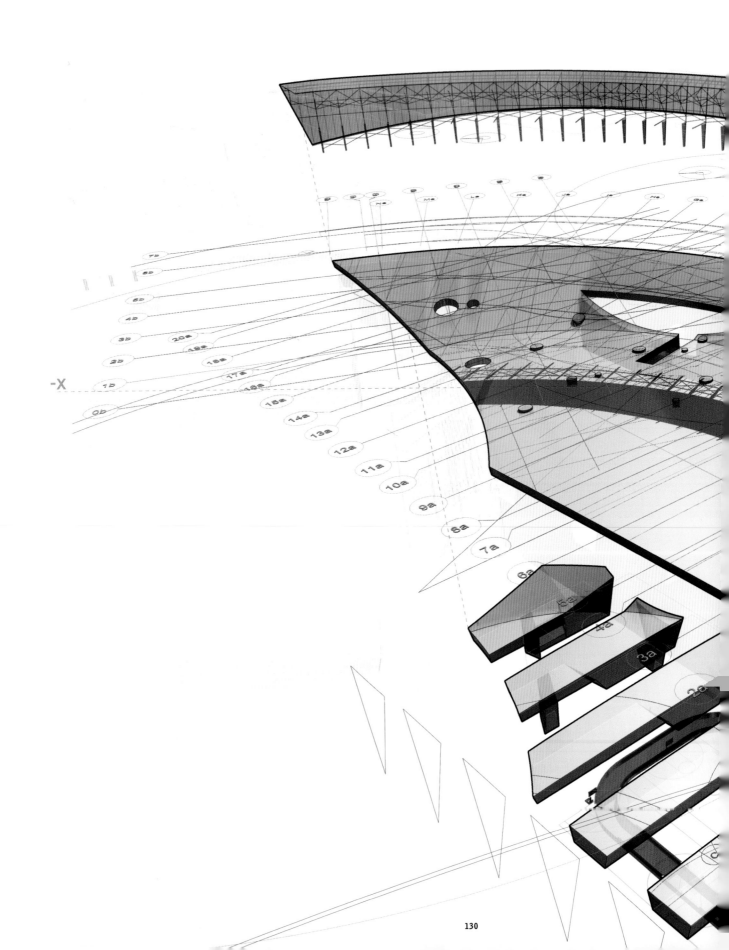

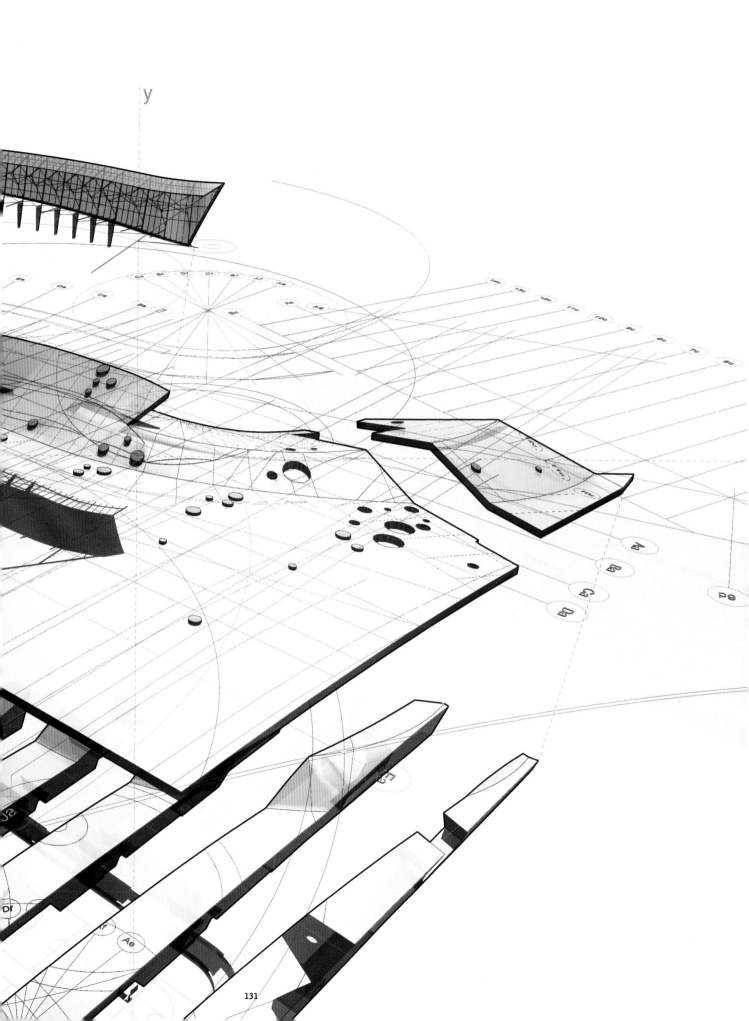

y

131

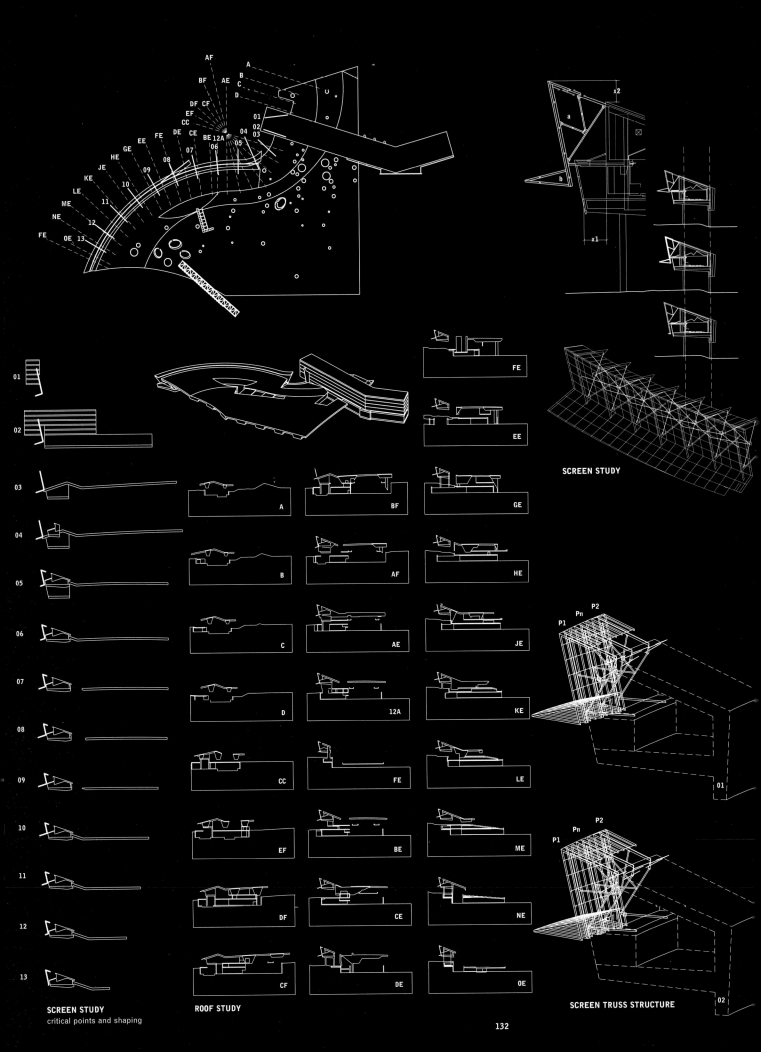

SCREEN STUDY

ROOF STUDY

SCREEN STUDY

SCREEN TRUSS STRUCTURE

SCREEN STUDY
critical points and shaping

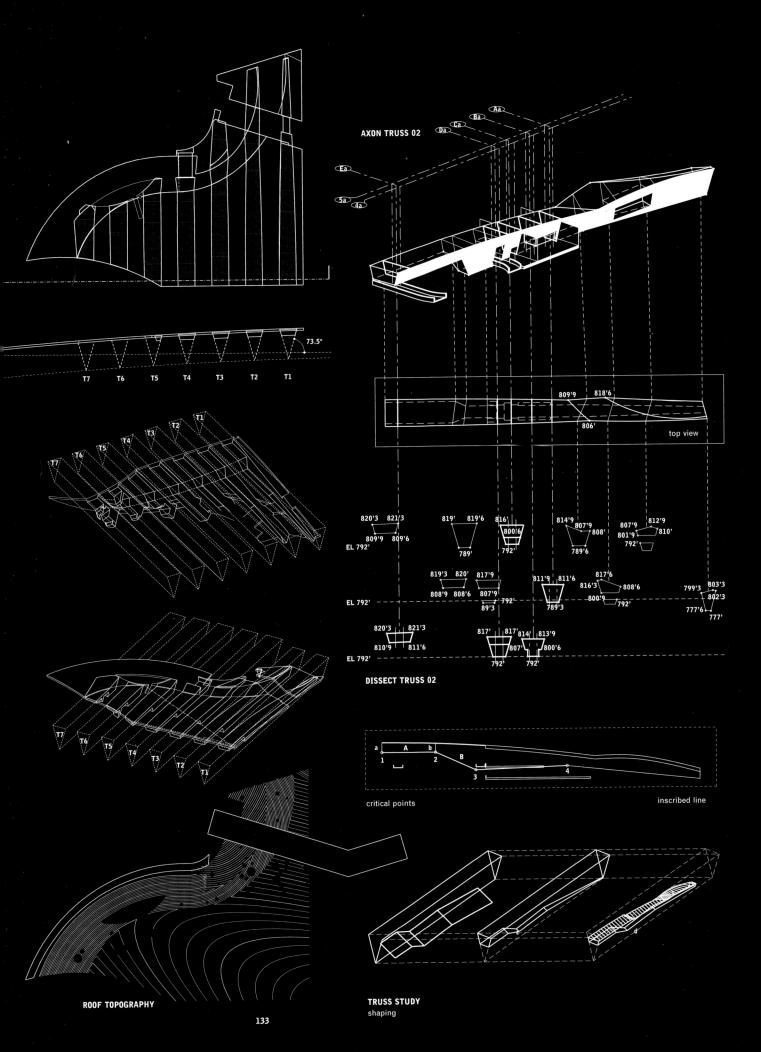

AXON TRUSS 02

73.5°

T7   T6   T5   T4   T3   T2   T1

T7 T6 T5 T4 T3 T2 T1

T7 T6 T5 T4 T3 T2 T1

809'9   818'6
806'
top view

820'3 821'3   819' 819'6   816'   814'9 807'9   807'9 812'9
809'9 809'6   800'6   808'   801'9 810'
EL 792'   789'   792'   789'6   792'
                                                         811'9 811'6
819'3 820' 817'9   817'6   799'3 803'3
808'9 808'6 807'9   816'3 808'6   802'3
EL 792'   792'   800'9 792'   777'6
                 89'3   789'3   777'

820'3   821'3   817' 817'814' 813'9
810'9   811'6   807' 800'6
EL 792'   792' 792'

DISSECT TRUSS 02

a   A   b
1   2   B
                    3   4

critical points   inscribed line

ROOF TOPOGRAPHY

TRUSS STUDY
shaping

134

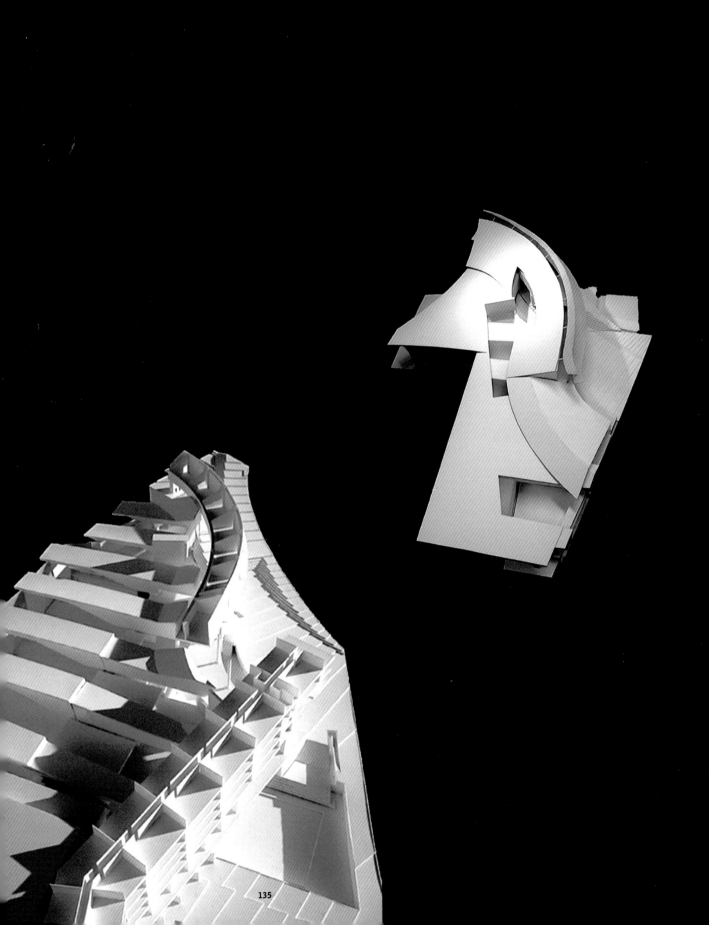

UNIVERSITY OF CINCINNATI STUDENT RECREATION CENTER

DATE: 1999-2005 LOCATION: Cincinnati, Ohio STATUS: In Process SITE AREA: 110,000 sf/10,219 m² PROJECT SIZE: 350,000 sf/32,516 m² PROGRAM: Multiuse recreational complex, including a food court, classrooms, student housing, convenience store, and varsity gymnasium facilities.

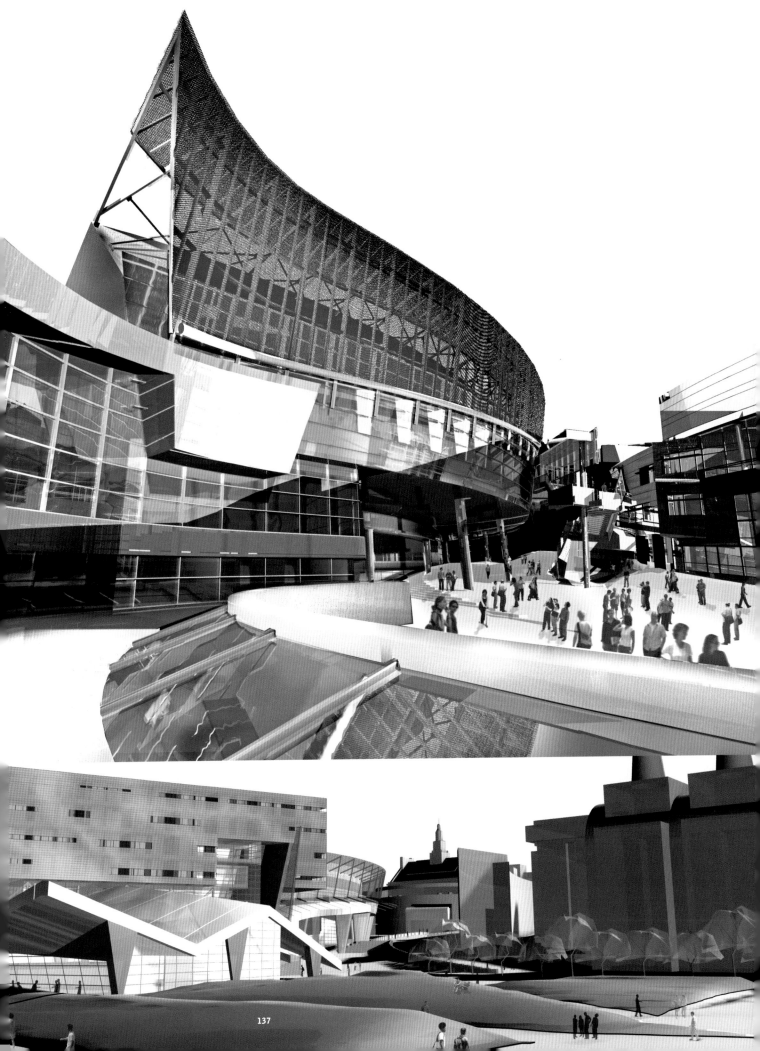

WAYNE L. MORSE UNITED STATES COURTHOUSE

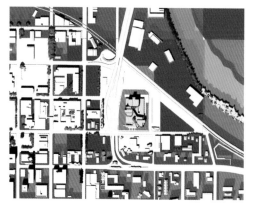

SITE PLAN

American courthouse architecture has moved away from the use of symbolic iconography to communicate the importance of the judicial process. Courtrooms are now routinely located in generic office towers—effectively repositioning the proceedings as *business as usual*—thus obscuring the gravity of the judicial process by excising the symbolism inherent in the traditional courtroom. The Eugene Federal Courthouse seeks to challenge this trend by expressing the courtrooms as discrete object buildings —a reference back to an earlier single-room courthouse model. The building is composed of two distinct strata, the honorific and the quotidian. The iconic elements are the courtrooms themselves, located in articulated pavilions that float above an orthogonal two-story plinth that houses office and administrative spaces. Their forms refer to the fluid nature of the American judicial system, a system that is designed to remain flexible by being continuously challenged and reinterpreted by the proceedings of the courts. The formal and structural organization of the plinth is mimetic of the Cartesian layout of the city, and thus represents the more static nature of Eugene's urban fabric upon which the organic and independent shapes of the courthouses rest.

Ribbons of steel envelop the pavilions, articulating the movement sequence among the three courtroom clusters. The waiting areas and public corridors that connect the courtroom pavilions provide views to the surrounding mountains and a perception of light and the passage of time. The entry occurs at the moment where the two systems collide, in a large open atrium, framed by the base's strict grid and sculpted by the fluid forms above.

The shapes of the pavilions emanate from the autonomous courtrooms themselves, whose soft forms are constricted to direct the focus to the witness stand and judge's bench. The jury boxes are partially recessed, isolated in an articulated space that refers to the juror's role as both observer and participant. In the courtrooms, natural light is admitted through two large, thick-walled apertures above the judge's bench. The effect is that of a freestanding building, a unique and dignified place in which the court's raison d'être is architecturally legible.

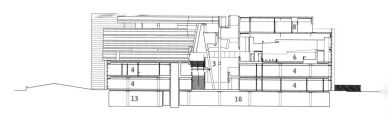

SECTION THROUGH ATRIUM AND COURTROOM LOOKING NORTH

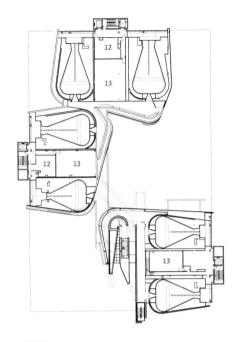

LEVEL 4

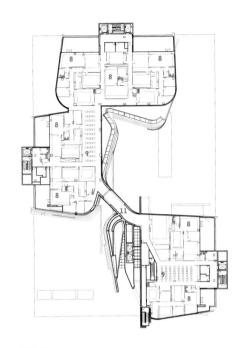

LEVEL 5

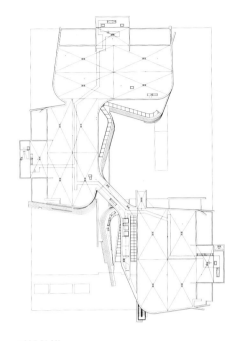

ROOF PLAN

LEVEL 1

LEVEL 2

LEVEL 3

1 loading dock 2 lobby 3 atrium 4 offices 5 jury assembly room 6 courtroom 7 ancillary facilities
8 judges chambers 9 library 10 parking 11 judges chambers bridge 12 jury suites 13 mechanical

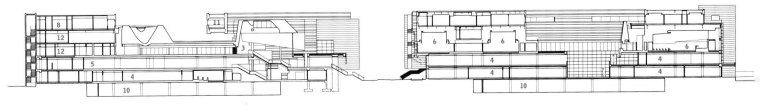

SECTION THROUGH ATRIUM AND PUBLIC CIRCULATION LOOKING EAST

SECTION THROUGH COURTROOMS LOOKING WEST

EARLY CONCEPT MODELS

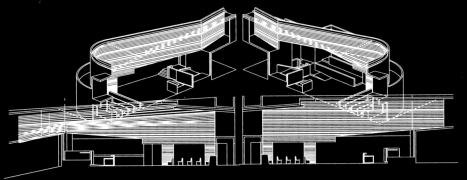

COURTROOM SPLIT AXONOMETRIC AND ELEVATION
early study

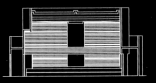

courtroom section and public seating

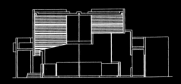

courtroom section through well

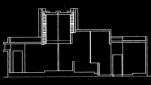

courtroom section through judge's bench

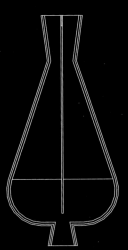

upper courtroom
reflected ceiling plan

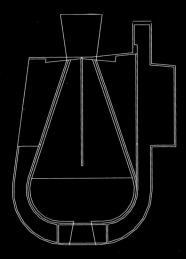

lower courtroom
reflected ceiling plan

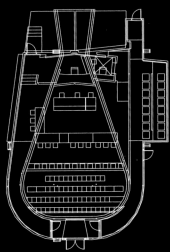

courtroom plan

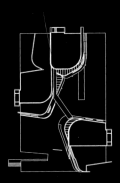

earlier scheme roof plan

figure ground diagram
of earlier scheme

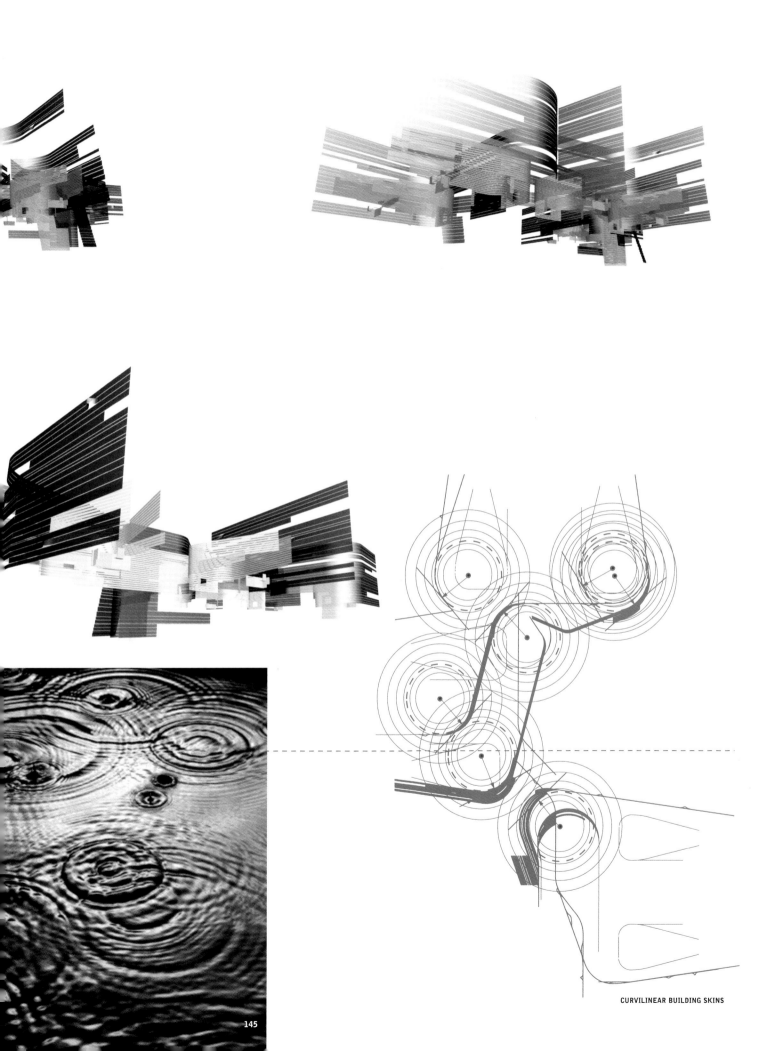

CURVILINEAR BUILDING SKINS

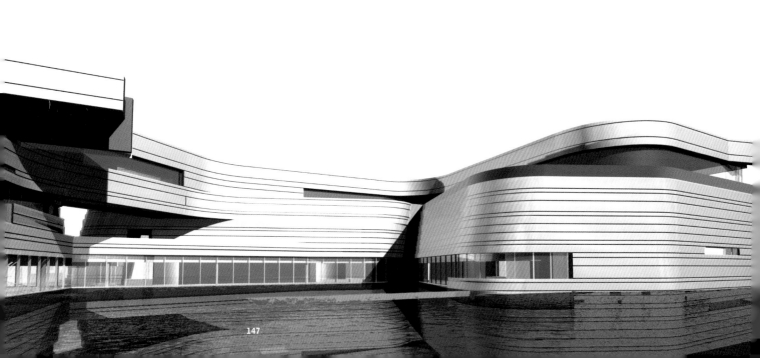

WAYNE L. MORSE UNITED STATES COURTHOUSE

DATE: **1999-2006** LOCATION: **Eugene, Oregon** STATUS: **In Process** SITE AREA: **5.17 acres/2.1 ha** PROJECT SIZE: **270,000 sf/25,084 m²** PROGRAM: **Six federal courtrooms with judges' chambers, support offices, lobby, jury assembly areas, and cafeteria.**

TIME CAPSULE

DATE: 2000 LOCATION: Central Park, New York City STATUS: Unbuilt SITE AREA: Central Park
PROJECT SIZE: N/A PROGRAM: Capsule competition, commissioned by the *New York Times*,
challenged designers to chronicle life in the late-twentieth century. The designers were
encouraged to consider two approaches. One was the pragmatic: capsules that could be
realized with available technology, on attainable sites and within a budget of $60,000.
The other was the fantastic: those that zoomed off the charts of imagination and cost.

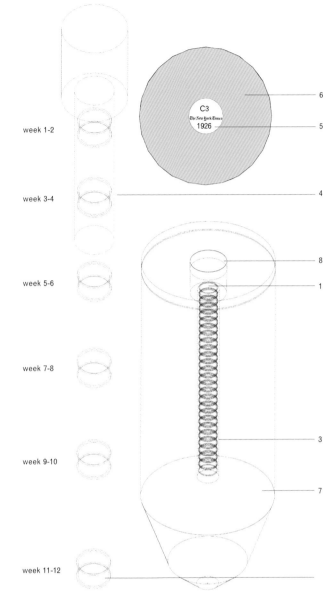

week 1-2

week 3-4

week 5-6

week 7-8

week 9-10

week 11-12

6

5

4

8

1

3

7

C3
The New York Times
1926

y
x
w
v
u
t
s
r
q
p
o
n
m
l
k
j
i
h
g
f
e
d
c
b
a

1 2 3 4

CENTRAL PARK

CAPSULE DIAGRAM

For the turn of the third millennium, on New Year's Eve 2000, one hundred aircraft spotlights point toward the sky, forming a grid across Central Park and illuminating the dense blanket of firework smoke drifting above Manhattan. The next day, and into the next century, the grid remains: concrete capsules each encase a vacuum-sealed cylinder containing one year of the complete *New York Times* on microfilm, with a magnifying glass in each dated cap. In total, one hundred years of newspaper are buried in the park, encapsulating every facet of our culture in a minefield of information. A map of the time capsule grid is printed on 9.5 billion millennium-issue Coca-Cola cans— its distribution worldwide.

In the near future, the markers take on significance for New York's collective memory. The capsules, with the newspapers' respective years cast in brass on the lids, become monuments to the events of those years. Groups gather around the year stones, remembering Jimi Hendrix or the Oklahoma bombing, *Star Wars*, JFK, or a birthday.

Over time, the markers become buried and their memory lost. Long into the next millennium, in some garbage heap—the archeological sites of the world—someone finds an ancient Coca-Cola can with a locator map of these long-forgotten markers. Our distant descendants will locate and excavate the capsules; they will open them to find news suspended in time from a world they don't remember and could never imagine.

DIAMOND RANCH HIGH SCHOOL

SITE PLAN

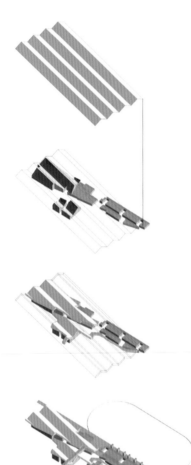

Diamond Ranch High School engages architecture in the act of education; it speaks to students experientially through a physically kinetic architectural language that makes no references to traditional typology, but rather looks elsewhere to encourage student inquiry and provoke curiosity. The opportunity existed, by virtue of the steeply sloped site, to explore the hybrid territory of an augmented landscape wherein building and site would be perceptually interchangeable. The jagged and inherently unstable forms of the Los Angeles foothills inform the language of the buildings as the scheme takes its organizational cues from the natural topography.

Two rows of fragmented, interlocking forms are set tightly on either side of a long central "canyon," or street, which cuts through the face of the hillside as might a geologic fault line. The street provides the primary opportunity for students to interact haphazardly or by plan with one another, with teachers, and with administrators as they move about the campus. Seeking to create a counterpoint to Diamond Ranch's suburban context, the

sense of an urban experience is intensified via the compression of the street. A monumental stairway that functions doubly as an outdoor amphitheater is embedded in the hillside, leading from the school's main academic areas to the roof terrace and football field above.

The site plan defines three distinct "schools within a school"—clusters of semi-independent units that each integrate a full curriculum segregated by grade level to foster team teaching in a more intimate educational setting. Landscaped outdoor teaching areas act as courtyard buffers between buildings and punctuate the classroom units with views of mountains and sky. The intention of the whole is to challenge the message sent by a society that routinely communicates its disregard for the young by educating them in cheap institutional boxes surrounded by impenetrable chain-link fencing.

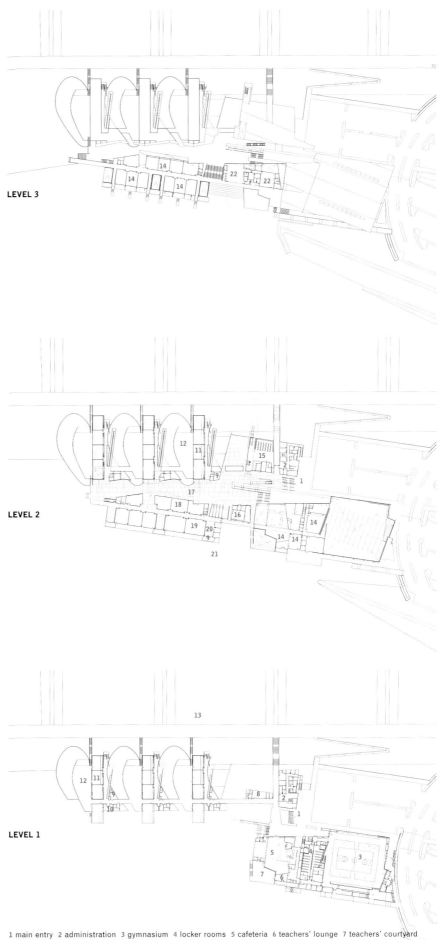

LEVEL 3

LEVEL 2

LEVEL 1

1 main entry 2 administration 3 gymnasium 4 locker rooms 5 cafeteria 6 teachers' lounge 7 teachers' courtyard
8 storage 9 teachers' workroom 10 restrooms 11 lower school classrooms 12 lower school courtyards 13 lower
playing fields 14 classrooms 15 library 16 school store 17 pedestrian street 18 labs 19 upper school classrooms
20 upper school courtyard 21 upper playing fields 22 visual/performing arts

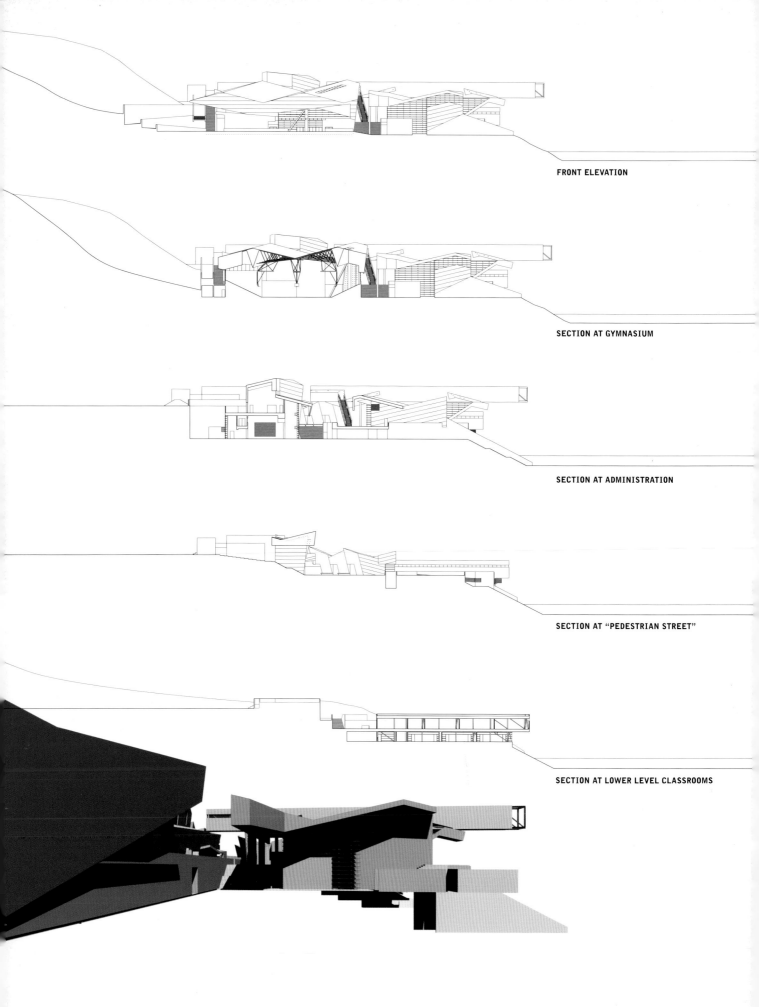

FRONT ELEVATION

SECTION AT GYMNASIUM

SECTION AT ADMINISTRATION

SECTION AT "PEDESTRIAN STREET"

SECTION AT LOWER LEVEL CLASSROOMS

DIAMOND RANCH HIGH SCHOOL

DATE: 1996-2000 LOCATION: Pomona, California STATUS: Built SITE AREA: 72 acres/29 ha PROJECT SIZE: 150,000 sf/13,935 m² PROGRAM: Public high school with 50 classrooms, a gymnasium, cafeteria, administration, and parking for 770 automobiles.

UNIVERSITY OF TORONTO
GRADUATE STUDENT HOUSING

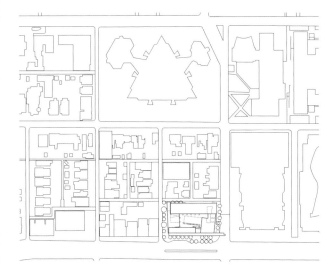

CONTEXT PLAN

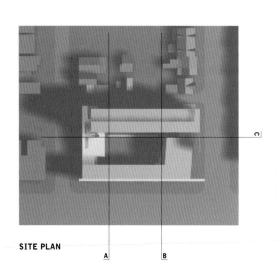

SITE PLAN

A long-standing interest in challenging the boundaries between public and private—between community and university—informs this graduate student housing project. Located on the edge of the University of Toronto's campus, bordering a bustling urban district, the building establishes a gateway to the campus and an iconic identity for the university.

The massing and exterior articulation responds to both contingent site characteristics and to intense programmatic needs. Organized around an open central courtyard, each of the building elements corresponds to the scale of its adjacencies. The two main components, a ten-story block on the east-ern edge of the site and a seven-story block along the western edge, wrap and engage one another. Skip-stop elevator configurations allow for a higher density within the building envelope than would a standard double-loaded corridor, while also providing additional space for student rooms that benefit from through-ventilation via windows that overlook both city and courtyard. At street level there are retail spaces that form an urban node to augment public activity and connect this campus entry point with the surrounding city.

Along the top floors of the western wing, a glazed light bar, visible for miles, projects beyond the building's edge to terminate at the halfway point across Harbord Street, forty-five feet above ground level. The final steel "O" of the glazed corridor's "UNIVERSITY OF TORONTO" sign dangles from the end, registering a shift from two dimensions to three and from ground to figure. The trajectory of this elevated, human-scaled cornice breaks through the boundary between private and public, defining a threshold that may stimulate further consideration of the university's civic role and of the boundaries between institution and city.

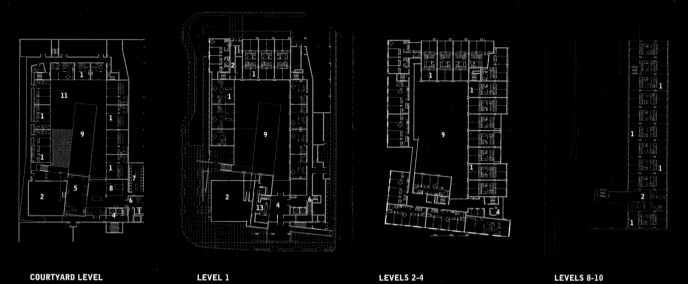

COURTYARD LEVEL   **LEVEL 1**   **LEVELS 2-4**   **LEVELS 8-10**

1 residential 2 retail 3 mechanical 4 lobby 5 common room 6 music room 7 laundry 8 open to above 9 courtyard 10 mailroom 11 reflecting pool

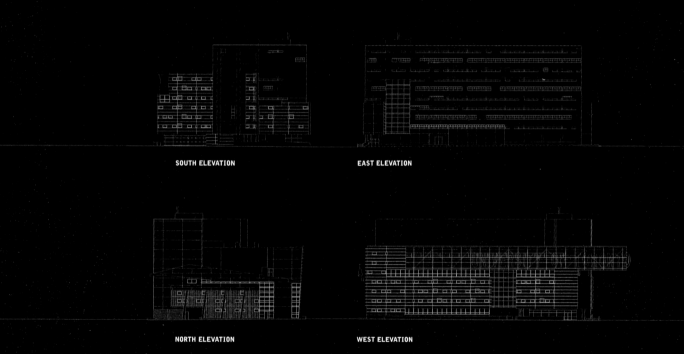

SOUTH ELEVATION   **EAST ELEVATION**

NORTH ELEVATION   **WEST ELEVATION**

SECTION A   **SECTION B**   **SECTION C**

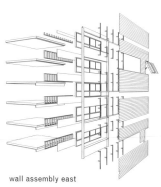

wall assembly east
CLADDING STUDY

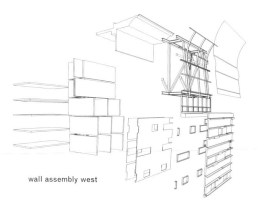

wall assembly west

UNIVERSITY OF TORONTO GRADUATE STUDENT HOUSING

DATE: 1997-2000 LOCATION: Toronto, Ontario, Canada STATUS: Built SITE AREA: 0.79 acres/.32 ha PROJECT SIZE: 230,000 sf/21,368 m² PROGRAM: 464 beds in a 121-unit dormitory facility, 153 parking spaces, and 3,200 sf/2,973 m² of commercial retail space.

SAN FRANCISCO FEDERAL OFFICE BUILDING

SAN FRANCISCO AERIAL VIEW

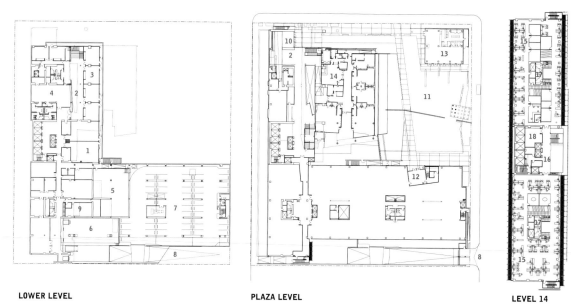

LOWER LEVEL   PLAZA LEVEL   LEVEL 14

1 auditorium 2 lobby 3 conference facility 4 fitness center 5 service 6 loading 7 parking 8 auto ramp access 9 mailroom 10 tower entry
11 plaza 12 annex entrance 13 cafe pavilion 14 daycare 15 office space 16 elevator lobby 17 restroom cores 18 conference room

*Without an active sidewalk life, without the
frequent, serendipitous interactions of many
people, "there is no public acquaintanceship,
no foundation of public trust, no cross connections with the necessary people—and no
practice or ease in applying the most ordinary
techniques of public life at lowly levels."*
Malcolm Gladwell on Jane Jacobs's *The Death and Life
of Great American Cities*

Broadly understood, the project has developed
around three primary objectives: the establishment of a benchmark for sustainable building design through the efficient use of natural
energy sources; the redefinition of the culture
of the workplace through office environments
that boost workers' health, productivity, and
creativity; and the creation of an urban landmark that engages with the community.

A slender eighteen-story tower punctuates
the skyline, and a public plaza and four-story
annex connect to the scale and fabric of
the city. The large, open plaza at the intersection of Mission and Seventh is a valuable
asset in the South-of-Market district, identi-
fied by the city as deficient in public space.

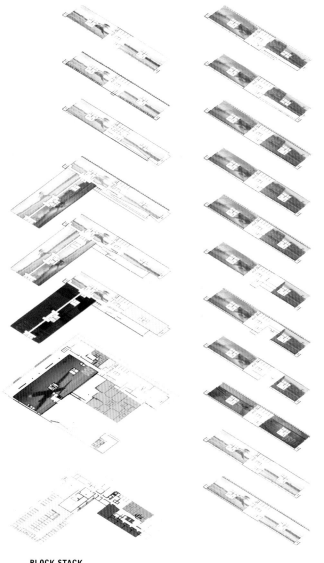

BLOCK STACK

The placement of the freestanding cafeteria pavilion and the public nature of the facilities housed within the tower's lower levels (including a conference center, fitness center, and day-care center for both local residents and employees) enliven the urban plaza with a steady stream of visitors.

The redefinition of circulation and vertical movement paths provides opportunities for chance encounters, a critical mass in circulation, and places for employees to gather across the typical confines of cubicles, departments, or floor plates. The democratic layout locates open work areas at the building perimeter and private offices and conference spaces at the central cores. As Gladwell's article points out, "one study after another has demonstrated [that] the best ideas in any workplace arise out of casual contact among different groups within the same company." Skip-stop elevators, sky gardens, tea salons, large open stairs, flexible floor plans, and the elimination of corner offices endow the tower with a Jacobsian "sidewalk life" of cross-sectional interactions.

Many of the same design decisions that create high-quality workspace also maximize energy efficiency. The Federal Building is the first office tower in the United States to forgo air conditioning in favor of natural ventilation. As a result of the tower's narrow profile and strategic integration of structural, mechanical, and electrical systems, the building provides natural ventilation to 70 percent of the work area in lieu of air conditioning, and affords natural light and operable windows to 90 percent of the workstations. A folded, perforated metal sunscreen shades the full-height glass window wall system, and a mutable skin of computer-controlled panels adjusts to daily and seasonal climate fluctuations. With an energy performance that surpasses the GSA's criteria by more than 50 percent, the project sets new standards for applications of passive climate control, while physically democratizing the workplace and enhancing employees' health, comfort, and sense of control over their environment.

SECTION THROUGH ELEVATOR LOBBY

SKIP STOP ELEVATOR

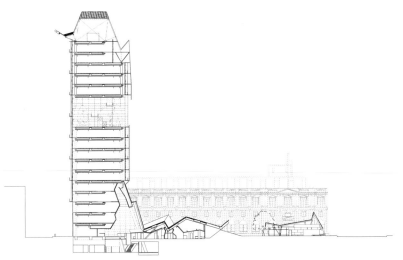

SECTION THROUGH SKY GARDEN

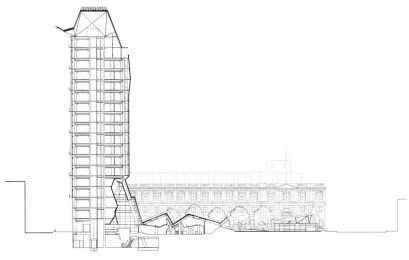

SECTION THROUGH MAIN LOBBY AND DAYCARE

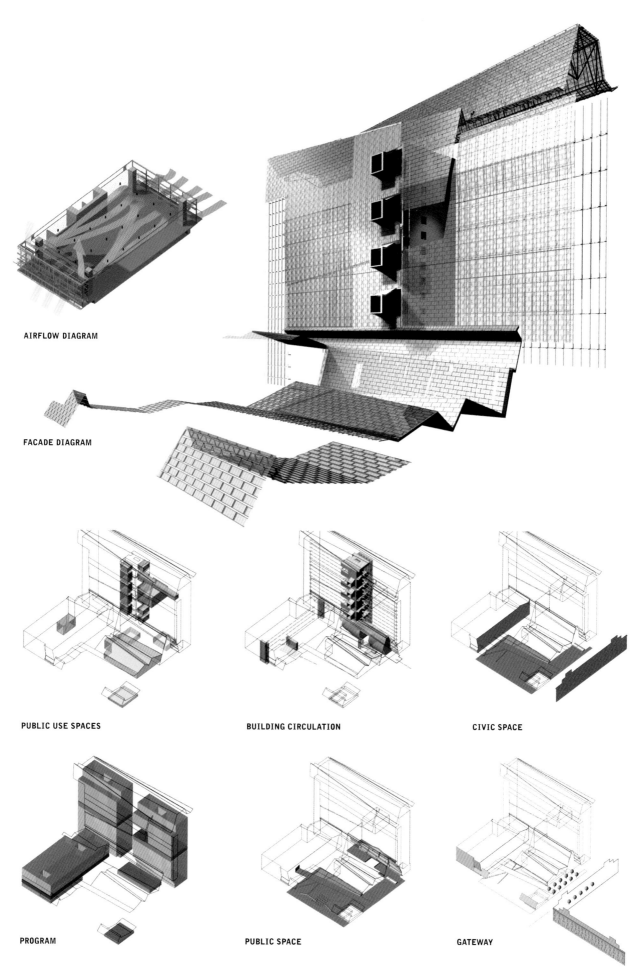

AIRFLOW DIAGRAM

FACADE DIAGRAM

PUBLIC USE SPACES

BUILDING CIRCULATION

CIVIC SPACE

PROGRAM

PUBLIC SPACE

GATEWAY

SAN FRANCISCO FEDERAL OFFICE BUILDING

DATE: 2000-2006 LOCATION: San Francisco, California STATUS: In Process SITE AREA: 91,000 sf/2,880 m² PROJECT SIZE: 605,000 sf/56,207 m² PROGRAM: Federal office building including offices for the Department of Health and Human Services, Social Security Administration, Department of State, Department of Labor, and the Department of Agriculture. Additional program includes a conference/community center, day care, fitness center, public sky lobby, public plaza, and café.

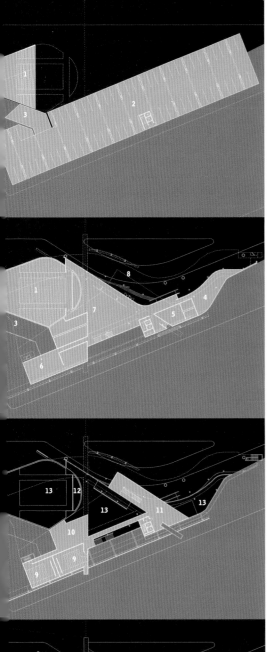

The transparency of film and its dematerialization in the projected image inform the concept for this intervention. An iconic, supergraphic "IFP/West Center" sign is projected onto the building from an angle so that its letter forms distort, exposing the various architectural elements of the facade. Some of the letters read as shadows, others as screens, while still others as sculptural entities emerging from the facade's surface.

The facade delaminates to form a canopy that shelters the public entrance to a central, multifunctional lobby. A series of stills from *Citizen Kane*—an instantly recognizable symbol—is printed on segments of the undulating, perforated metal facade. The fusion of graphic and spatial systems connects this project with our explorations at Tsunami in Las Vegas. Both explore the power of two-dimensional surface to dematerialize architectural substance.

1 cinema with 500 seats 2 parking garage 3 parking ramp 4 cafe 5 kitchen 6 bookstore 7 lobby 8 covered entrance area 9 screening room with 75 seats 10 reception 11 library with 25 computers 12 projection room 13 open to below 14 production offices 15 IFP West offices 16 production offices for members 17 roof garden

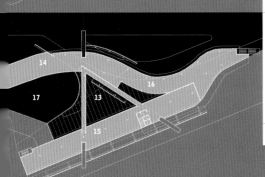

EL+40'
EL+26'
EL+14'
EL+2'
EL-9'

IFP WEST FILM CENTER

DATE: 2001 LOCATION: Culver City, California STATUS: Unbuilt SITE AREA: 7,500 sf/697 m² PROJECT SIZE: 7,000 sf/650 m² PROGRAM: Temporary office space, with 55-seat theater, restaurant/cafe, bookstore, library, two 75-seat screening rooms, an open gallery space for small receptions.

CHILDREN'S MUSEUM OF LOS ANGELES

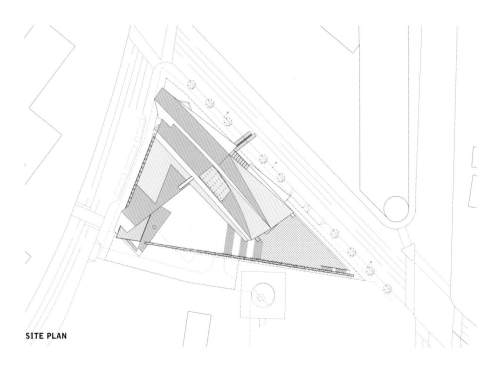

SITE PLAN

It comes as a mild shock, having passed through the echoing, disorienting passages, then suddenly to emerge outdoors, amid wind and light, high above the ground, with a dizzying panorama of Florence and the surrounding hills at your feet.

Ross King, *Brunelleschi's Dome*

The Children's Museum building is itself didactic—an exhibit on an urban scale that engages its young visitors. The museum draws kids, very few of whom live downtown, to L.A.'s bourgeoning city center and plays a role in teaching them about the life of the building and about the city.

A system of ramps functions as transitional exhibit space, guiding the visitors' procession in and out of the building envelope, repeatedly passing from inside to outside, from enclosed glazed volume to open air. The ramps span the central atrium, connect exhibit and performance volumes, pierce through the exterior wall to allow glimpses to the inside, hover above the busy street outside, and double back into the museum. From one ramp inside the atrium, visitors can manipulate a video camera located in another cantilevered outdoor ramp, which in turn projects imagery of the urban streetscape onto the full height of the atrium wall.

Children are encouraged to act upon the architecture both through movement and through more primitive markings: the cladding materials allow children to draw or paint directly on the building. At other locations children's drawings texture the building in tiled patterns; the building thus becomes a canvas on which children apply their own creative ideas and imagery.

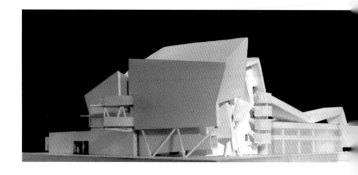

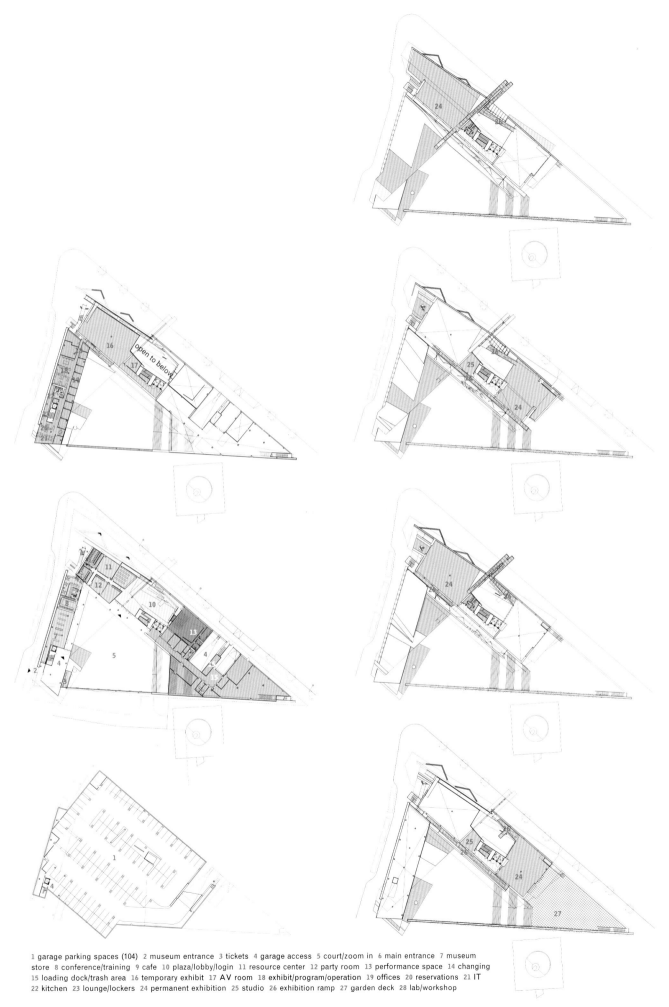

1 garage parking spaces (104) 2 museum entrance 3 tickets 4 garage access 5 court/zoom in 6 main entrance 7 museum store 8 conference/training 9 cafe 10 plaza/lobby/login 11 resource center 12 party room 13 performance space 14 changing 15 loading dock/trash area 16 temporary exhibit 17 AV room 18 exhibit/program/operation 19 offices 20 reservations 21 IT 22 kitchen 23 lounge/lockers 24 permanent exhibition 25 studio 26 exhibition ramp 27 garden deck 28 lab/workshop

SECTION THROUGH CORE LOOKING EAST

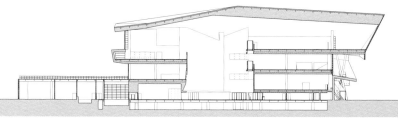

SECTION THROUGH ATRIUM AND GALLERIES LOOKING SOUTH

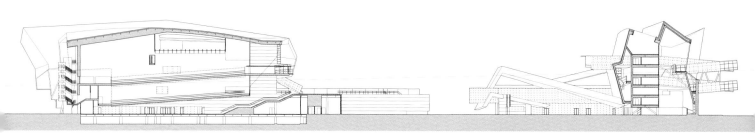

SECTION THROUGH RAMPS LOOKING NORTH

SECTION THROUGH ATRIUM LOOKING WEST

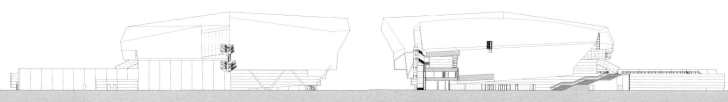

NORTH ELEVATION

SOUTH-WEST ELEVATION

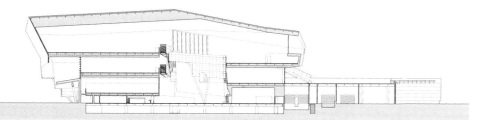

SECTION THROUGH ATRIUM AND GALLERIES LOOKING NORTH

SECTION THROUGH WEST GALLERIES

SECTION THROUGH EAST GALLERIES

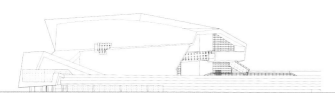

SOUTH ELEVATION

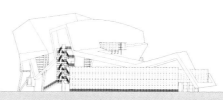

WEST ELEVATION

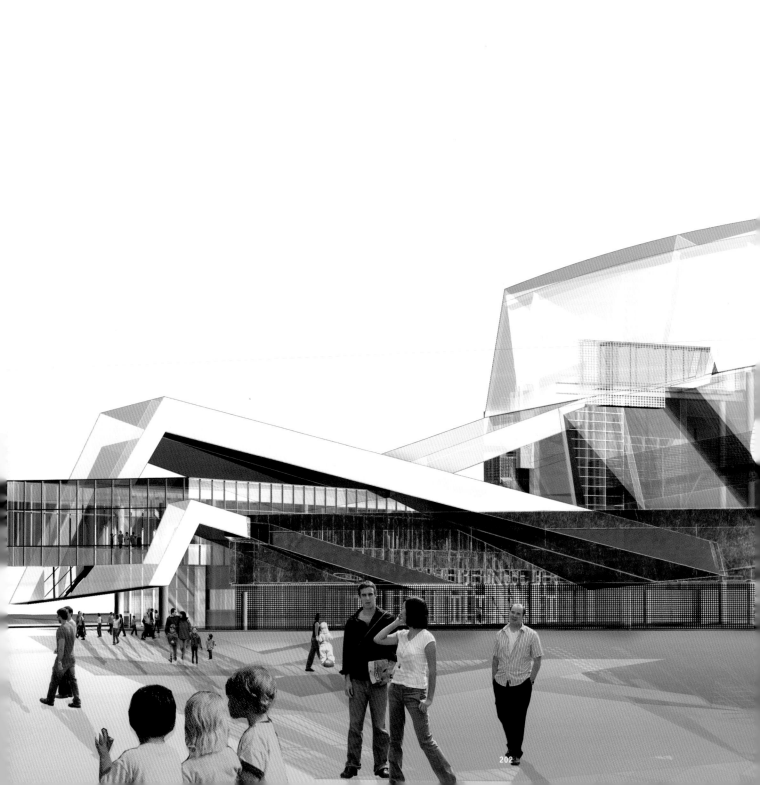

CHILDREN'S MUSEUM OF LOS ANGELES

DATE: 2001 LOCATION: Los Angeles, California STATUS: Competition SITE AREA: 2 acres/.81 ha BUILDING AREA: 95,000 sf/8,825 m² PROGRAM: Museum and cultural center including permanent and temporary exhibition spaces, theater, shop, storage, classrooms, café, retail store, and underground parking.

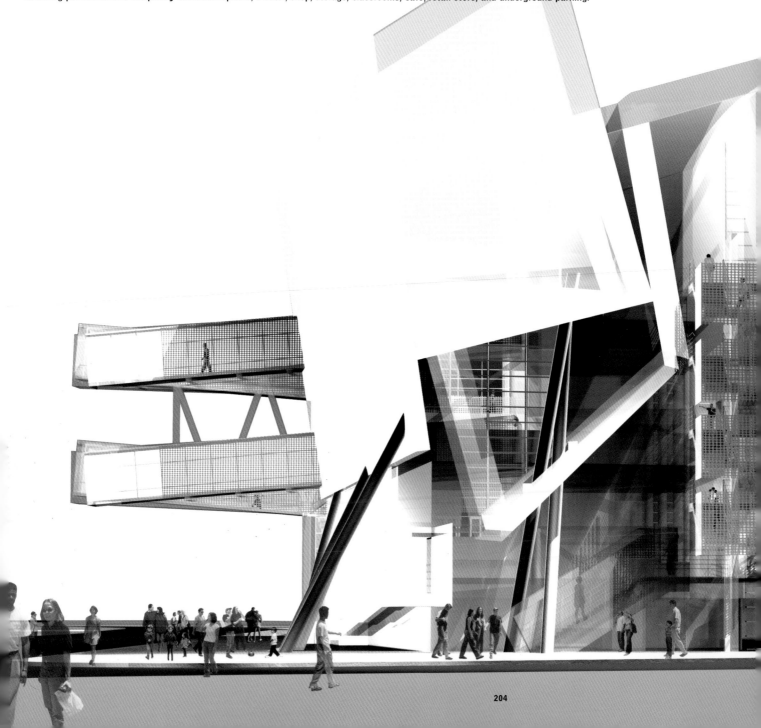

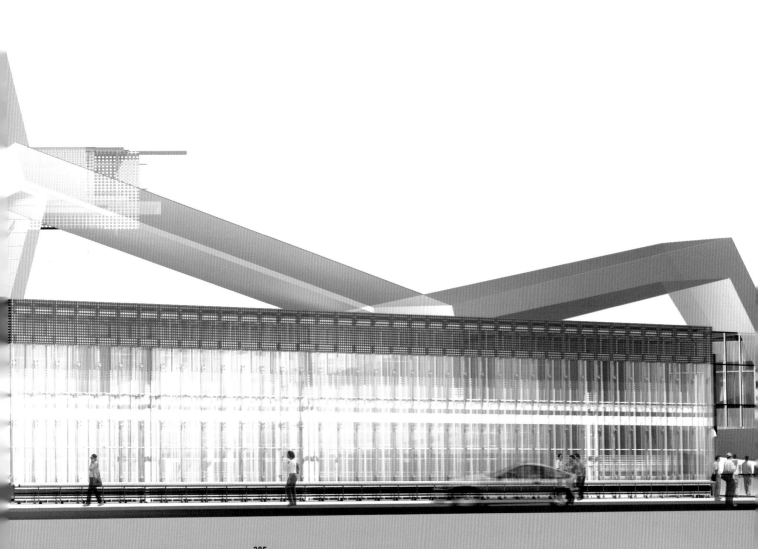

205

LOS ANGELES COUNTY MUSEUM OF ART

Through this project, which defines a new organization of site circulation and landscape, we explored the changing role of the museum through architectural language. The organizational overlay weaves LACMA's series of disconnected buildings into a singular, cohesive campus. This new connective tissue integrates the existing site with potential future development, connects isolated sectors of the museum, and makes space for new galleries.

Blurring distinctions between building and landscape, the gardens and the structural pieces develop in parallel as strands of movement on the site. The landscape and the urban facade become sites for exhibiting art so that museum visitors along with pieces of art from the permanent collection flow outside to "roofless galleries."

Based on LACMA's efforts to stimulate interdisciplinary dialogue among its encyclopedic collections, cross-stitches in the circulation routes allow curators and visitors to forge new connections between pieces. In response to the contemporary development of hybrid artistic genres, the texture of flowing landscape and architecture promotes fluid circulation, and engagement with art from multiple perspectives.

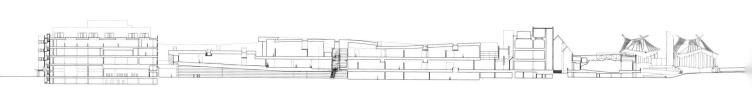

SECTION A

SITE PLAN

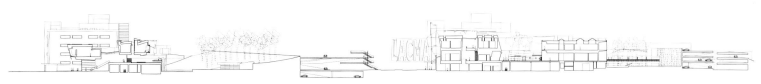

SECTION B   **SECTION C**

PHASE 1

PHASE 2

PHASE 3

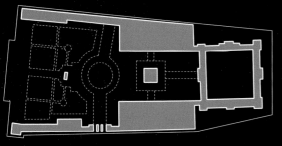
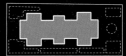

GRAND LOUVRE 1190-2001
40-acre site 7,618,300 sf
890,065 sf of exhibition space

THE J. PAUL GETTY CENTER 1997
24-acre site 945,000 sf
64,500 sf of exhibition space

NATIONAL GALLERY OF ART, WASHINGTON, D.C. 1978
22-acre site 1,076,000 sf
217,445 sf of exhibition space

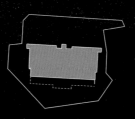
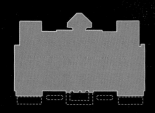

MODERN MUSEUM, STOCKHOLM 1997
21-acre site 275,556 sf
64,583 sf of exhibition space

L.A. COUNTY MUSEUM 1965-2001
19.1-acre site 640,000 sf
240,000 sf of exhibition space

MUSEO DEL PRADO, MADRID, SPAIN 1819
18.7-acre site 50,537 sf

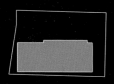

THE METROPOLITAN MUSEUM OF ART, NEW YORK 1880-1990
17-acre site 2,100,000 sf
850,000 sf of exhibition space

TATE GALLERY, LONDON 1999
8.48-acre site 371,860 sf
107,639 sf of exhibition space

THE GUGGENHEIM MUSEUM, BILBAO 1997
8.03-acre site 256,000 sf
112,000 sf of exhibition space

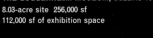

CENTRE POMPIDOU, PARIS 1976
7.5-acre site 1,000,000 sf
183,000 sf of exhibition space

MUSEUM OF FINE ARTS, HOUSTON 1999
6-acre site 197,000 sf
57,020 sf of exhibition space

HIRSHHORN MUSEUM AND SCULPTURE GARDEN 1974
4.5-acre site 162,700 sf
61,800 sf of exhibition space

THEATRE SQUARE, ROTTERDAM 1992
3.03-acre site

RODIN SCULPTURE GARDEN, PARIS 1919
2.9-acre site

NEUE STAATSGALERIE, STUTTGART 1983
2.2-acre site 164,690 sf
67,920 sf of exhibition space

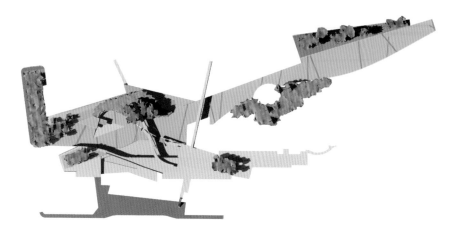

ARTSCAPE
Designed both as "roofless galleries" and as an infrastructure
for further development. It supports urbanistic and artistic expansion.

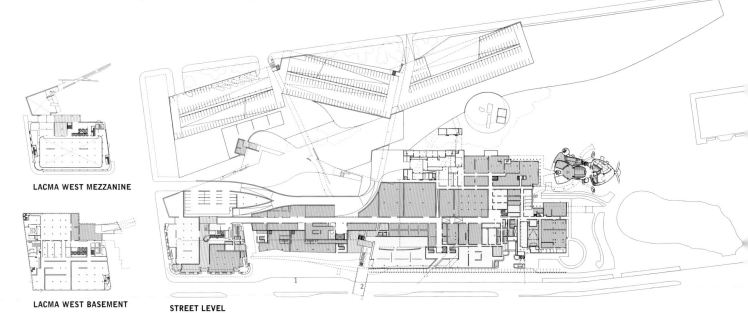

LACMA WEST MEZZANINE

LACMA WEST BASEMENT

STREET LEVEL

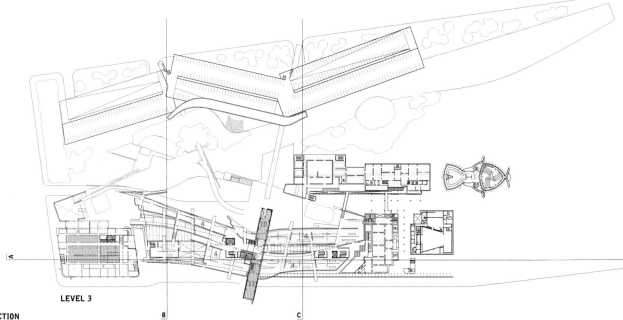

LEVEL 3

▓ **PUBLIC NON-COLLECTION**

PUBLIC COLLECTION

▓ **NON PUBLIC COLLECTION**

NON-PUBLIC NON-COLLECTION

▓ **REVENUE GENERATING PROGRAM**

1 entrance plaza 2 main entry 3 entrance hall and orientation gallery 4 modern art galleries 5 restaurant 6 ticket kiosk
7 public plaza/connective tissue 8 roofless galleries/park space 9 water feature 10 cafe 11 bar

ROOFLESS GALLERIES
sculpture, land art, installation, performance,
cafes, contemplation

ART AND COMMERCE
public non-collection spaces, art spaces

PUBLIC ACCESS
museum entrance from parking structure
and Wilshire Blvd.

SERVICE BASEMENT
service art and non-art, service infrastructure

FLOW AND STITCHES
plaza level, new gallery circulation

FLOW AND STITCHES
level 3, new gallery circulation

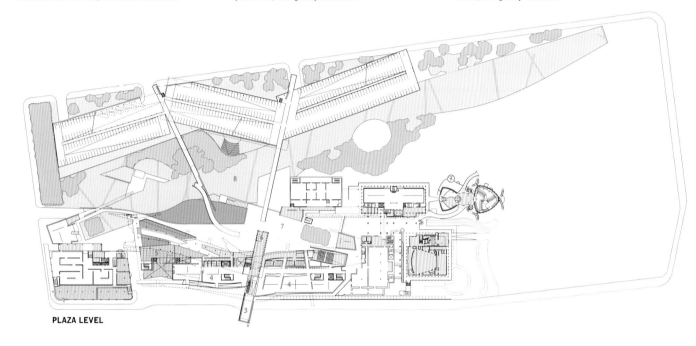

PLAZA LEVEL

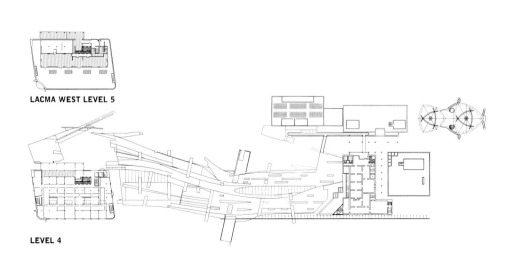

LACMA WEST LEVEL 5

LEVEL 4

214

LOS ANGELES COUNTY MUSEUM OF ART

DATE: 2001 LOCATION: Los Angeles, California STATUS: Competition SITE AREA: 18 acres/7.28 ha PROJECT SIZE: 640,000 sf/59,458 m² PROGRAM: Renovation and expansion to existing museum, which includes a new contemporary art structure to act as the primary entrance to the campus.

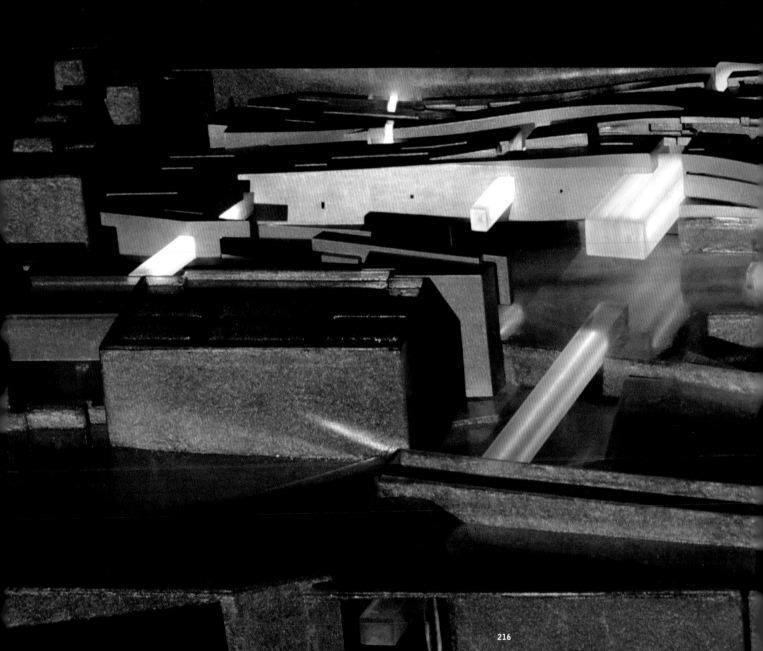

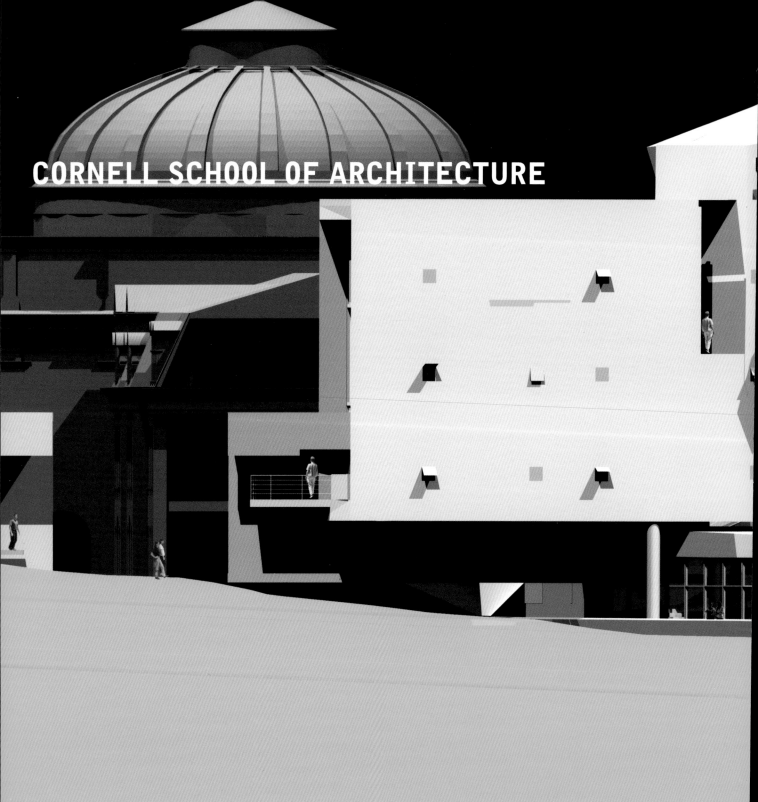

CORNELL SCHOOL OF ARCHITECTURE

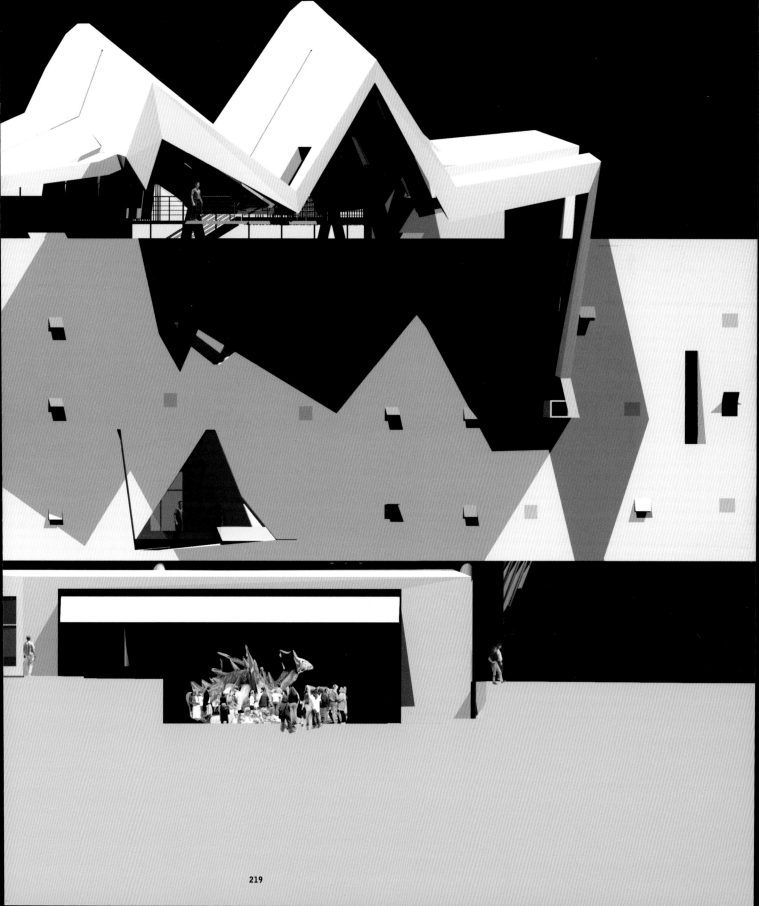

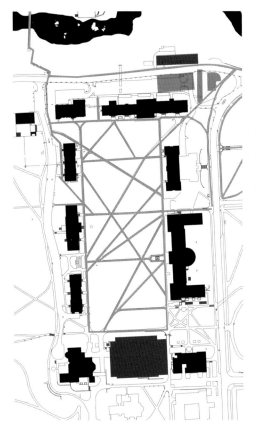

SITE PLAN

DRAGON DAY PARADE ROUTE

Each spring since 1901, first-year architecture students at Cornell spend months constructing a giant dragon to parade from Sibley Hall through campus to the Arts Quad, where, if it has survived the traditional assaults from the Engineering School's rival creature, it is consumed by a bonfire. To celebrate and encourage this tradition, space at the new School of Architecture was made specifically for this activity. The new outdoor, submerged workshop area is connected to the main pedestrian walkway and positioned as a primary focal point in the design of the new architecture school. Lit late into the night, dragon making, along with the more prosaic undertakings of the architecture department,

are on continual display to the university at large.

In reference to the school's stated pedagogical approach emphasizing the process of making, the building is itself didactic, offering lessons for students both within and outside the discipline of architecture. Glazed facades allow views into studio spaces, gallery and exhibition space, and the shop's indoor and outdoor workspaces. Neutral, flexible design studios support social interaction, opportunities for informal learning, and increased engagement among faculty and students. Common jury rooms are suspended within the large, open space,

so that students can view each other's critiques from the design studios. By contrast, an opaque linear bar structure housing faculty offices pierces the studio space—the only area in the building where there is a quiet, more private zone.

The primary intersection, where the faculty bar crosses the studio space and cantilevers over the main pedestrian walkway at University Avenue, defines the new entrance for the school. This seam resolves tension between the new building and Sibley Hall, between faculty and student environments, and between the architecture department and the general university population.

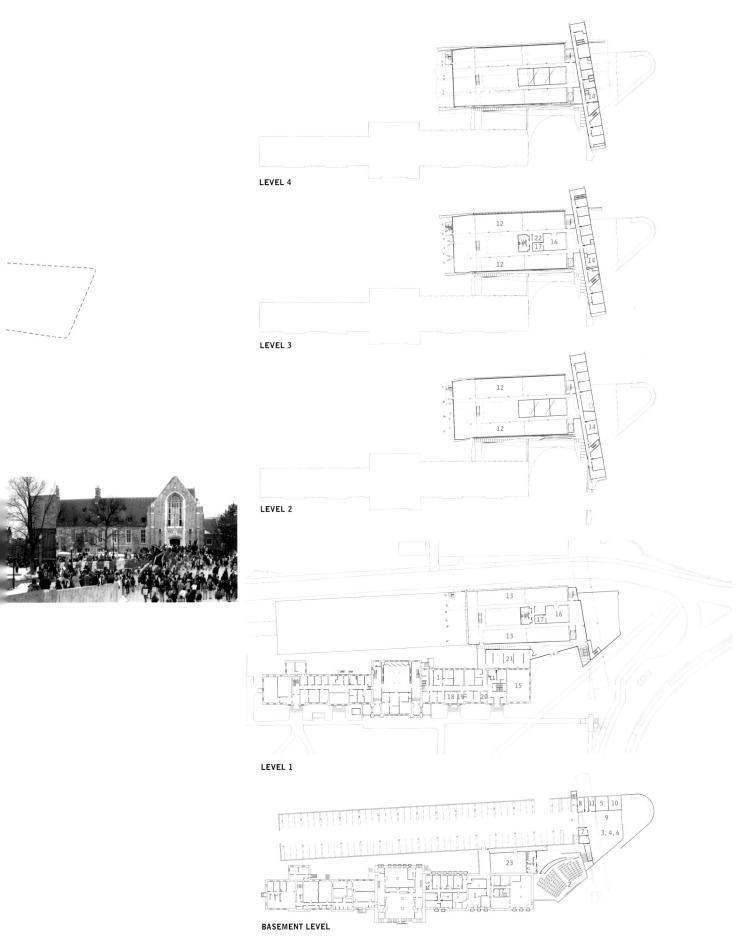

LEVEL 4

LEVEL 3

LEVEL 2

LEVEL 1

BASEMENT LEVEL

1 graduate studio offices 2 auditorium 3 large powertool area 4 general work area 5 welding room 6 paint booths/paint staging
7 office of shop coordinator 8 maintenance/workroom 9 high bay project assembly classroom 10 building system resource center
11 lecture room 12 undergraduate design studios 13 first-year graduate design studios 14 faculty studio offices 15 multimedia
room 16 computer lab 17 printer/scanner room 18 department chair's office 19 reception/waiting 20 rome program 21 exhibition
gallery 22 model/paint room

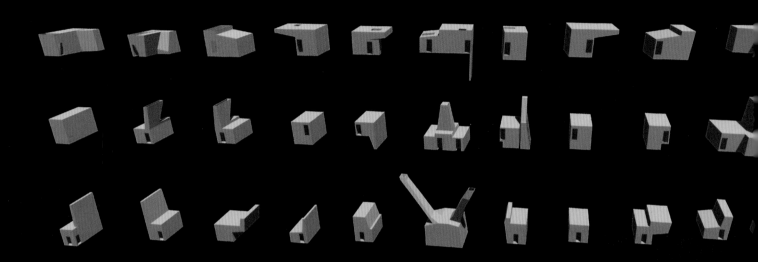

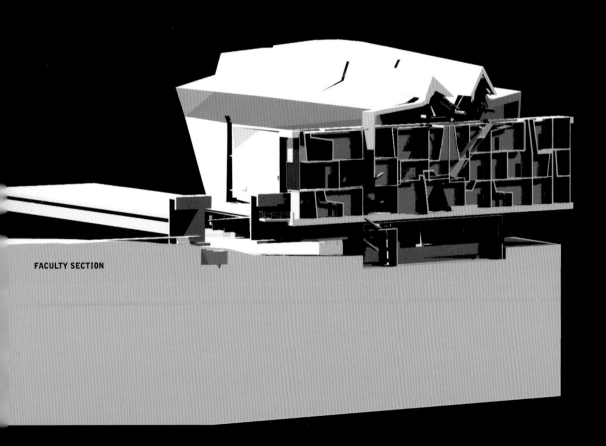

FACULTY SECTION

190

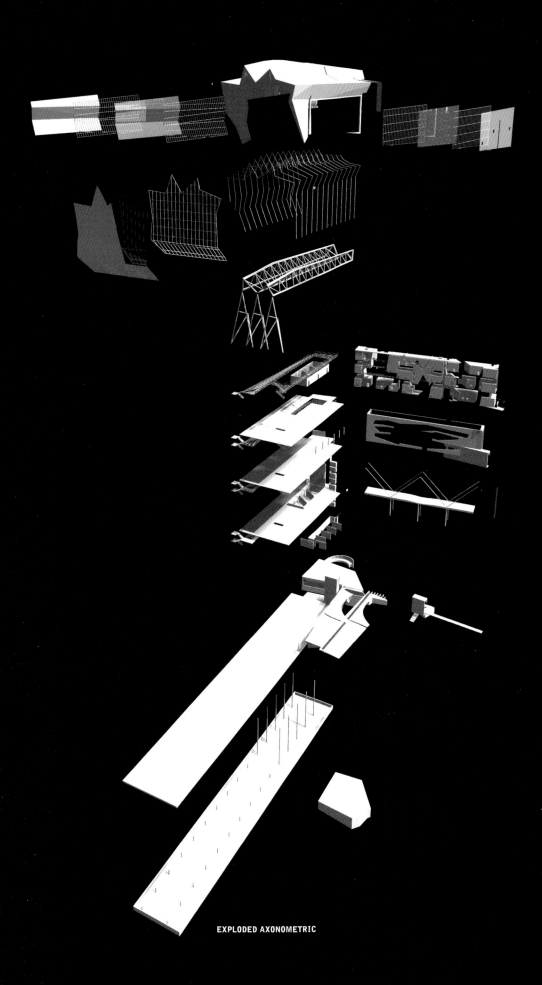

EXPLODED AXONOMETRIC

JURY SECTION

LONG JURY SECTION

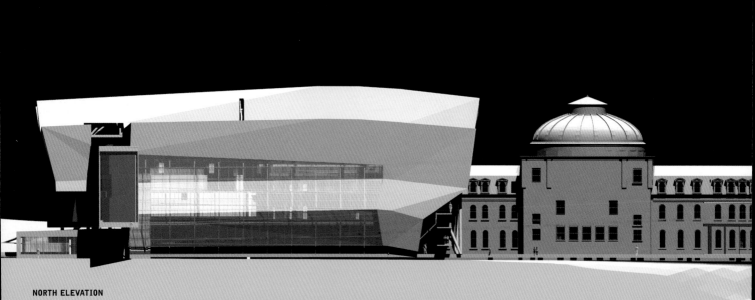

NORTH ELEVATION

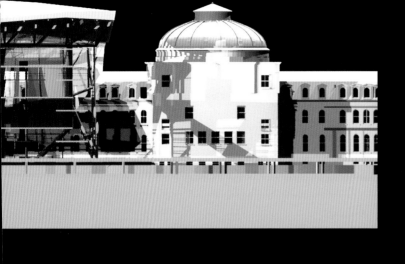

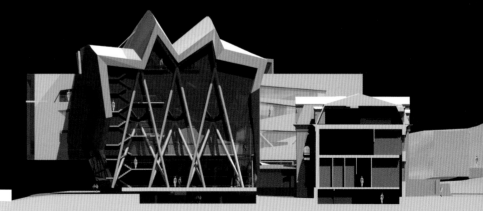

WEST ELEVATION

CORNELL SCHOOL OF ARCHITECTURE

DATE: 2001 LOCATION: Ithaca, New York STATUS: Competition SITE AREA: 72,000 sf/6,689 m² BUILDING AREA: 75,000 sf/6,968 m² and 29,000 sf/2,694 m² parking
PROGRAM: Renovation of existing 12,000-sf/1,115-m² facility and addition of a 75,000-sf/6,968-m² School of Architecture.

SOUTH ELEVATION

RENSSELAER ELECTRONIC MEDIA
AND PERFORMING ARTS CENTER

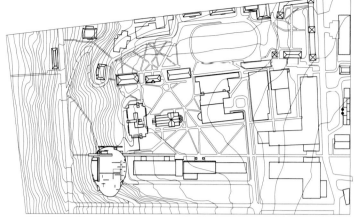

CONTEXT PLAN

The Electronic Media and Performing Arts Center's articulated ovoid form absorbs the theater's fly assembly, with zinc-clad skin slumped over the interior space. Orthogonal glazed blocks intersect and wrap the singular form, and act as connections to existing university buildings. An elevated pedestrian path functions as the primary processional walkway through campus, leading to the building, piercing the structure, and terminating in a viewing platform overlooking the Hudson River Valley. Prominently located on axis with this pedestrian path, and visible from the far reaches of the campus and the town of Troy, the building presents an iconic identity for Rensselaer.

The monolithic exterior of the building possesses transformative qualities that serve to activate and engage the building. The glazed facade, for example, affords "ticketless" views of impromptu performances to passersby, while the atrium's eighteen-thousand-square-foot media wall gives art students an opportunity to break out of the conventional gallery or theater to project works on its large blank surface.

The plan aligns all program and theater spaces on an efficient interior grid. Twin black-box performance spaces, small performance chambers, rehearsal rooms, and production studios float within a core of public circulation. Interstitial spaces that slip between the skin and the programmatic boxes blur boundaries and foster hybrid forms among the creative disciplines.

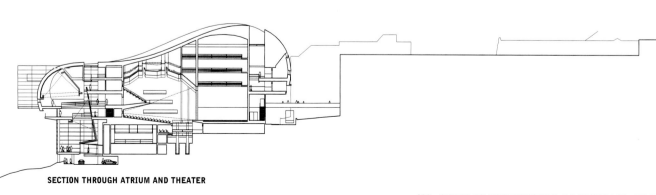

SECTION THROUGH ATRIUM AND THEATER

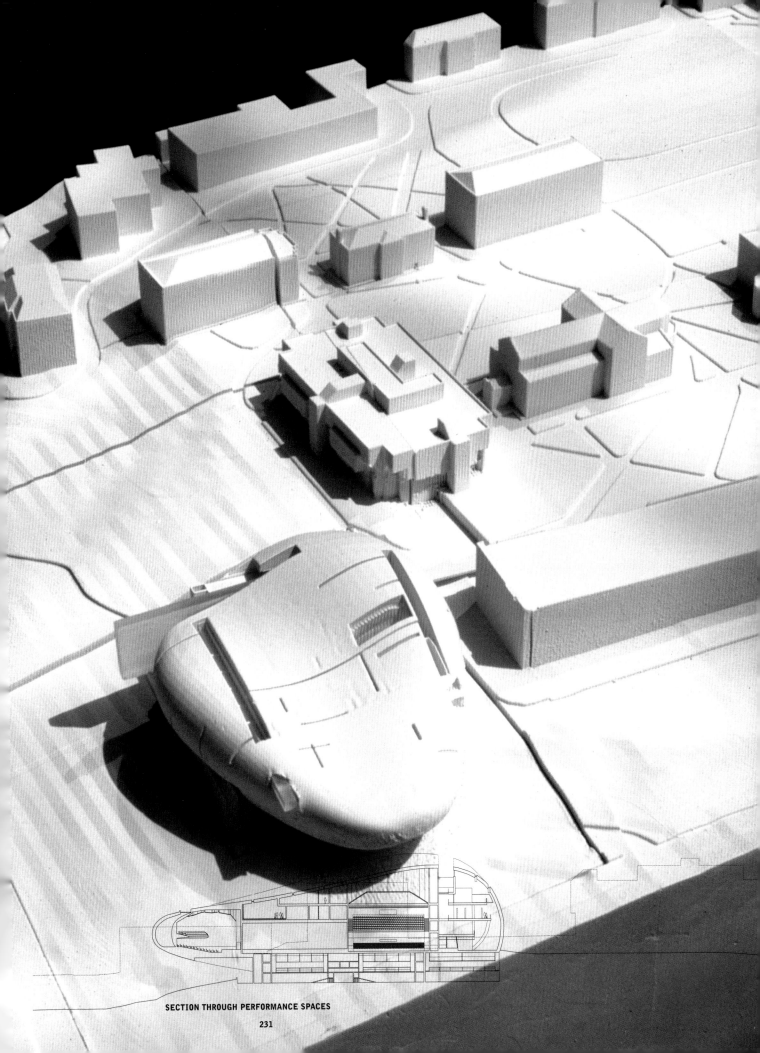

SECTION THROUGH PERFORMANCE SPACES

SOUTH ELEVATION

1 parking 2 8th street stair 3 footpath entry 4 core connection 5 mechanical room 6 natural air cooling ducts 7 lobby 8 black box theater (2) 9 black box theater with projection space 10 support space 11 atrium 12 workshop and storage area 13 orchestra pit 14 wardrobe 15 dressing rooms 16 green room 17 lockers and showers 18 rehearsal space 19 room for musicians 20 laundry 21 recital hall 22 technical director's office 23 set shops 24 main entry 25 campus path 26 viewing platform 27 cafe 28 kitchen 29 media wall 30 theater balcony 31 recital hall balcony 32 choir and orchestra rehearsal room 33 library 34 dance studios 35 administrative and curatorial offices 36 gallery 37 founder's room 38 postproduction studio 39 recording studio 40 video production 41 WRPI—student radio station 42 backstage 43 theater 44 fly tower 45 rehearsal rooms

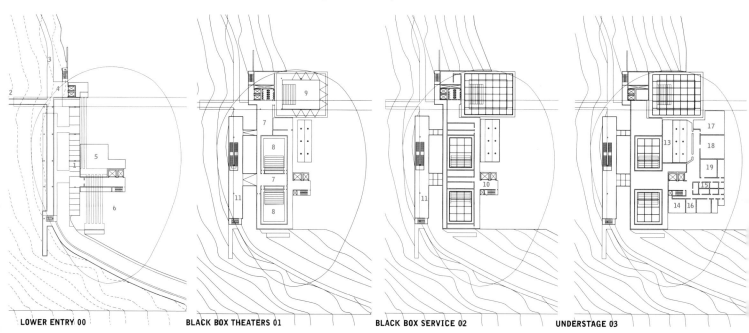

LOWER ENTRY 00   **BLACK BOX THEATERS 01**   **BLACK BOX SERVICE 02**   **UNDERSTAGE 03**

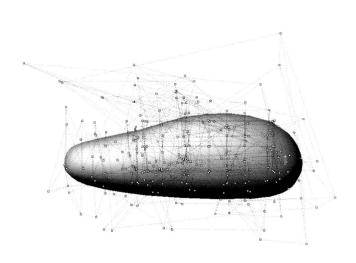

EGG MORPHOLOGY SIDE VIEW

NORTH ELEVATION

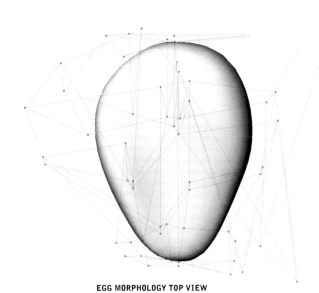

EGG MORPHOLOGY TOP VIEW

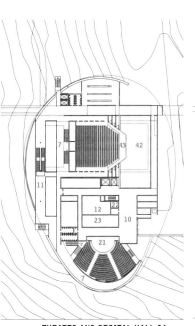

THEATER AND RECITAL HALL 04

ENTRY AND CAFE 05

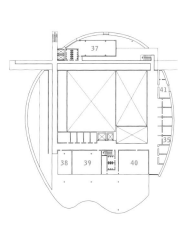

MUSIC AND DANCE AND
ADMINISTRATION 06

FOUNDER'S ROOM AND AV DEPT. 07

RENSSELAER ELECTRONIC MEDIA AND PERFORMING ARTS CENTER

DATE: 2001 LOCATION: Troy, New York STATUS: Competition SITE AREA: 3 acres/1.2 ha PROJECT SIZE: 129,000 sf/11,985 m² PROGRAM: Electronic media and performing arts center including black box theater, theater and recital hall, café, rehearsal spaces, and support space.

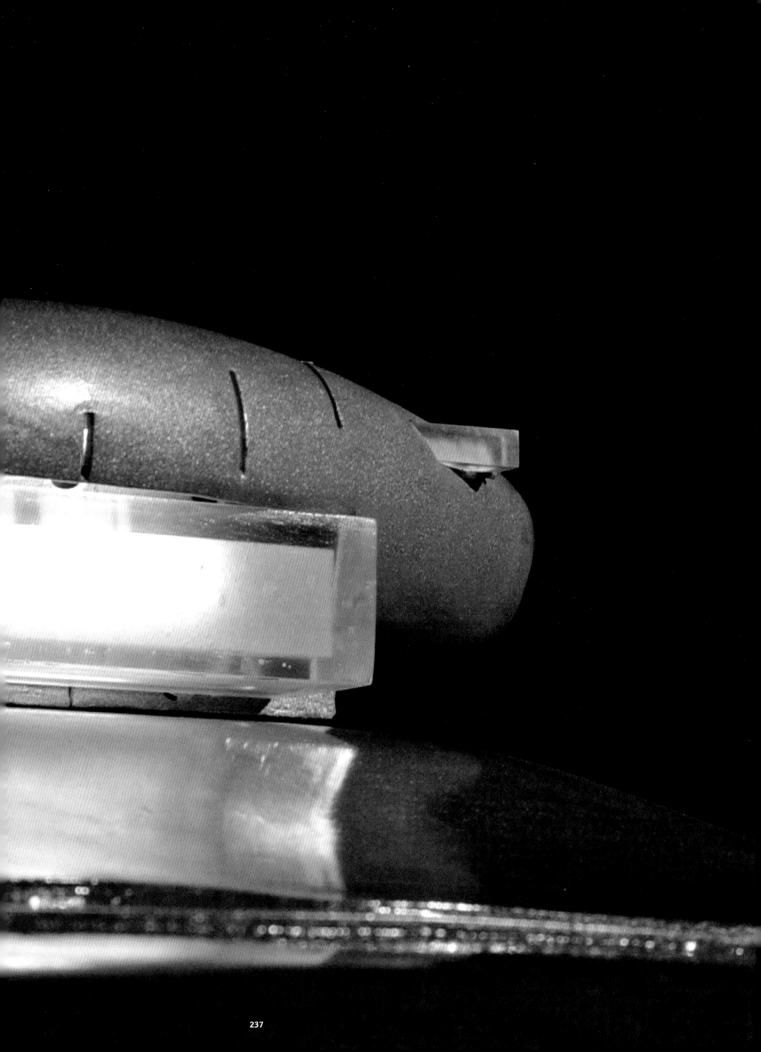

BMW EVENT AND DELIVERY CENTER

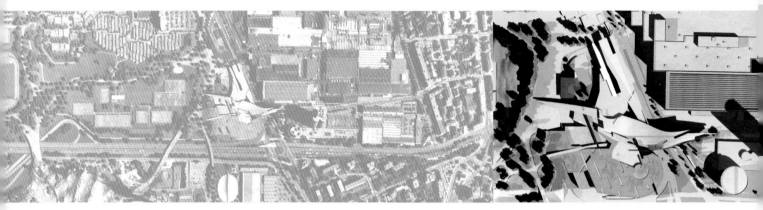

AERIAL VIEW

SITE PLAN

The Event and Delivery Center for BMW focuses on the resolution of critical issues of urbanism, technology, and environmental sustainability in alignment with the company's core values. By overlaying the multiple circulation exigencies on the site, a complex pattern of infrastructure emerges that is further informed by an urban strategy pulled from the site's existing grid. The site plan emphasizes connections among BMW, the Olympic Park, and the city of Munich, while the structure creates a new, instantly recognizable urban landmark.

The principal space, which functions as a proscenium for the transference of car to new owner, meets the street as a transparent volume. As new automobiles spiral up from below the ground and move out into a void in a thick, glass wall, their motion animates the building. The theatricality of the building dynamically defines the corner site, while incisions in the building reveal views of the BMW tower and the mountains and city of Munich beyond. This project weaves dis-

parate parts of the existing urban fabric together with fluid, large-scale gestures evocative of movement, transforming the BMW Center into an extension of the adjacent park and integrating it with the surrounding buildings, open spaces, and traffic facilities.

Advanced building systems, kinetic plan elements, and new circulation paths and bridges reflect the legacy of technological innovation and dynamism at BMW. Efficient and responsible use of natural resources is achieved via the integration of energy-saving lighting, ventilation, and solar heat generation, while an eight-thousand-square-meter occupiable earth roof acts as an insulating element and connects the building seamlessly with the park to the west. Emerging from its context, the building is an extension of nature—appropriate to BMW's ecological aspirations for the future of the automobile.

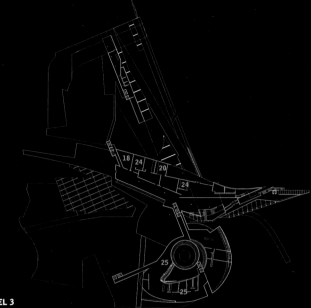

LEVEL 3

1 operations hall 2 parking 3 BMW world 4 BMW premiere 5 group center
6 briefing center 7 function hall 8 TV studio 9 auditorium 10 reception
11 museum/mobile tradition 12 BMW automobile 13 BMW group 14 R+D
competence 15 BMW individual 16 BMW motor sport 17 motorcycle delivery
18 catering 19 BMW motorcycle 20 BMW brand shops 21 BMW premiere
22 MINI 23 factories/manufacturing 24 shops 25 customer lounge

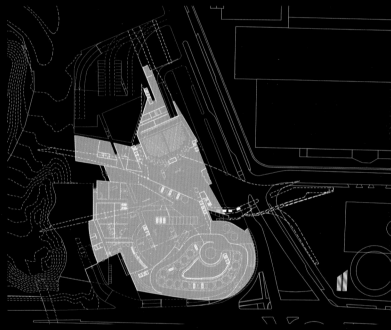

GROUND LEVEL

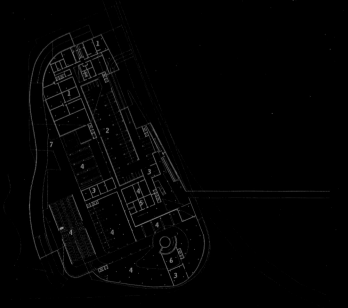

BASEMENT LEVEL 1

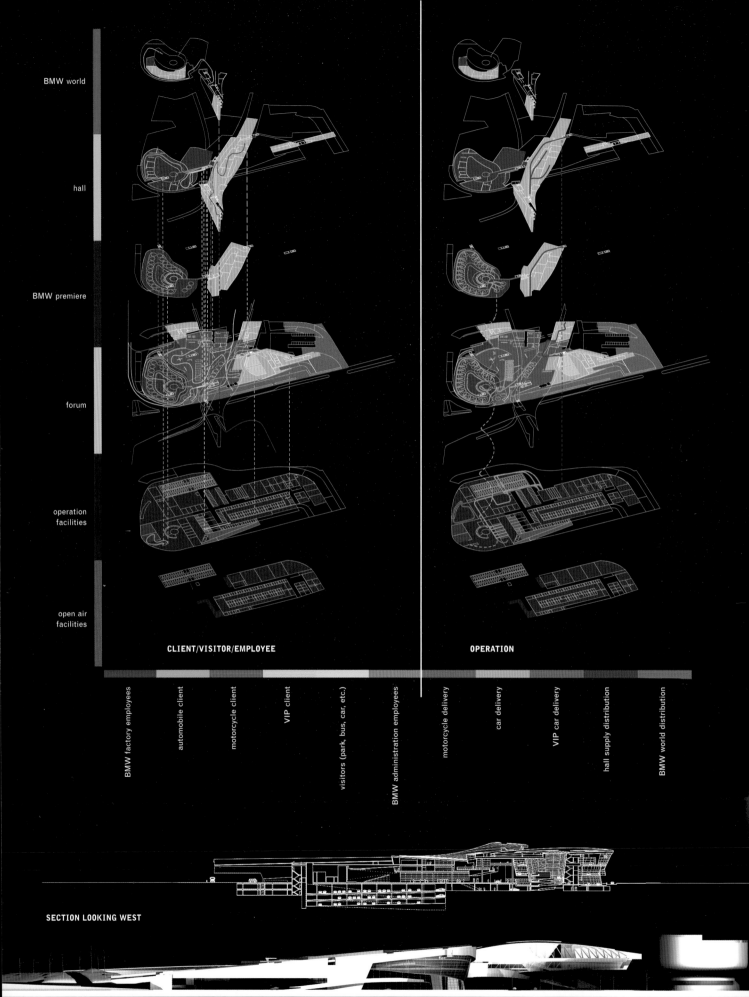

BMW world

hall

BMW premiere

forum

operation
facilities

open air
facilities

CLIENT/VISITOR/EMPLOYEE

OPERATION

BMW factory employees

automobile client

motorcycle client

VIP client

visitors (park, bus, car, etc.)

BMW administration employees

motorcycle delivery

car delivery

VIP car delivery

hall supply distribution

BMW world distribution

SECTION LOOKING WEST

SECTION LOOKING NORTH

EAST-WEST ELEVATION

BMW EVENT AND DELIVERY CENTER

DATE: 2001 LOCATION: Munich, Germany STATUS: Competition SITE AREA: 275,139 sf/25,561 m² PROJECT SIZE: 651,739 sf/60,548 m² PROGRAM: Event and delivery center distributed across 6 zones: BMW world (69,966 sf/6,500 m²), hall (63,884 sf/5,935 m²), BMW premiere (78,900 sf/7,330 m²), forum (28,524 sf/2,650 m²), operational facilities (331,531 sf/30,800 m²), open air facilities (331,531 sf/7,333 m²).

NOAA SATELLITE OPERATION FACILITY

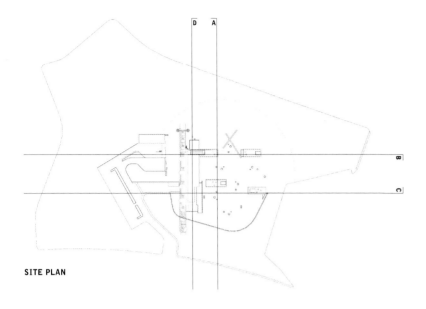

SITE PLAN

SATELLITE IMAGE OF SITE

Those who dwell, as scientists or laymen, among the beauties and mysteries of the earth are never alone or weary of life.

Rachel Carson, *The Sense of Wonder* (1956)

In light of NOAA's mission to monitor and safeguard the earth, we reexamined the traditional relationship between building and landscape, figure and ground. A reflection of the Satellite Operation Facility's environmental mandate, the design scheme prioritizes open space, reduces the presence of built form, and integrates architecture with landscape.

A field of antennae—the "eyes and ears" of the operation—crowns the three-story bar building, pitching and sweeping to receive information (visible data, radiance, sea surface, snow and ice cover, and moisture content of the atmosphere) from the sixteen satellites it monitors. The iconic antennae comprise the dominant visual register of the project. The departments that operate as "the brain" of the operation—mission control, launch control, and computer processing— are housed in the slender bar.

Beneath the bar lies the "body," a disc-shaped building that slips into the thickened landscape of lifted ground. This partially submerged, double-high space accommodates offices and support services. Long swaths of interior walls are wrapped in imagery of the earth taken by NOAA's satellites, while the convex ceiling plane simulates the planet's curvature as seen from space. Slots in the traversable, undulating green roofscape admit natural light and create niches for large courtyards. A glass lobby, with a security control point, mediates between the two main architectural components of body and brain.

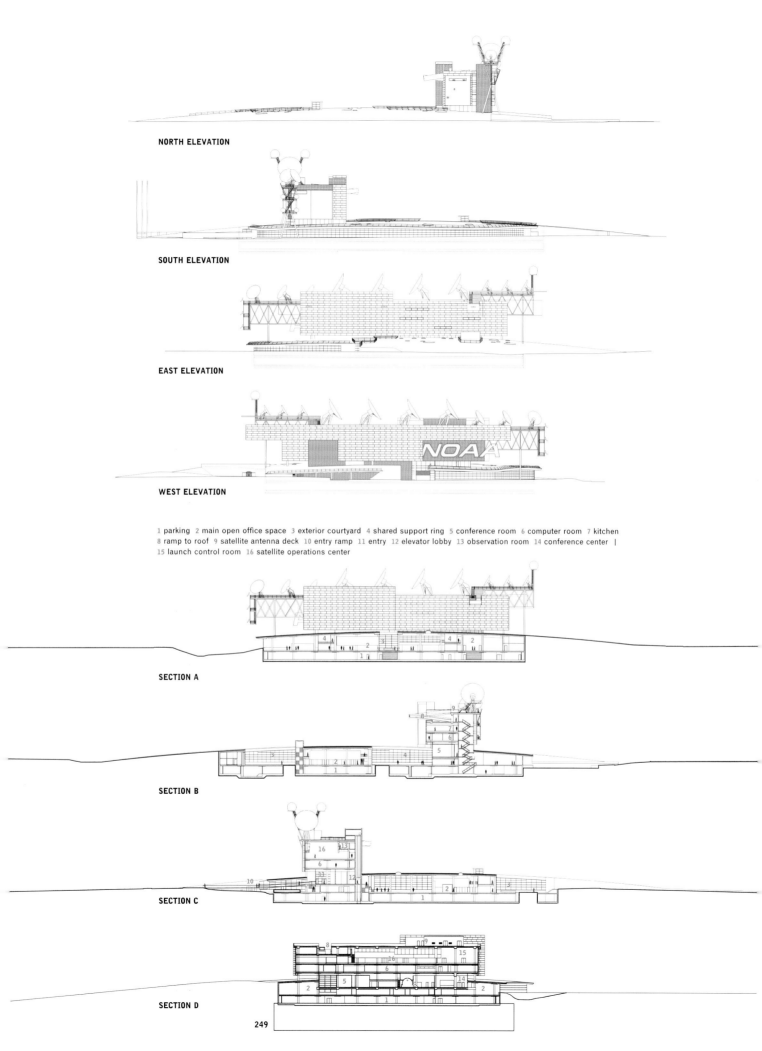

NORTH ELEVATION

SOUTH ELEVATION

EAST ELEVATION

WEST ELEVATION

1 parking 2 main open office space 3 exterior courtyard 4 shared support ring 5 conference room 6 computer room 7 kitchen
8 ramp to roof 9 satellite antenna deck 10 entry ramp 11 entry 12 elevator lobby 13 observation room 14 conference center |
15 launch control room 16 satellite operations center

SECTION A

SECTION B

SECTION C

SECTION D

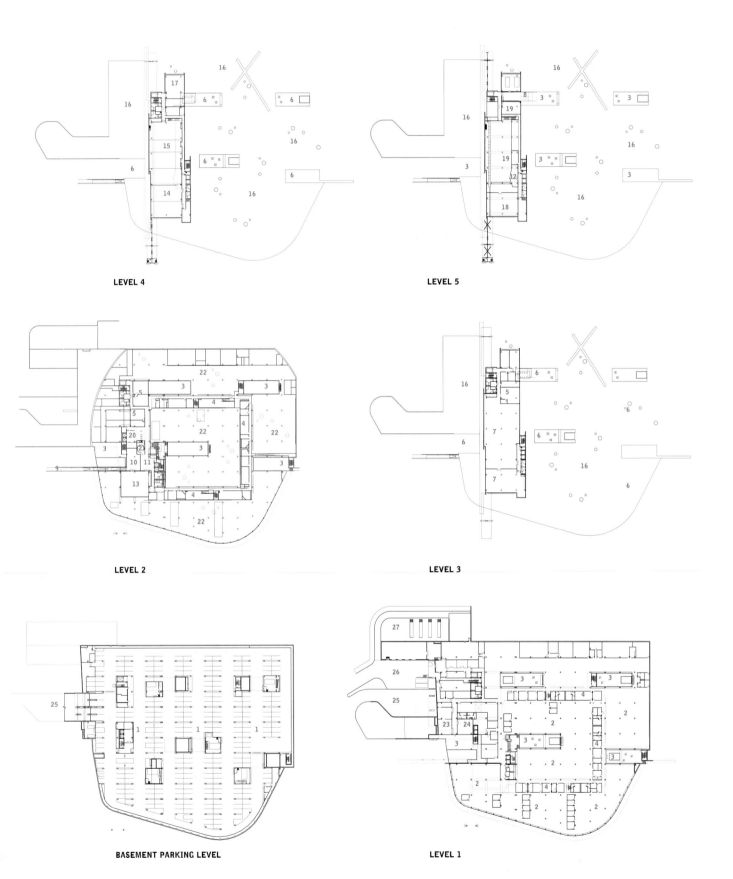

LEVEL 4

LEVEL 5

LEVEL 2

LEVEL 3

BASEMENT PARKING LEVEL

LEVEL 1

1 parking 2 main open office space 3 exterior courtyard 4 shared support ring 5 conference room 6 exterior courtyard 7 computer room 8 ramp to roof
9 entry ramp 10 entry 11 elevator lobby 12 observation room 13 conference center 14 launch control room 15 satellite operations center 16 green roof
17 support space 18 open to launch control room 19 open to satellite operations center 20 security lobby 21 art room 22 open to open office below
23 cafe 24 gym 25 ramp to parking 26 service area 27 utility yard

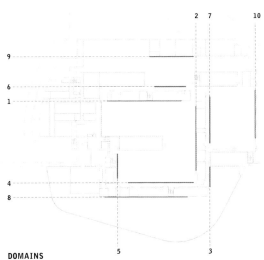

DOMAINS

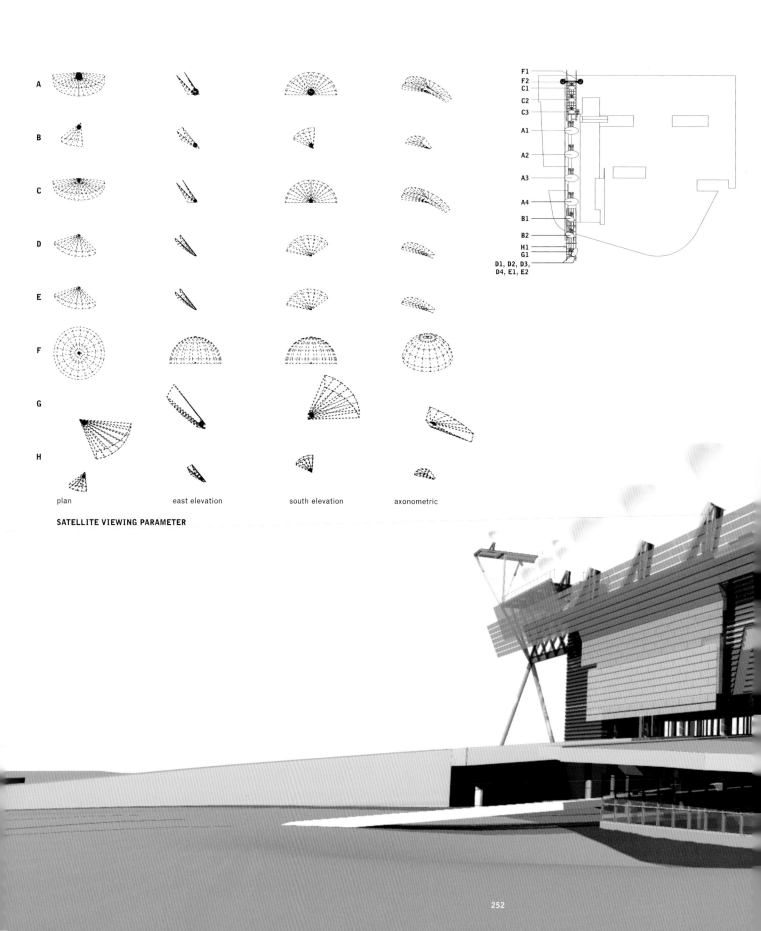

A

B

C

D

E

F

G

H

plan　　　　　　　　east elevation　　　　　south elevation　　　axonometric

SATELLITE VIEWING PARAMETER

F1
F2
C1
C2
C3
A1
A2
A3
A4
B1
B2
H1
G1
D1, D2, D3,
D4, E1, E2

NOAA SATELLITE OPERATION FACILITY

DATE: 2001-2005 LOCATION: Suitland, Maryland STATUS: In Process SITE AREA: 20 acres/8.09 ha PROJECT SIZE: 208,000 sf/19,324 m² PROGRAM: Satellite operations control center including office space, computer rooms, satellite control rooms, conference center, conference rooms, exercise facility, café with 24-hour, 7-day operational capability.

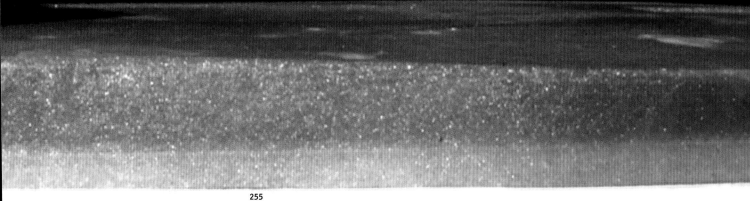

HYPO ALPE-ADRIA-CENTER

SITE PLAN

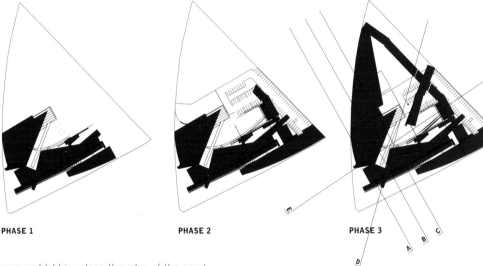

PHASE 1   PHASE 2   PHASE 3

This building integrates inherent complexities at the shifting border between rural and urban typologies; its form emanates from both the pre-Alpine contoured landscape and the narrow, twisting passages and plazas of a small village. The center is located just east of Klagenfurt, Austria, where the city extends into its outlying suburban and agricultural regions. As with many contemporary edge-city conditions, the site is surrounded by dislocated buildings, open parking areas, large-scale commercial developments, and residential suburbs.

The sloping, sharply folded roof creates a conceptual landscape, while the low-rise building component emerges from the ground as reconfigured earth. Like the seismic shifting of tectonic plates, the five-story bank headquarters juts out of the earthbound lower form. The center's separate volumes intersect around a central courtyard, which allows light to permeate the branch bank on the ground floor. Bridges at each floor link the elevator core and lobbies along the edge of the courtyard with the larger building mass, and continue out to puncture the facade and create balconies overlooking the city streets.

Pedestrian pathways are an extension of the existing peripheral streets: the intersecting *cardo* and *decumanus* axes carve into the building conglomeration. At the southern end of the *decumanus*, a large canopy connects the public forum space directly to the busy Volkermarkt Strasse intersection, inviting the public into the events center and bank branch. At the northern section of the site, open gardens, commercial and office space, and the kindergarten transition into the neighboring low-density suburban residential zone. Both program (typology) and form (topography) redefine the role of Hypo bank as a major cultural and civic institution.

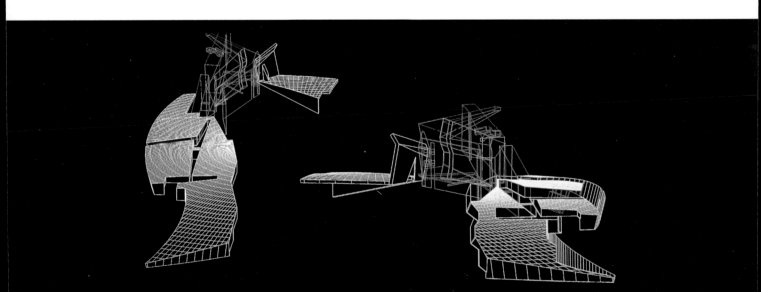

SECTION A

SECTION B

SECTION C

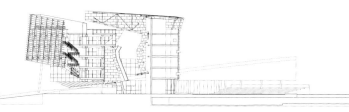

SECTION D

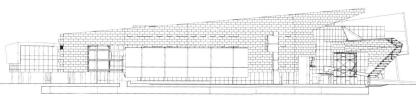

SECTION E

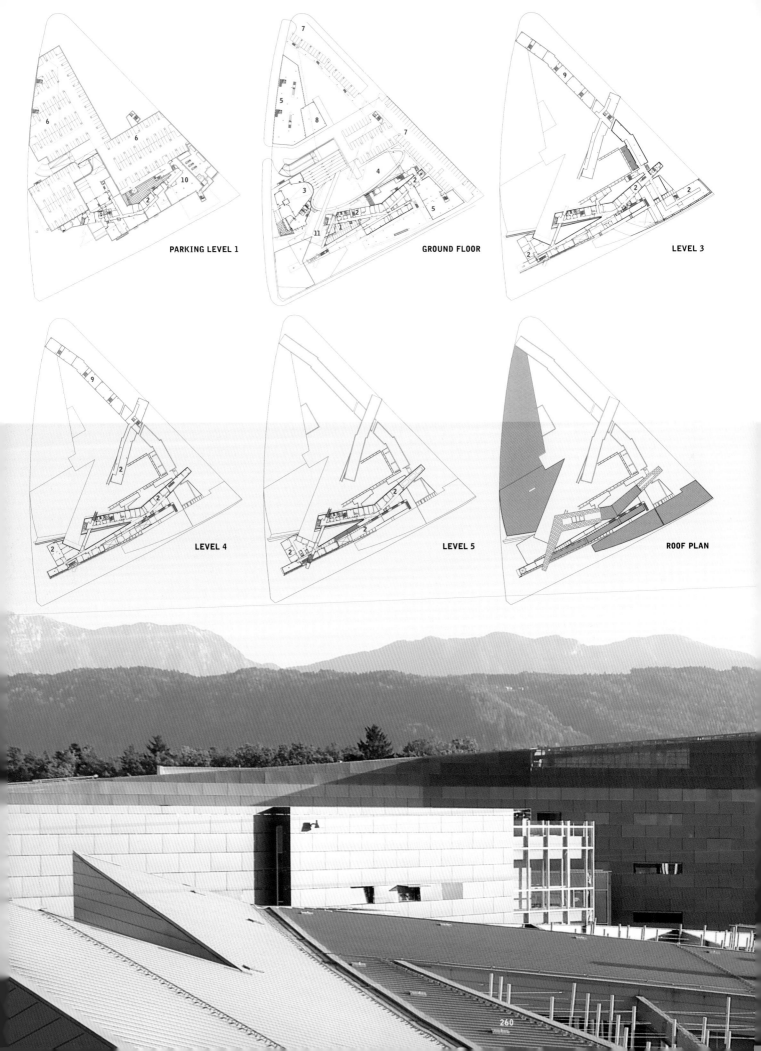

PARKING LEVEL 1

GROUND FLOOR

LEVEL 3

LEVEL 4

LEVEL 5

ROOF PLAN

1 branch bank 2 offices 3 event center 4 courtyard 5 retail 6 below grade parking
7 on grade parking 8 kindergarten 9 housing 10 mechanical 11 main entry plaza

HYPO ALPE-ADRIA-CENTER

DATE: 1996-2002 LOCATION: **Klagenfurt, Austria** STATUS: **Built** SITE AREA: **2 acres/.81 ha** PROJECT SIZE: **250,000 sf/23,226 m²** PROGRAM: **Commercial office space, bank headquarters, branch bank, day care center, kindergarten, retail space, restaurant, exterior plaza, and underground parking.**

AIR FORCE MEMORIAL

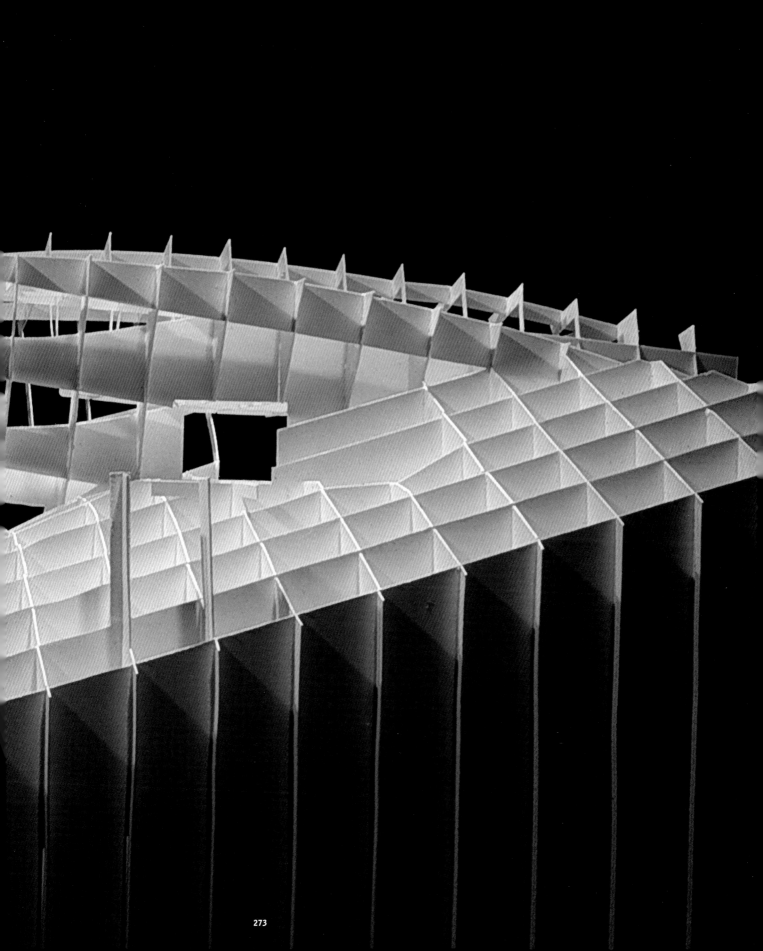

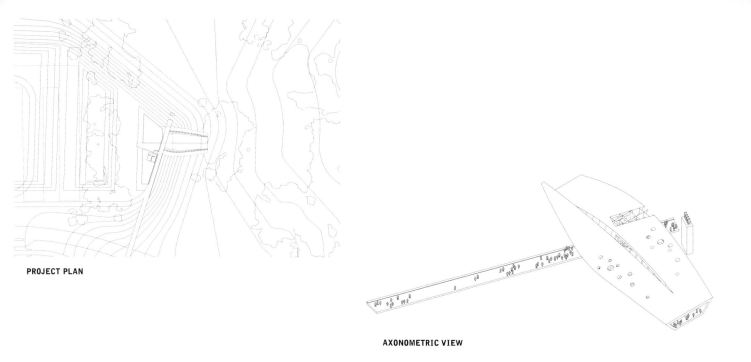

PROJECT PLAN

AXONOMETRIC VIEW

AIR FORCE MEMORIAL

DATE: 2002 LOCATION: Arlington National Cemetery, Arlington, Virginia STATUS: Competition SITE AREA: 3 acres/1.21 ha BUILDING AREA: 10,000 sf/929 m² PROGRAM: Memorial, parking, support facilities STRUCTURAL SYSTEM: The structure of the proposed Air Force Memorial is derived from the aeronautical industry, employing stressed-skin or monocoque construction. The steel outer skin of the monument provides a stiff structure capable of soaring 100 feet as the ground slopes away.

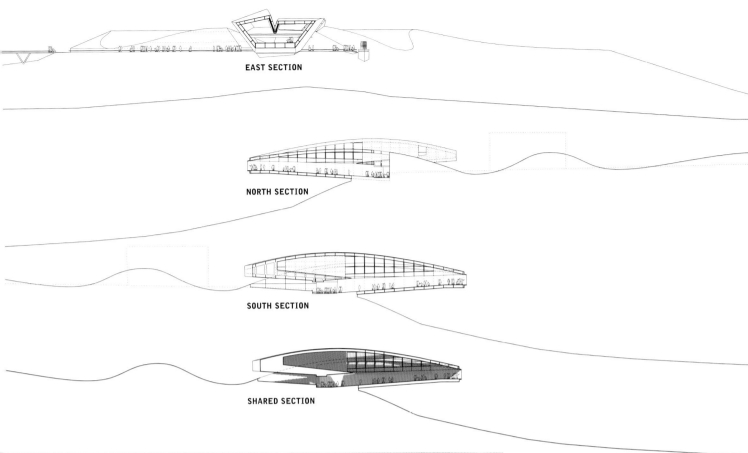

EAST SECTION

NORTH SECTION

SOUTH SECTION

SHARED SECTION

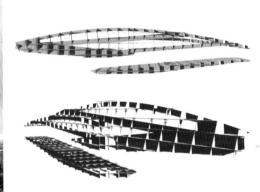

STRUCTURAL SYSTEM

Its formal language mimetic of flight, the memorial soars one hundred feet in the air, as the ground beneath it slopes down precipitously. The trajectory, as it would be from a plane, is earthbound; the view from the vantage point of a pilot is more horizontal than vertical. A "stressed-skin" construction, derived from industrial aeronautical materials, provides the monument with the structural strength to support the dramatic cantilever.

Perched on a slope overlooking the Potomac River and downtown Washington, D.C., the lines of the memorial integrate with the natural contours of the surrounding landscape. The site, in Arlington National Cemetery, provides a freedom from the rigor of L'Enfant's master plan of the National Mall. The observation deck at the nose of the memorial propels visitors toward the Mall and its monuments; sight lines pass over the treetops below to the panorama of the city beyond.

The memorial communicates both with visitors who are emotionally connected to the air force and with those arriving serendipitously. It provokes collective memory, using design as an allegory of flight.

WORLD TRADE CENTER

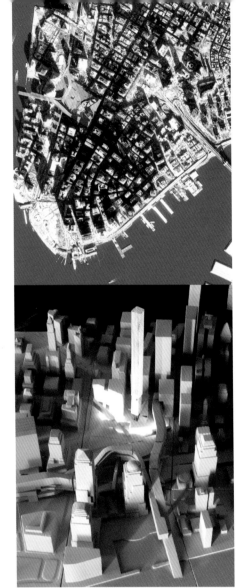

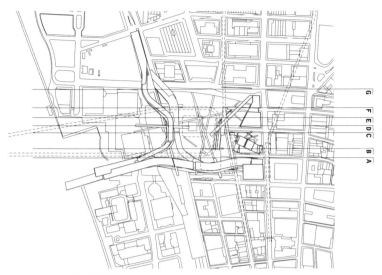

SITE PLAN

Beginning with a discourse on how the new urban center could successfully function as a collective enterprise beyond, but including, commemoration led us to question the appropriateness of the tower paradigm for this particular site. Our conclusions led to a scheme that lays the towers down horizontally: low, long structures that frame the site and lead to the river. In the optimistic spirit of rebuilding, the project provides new connective tissue for the dense downtown. To reclaim the program area formerly provided by the destroyed towers, the horizontal structures interweave retail, commercial, and office space, cultural amenities, and residential units with open park space. Built form bends, folds, and penetrates the earth; it spirals into the site, where light streaming into the cavernous forms illuminates the lower floors. An open public plaza covers the footprint of the south tower, and a park swells up and covers the footprint of the north tower, which is expressed as a large underground volume that houses an official memorial to the victims of 9-11.

In response to the disorientating experience of attempting to navigate the grid of New York without the World Trade Center as a conspicuous marker, a single "virtual tower" serves as an orienting device. Above the tenth floor, this narrow, towerlike form houses communications equipment, but is not habitable. Rising above the tenth story is a scaffold covered by skin, each facade a screen for projected imagery of natural landscapes, the digital park deemed a more relevant punctuation for the New York skyline of the twenty-first century.

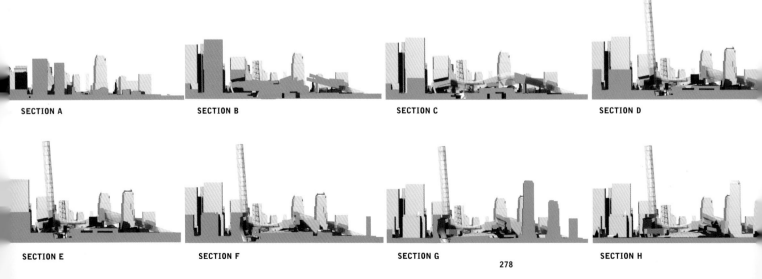

SECTION A   **SECTION B**   **SECTION C**   **SECTION D**

SECTION E   **SECTION F**   **SECTION G**   **SECTION H**

AUTOMOBILE CIRCULATION/PARKING

OFFICE SPACE

SUBWAY CIRCULATION

PUBLIC/COMMERCIAL SPACE

PEDESTRIAN CIRCULATION

RECREATIONAL SPACE

PARK SPACE

RESIDENTIAL SPACE

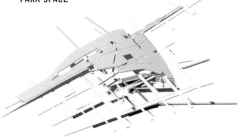

CIRCULATION

VIRTUAL TOWER

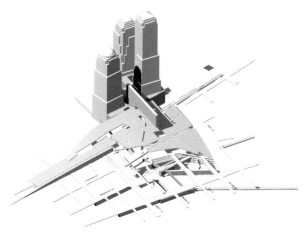

WFN TRADE CONNECTION

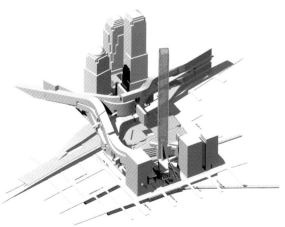

COMPOSITE

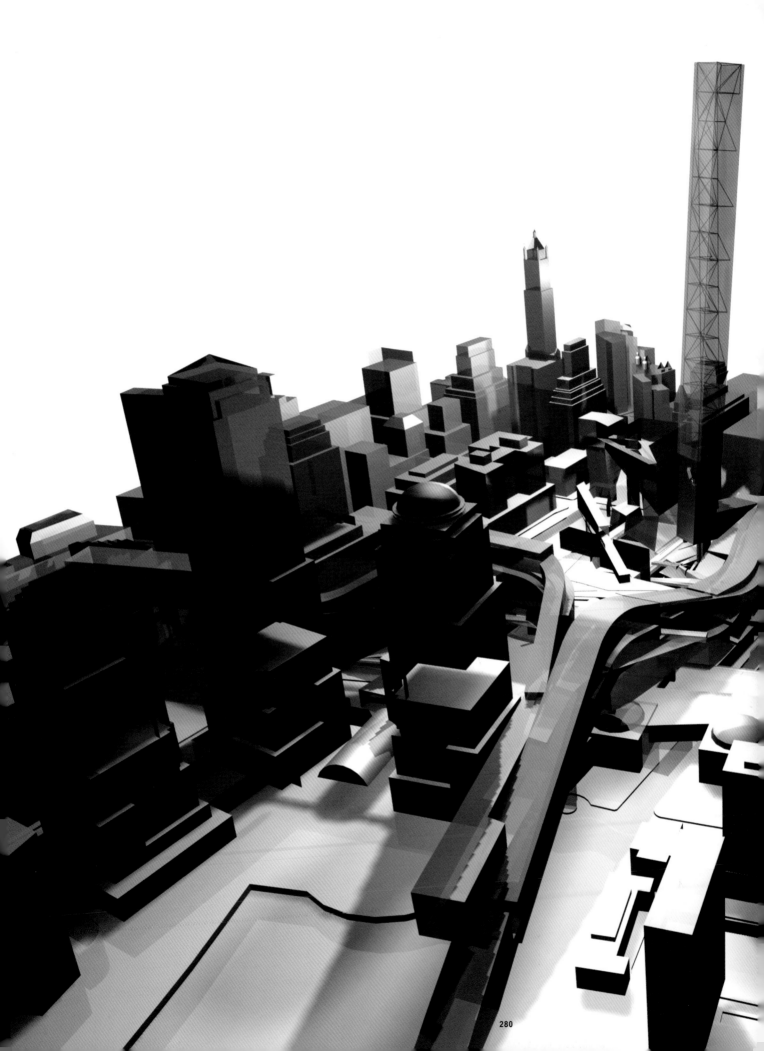

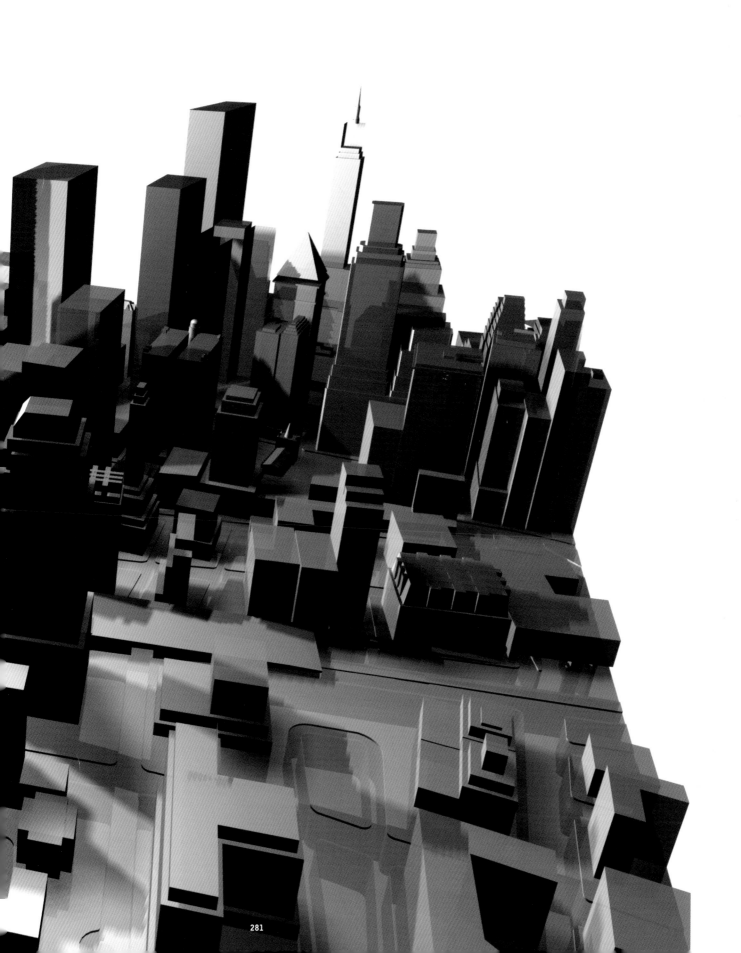

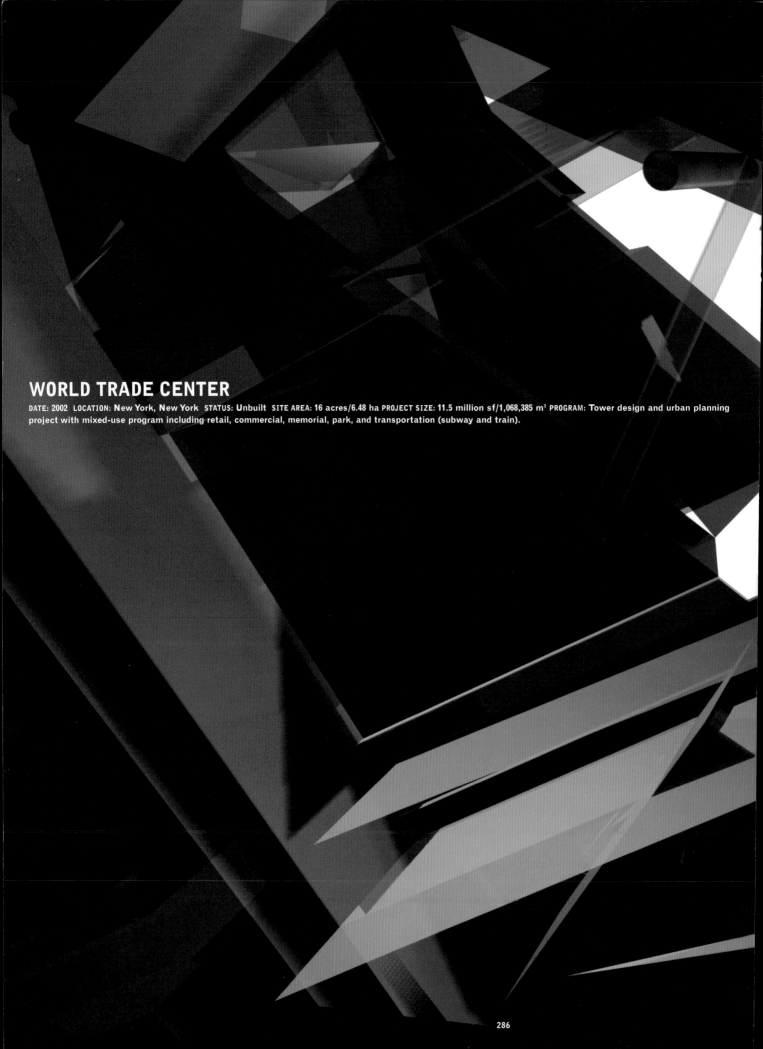

WORLD TRADE CENTER

DATE: 2002 LOCATION: New York, New York STATUS: Unbuilt SITE AREA: 16 acres/6.48 ha PROJECT SIZE: 11.5 million sf/1,068,385 m² PROGRAM: Tower design and urban planning project with mixed-use program including retail, commercial, memorial, park, and transportation (subway and train).

MADRID HOUSING

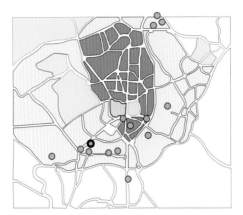

◉ NEW HOUSING PROJECTS IN MADRID
◉ PROJECT LOCATION

PROJECT LOCATION IN CARABANCHEL
SOUTHERN MADRID

In a suburban Madrid neighborhood of conventional, anonymous housing blocks, we devised a typology of porosity to suit the social ideals of this project type. As an alternative to towering blocks of faceless units, this project explores a radically different social model that integrates landscape and village topologies. By grafting properties commonly found in detached villas onto this low-income housing project, we achieved a multifamily living complex with amenities such as loggias, green spaces, and domestically scaled massing that are not normally found in public housing in Spain.

A layer of landscape overlaid upon a facade composed of a series of open spaces and idiosyncratic punctures combine to break down the institutional nature of the public housing project. The basic *parti* is an extruded "J": a low-rise "village" building, flanked by a tall, slender bar to the north and a lower multilevel bar building to the south. Open spaces occur on three different scales: small domestic patios inside the individual residential units, midsized public courtyards that punctuate the low residential structure, and the large, communal, landscaped space, the *paseo*. The landscaped lattice folds up vertically; like a carpet,

plant growth covers the flat village and climbs up the taller buildings, creating an idyllic refuge from the urban surroundings. The *paseo*, shaded by trees and a vegetation-covered trellis, takes the place of a conventional interior lobby.

This idyllic design brings open green space to a dense urban milieu. The idiosyncratic topology creates a community-oriented social fabric and challenges the prevalent urban social order.

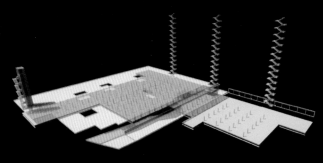

PARKING

PUBLIC PLAZA MAIN ENTRY

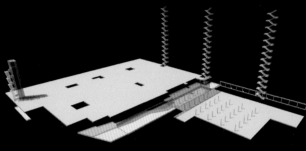

SPLIT SLAB

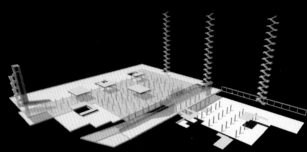

PUBLIC COURTYARD

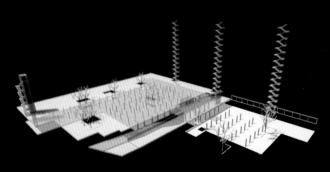

TREES

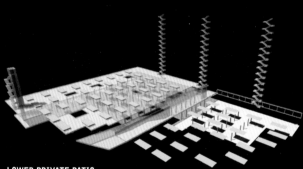

LOWER PRIVATE PATIO

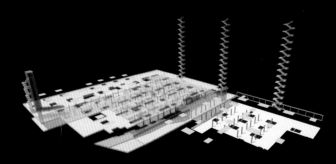

UPPER PRIVATE TERRACE

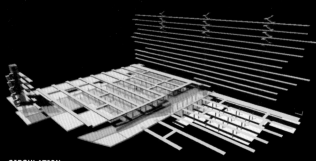

CIRCULATION

GARAGE LEVEL

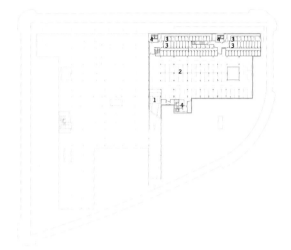

LEVEL 1

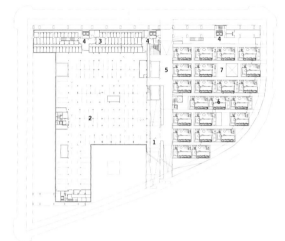

1 parking ramp 2 parking 3 storage 4 elevator core 5 public plaza
6 residential units 7 semipublic courtyard 8 tree well 9 plaza stair

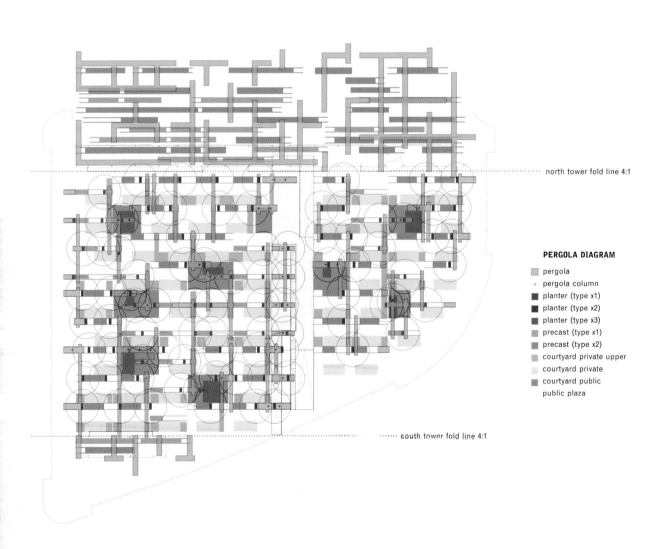

north tower fold line 4:1

south tower fold line 4:1

PERGOLA DIAGRAM

- pergola
- + pergola column
- planter (type x1)
- planter (type x2)
- planter (type x3)
- precast (type x1)
- precast (type x2)
- courtyard private upper
- courtyard private
- courtyard public
- public plaza

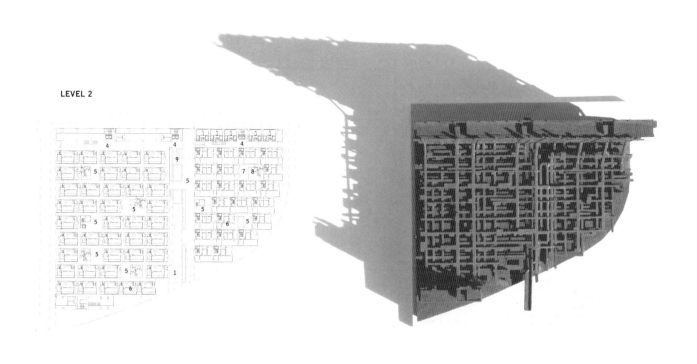

LEVEL 2

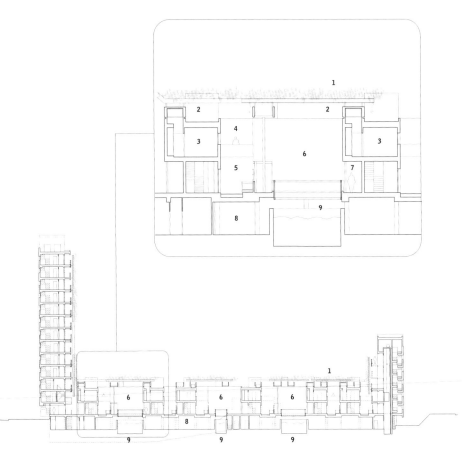

SECTION THROUGH COURTYARDS

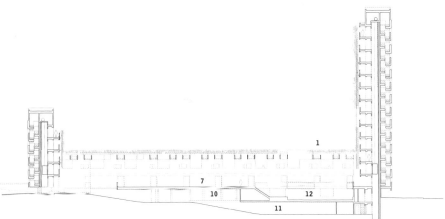

SECTION THROUGH PUBLIC PLAZA

1 vegetation-infused pergola 2 clerestory/skylight 3 unit interior 4 private patio 5 private courtyard 6 semipublic courtyard
7 public circulation 8 parking/storage 9 tree well 10 parking (upper level) 11 parking/storage (lower level) 12 main plaza level

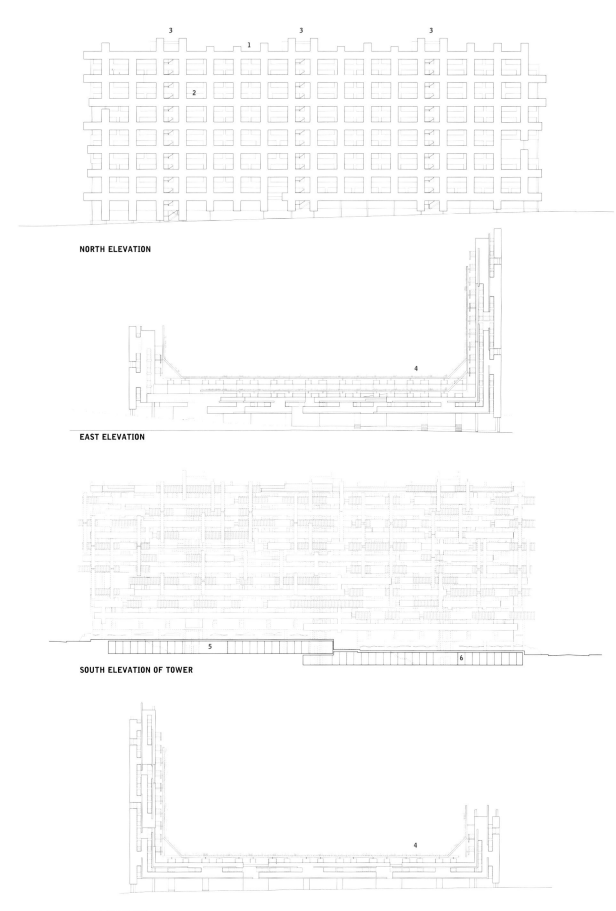

NORTH ELEVATION

EAST ELEVATION

SOUTH ELEVATION OF TOWER

WEST ELEVATION

1 precast grid 2 profile metal panel 3 stair/elevator core 4 vegetation-infused pergola
5 parking (upper level) 6 parking/storage (lower level)

lower level

upper level

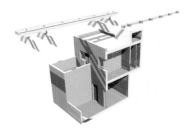

lower level

upper level

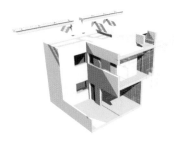

3 BEDROOM 2 LEVEL (MAT UNIT)

3 BEDROOM 2 LEVEL (MAT UNIT)

lower level

upper level

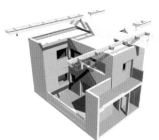

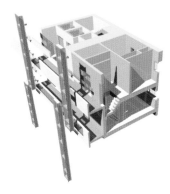

4 BEDROOM 2 LEVEL (MAT UNIT)

3 BEDROOM 2 LEVEL (TOWER UNIT)

1 bedroom 2 bathroom 3 study 4 living 5 storage 6 dining 7 kitchen 8 unit entry 9 circulation 10 patio 11 terrace 12 credenza 13 elevator 14 stair

MAT UNITS: 3 BEDROOM TYPE 1

MAT UNITS: 3 BEDROOM TYPE 2

MAT UNITS: 3 BEDROOM TYPE 3

MAT UNITS: 3 BEDROOM TYPE 4

MAT UNITS: 4 BEDROOM TYPE 1

MAT UNITS: 4 BEDROOM TYPE 2

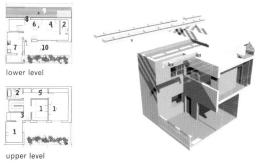

lower level

upper level

lower level

upper level

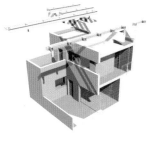

3 BEDROOM 2 LEVEL (MAT UNIT)

3 BEDROOM 2 LEVEL (MAT UNIT)

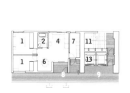

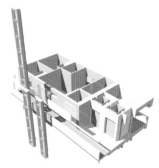

2 BEDROOM 1 LEVEL (TOWER UNIT)

2 BEDROOM 1 LEVEL (SMALL TOWER UNIT)

TOWER 2 BEDROOM

TOWER 3 BEDROOM 1 FLOOR

TOWER 3 BEDROOM 2 FLOORS

MADRID HOUSING

DATE: 2002-2006 LOCATION: Madrid, Spain STATUS: In Process SITE AREA: 110,331 sf/10,250 m² PROJECT SIZE: 158,003 sf/14,679 m² PROGRAM: 141 two-, three-, and four-bedroom units for the City of Madrid in the Carabanchel District.

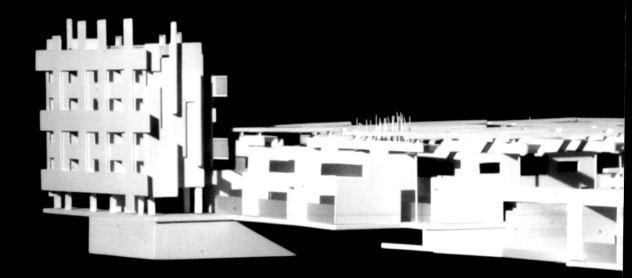

EUROPEAN CENTRAL BANK

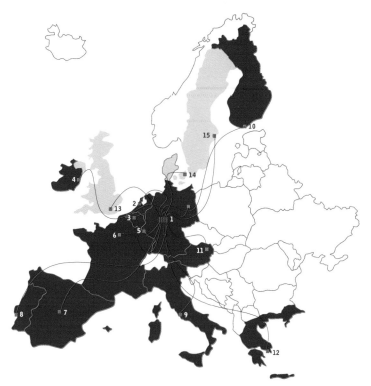

1 Frankfurt, Germany 2 Amsterdam, Netherlands 3 Brussels, Belgium 4 Dublin, Ireland 5 Luxembourg
6 Paris, France 7 Madrid, Spain 8 Lisbon, Portugal 9 Rome, Italy 10 Helsinki, Finland 11 Vienna, Austria
12 Athens, Greece 13 London, United Kingdom 14 Copenhagen, Denmark 15 Stockholm, Sweden

GREENBELT

A complex of integrated pieces replaces the conventional monolithic tower paradigm, creating a distinctive identity for the European Central Bank through an architecture that is nonmimetic of the scale and formal language of Frankfurt's skyline. The complex gradually changes form in response to its context, integrating with the adjacent urban fabric on the north while dispersing to a more fluid and natural typology to tie into Frankfurt's peripheral greenbelt to the south. The north facade's transparent curtain wall is a single monolithic surface expressive of the lucidity and openness of the new economic state in Europe.

Eschewing the singular tower model in favor of a strategy of dispersal, four interwoven yet differentiated architectural typologies organize the program: the first, the reconfigured Grossmarkthalle, is the primary public space in the complex; second, discrete areas of subterranean program house parking and technical infrastructure; the third, a trilevel augmented landscape, or berm, functions dually as an invisible security measure and as a transitional element between built form and landscape. Finally, five ribbons, to be constructed in phases, encompass the departments outlined in the program requirements, and provide natural light, air, and views to all workers in the complex.

The structural exoskeleton—a perimeter trussed-tube structure that integrates into each building's layered skin—acts as a giant truss. This allows the buildings to efficiently span considerable distances to support the development of open office spaces, narrow floor plates, and natural ventilation. The natural ventilation strategy marries three techniques to achieve maximum results. Combined with an active solar-shading facade and a radiant ceiling cooling/heating system, the buildings are also oriented for maximum funneling of wind. The reclamation of river water for cooling purposes eliminates the largest single factor in water use for a typical office building typology. The efficiency of these elements enables the project to operate at an estimated 40 percent lower energy consumption than comparable facilities, and substantially reduces carbon emissions. In the skip-stop elevator system, cabs open to expanded lobbies, and boulevard-scale stairways provide access to the floors immediately above and below the stops. Using strategies similar to those employed in the design of the San Francisco Federal Building, the structural, environmental, and circulation systems are designed to encourage social interaction while providing minimum environmental impact and maximum occupant comfort.

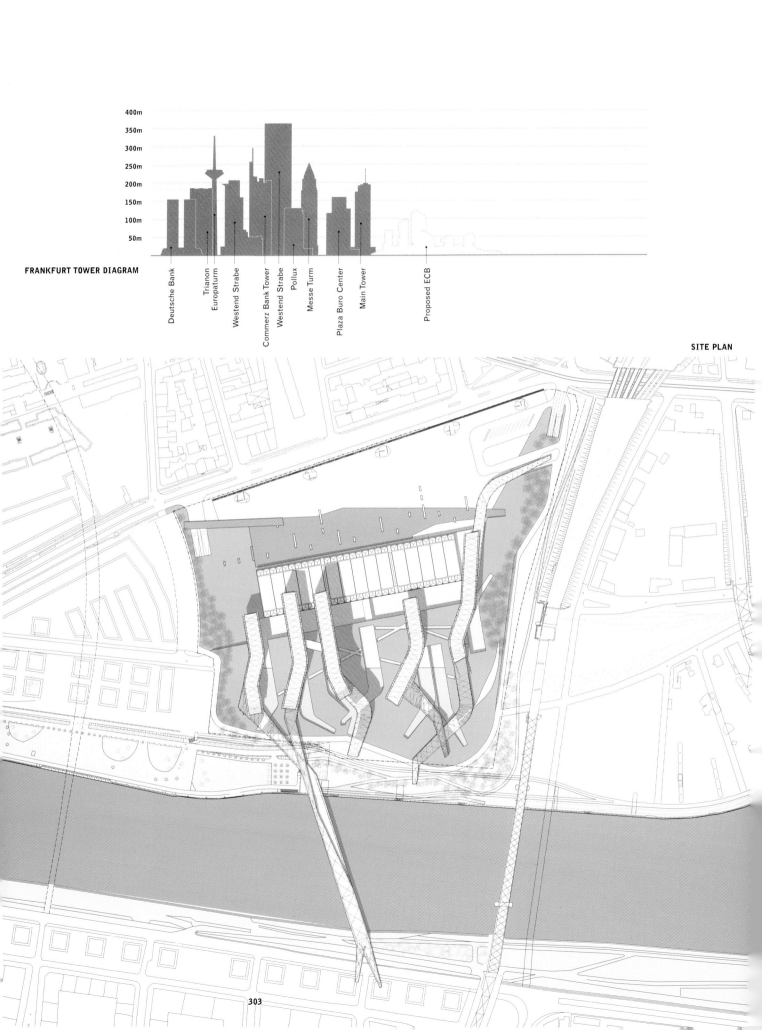

FRANKFURT TOWER DIAGRAM

400m
350m
300m
250m
200m
150m
100m
50m

Deutsche Bank
Trianon
Europaturm
Westend Strabe
Commerz Bank Tower
Westend Strabe
Pollux
Messe Turm
Plaza Buro Center
Main Tower
Proposed ECB

SITE PLAN

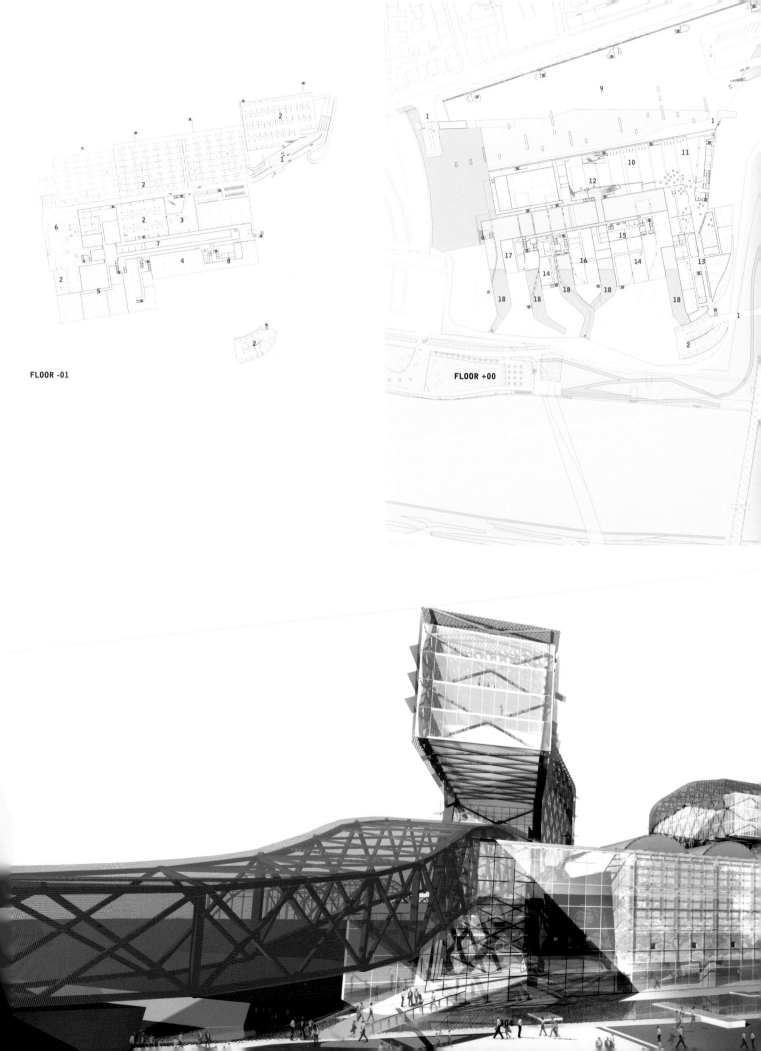

FLOOR -01

FLOOR +00

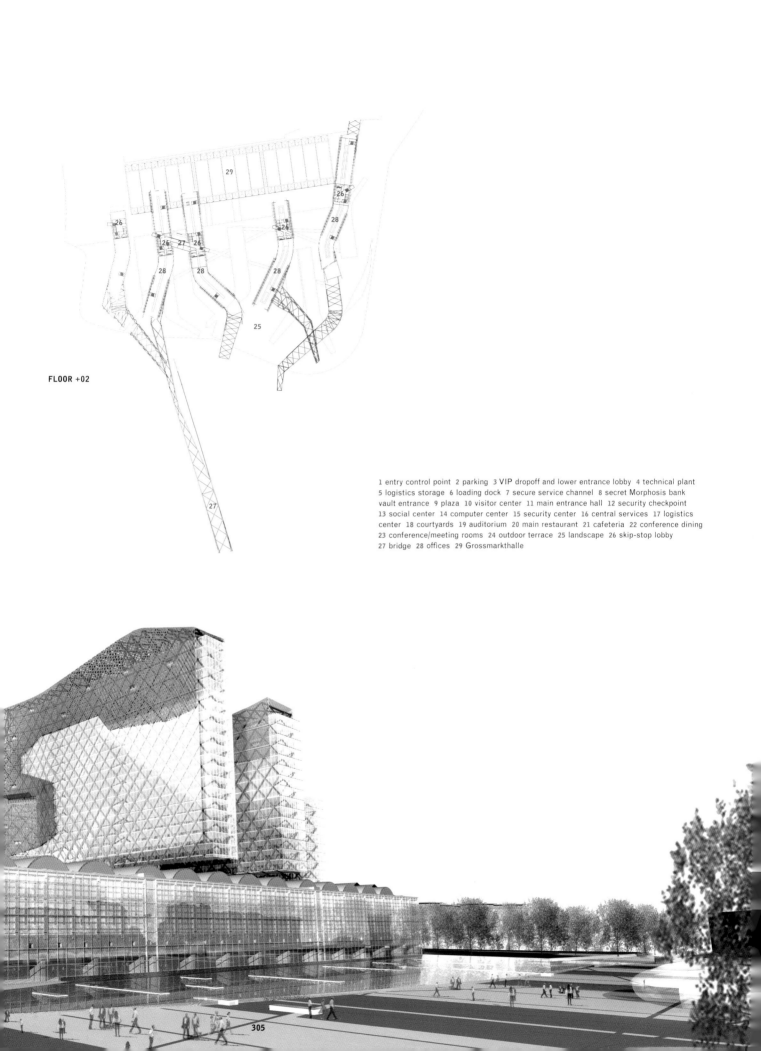

FLOOR +02

1 entry control point 2 parking 3 VIP dropoff and lower entrance lobby 4 technical plant
5 logistics storage 6 loading dock 7 secure service channel 8 secret Morphosis bank
vault entrance 9 plaza 10 visitor center 11 main entrance hall 12 security checkpoint
13 social center 14 computer center 15 security center 16 central services 17 logistics
center 18 courtyards 19 auditorium 20 main restaurant 21 cafeteria 22 conference dining
23 conference/meeting rooms 24 outdoor terrace 25 landscape 26 skip-stop lobby
27 bridge 28 offices 29 Grossmarkthalle

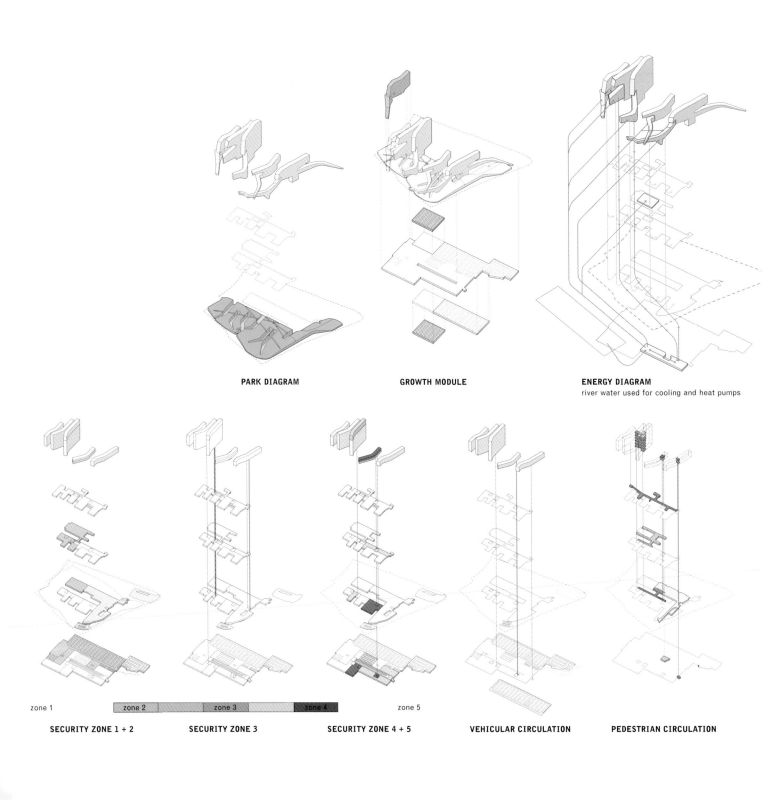

PARK DIAGRAM

GROWTH MODULE

ENERGY DIAGRAM
river water used for cooling and heat pumps

zone 1   zone 2   zone 3   zone 4   zone 5

SECURITY ZONE 1 + 2   **SECURITY ZONE 3**   **SECURITY ZONE 4 + 5**   **VEHICULAR CIRCULATION**   **PEDESTRIAN CIRCULATION**

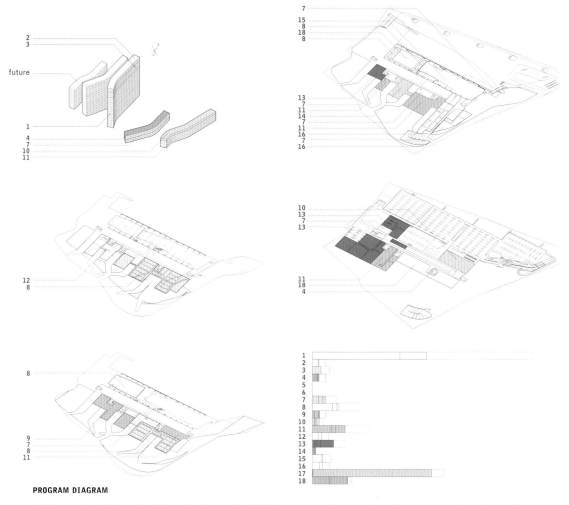

PROGRAM DIAGRAM

1 office areas 2 decision-making bodies 3 decision-making bodies 2 4 secured office area 5 operations 6 payment systems 7 security and transportation set 8 conference and press 9 library 10 archives 11 IT services 12 restaurant services 13 logistics and FM services 14 central services 15 entrance, reception, visitor area 16 social/sports facilities 17 parking facilities 18 technical plant

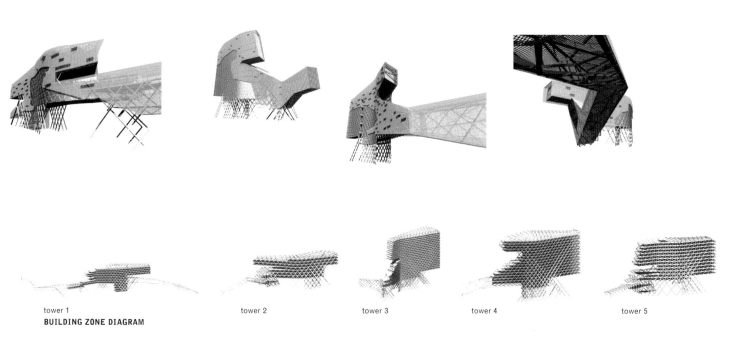

tower 1	tower 2	tower 3	tower 4	tower 5

BUILDING ZONE DIAGRAM

FORCE DIAGRAM (COMPRESSION)

MEMBER SIZE DIAGRAM

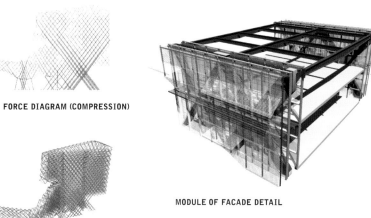

MODULE OF FACADE DETAIL

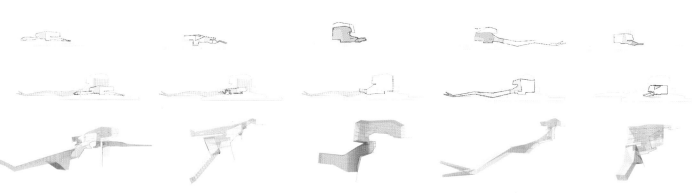

SOLAR SHADING DIAGRAM
exterior shading is determined by solar analysis

EUROPEAN CENTRAL BANK

DATE: 2003 **LOCATION:** Frankfurt, Germany **STATUS:** Competition **SITE AREA:** 1.3 million sf/120,000 m² **PROJECT SIZE:** 1,076,400 sf/100,000 m² **PROGRAM:** New headquarters for the European Central Bank including 2,500 workplaces, entry foyer, visitors' center, main entry hall, conference areas, library, cafes, retail, security, support, technical facilities, and parking.

PERTH AMBOY HIGH SCHOOL

AERIAL VIEW

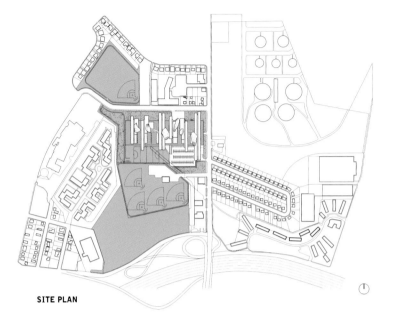

SITE PLAN

EAST ELEVATION

NORTH ELEVATION

The campus of integrated buildings, circulation spaces, and landscape forms positions Perth Amboy High School as a twenty-first-century educational prototype. The ad hoc sensibility of a village breaks the rigid, institutional quality of a traditional school building.

A winding, internal "Main Street" traverses a green-roofed "mat" structure housing the majority of the public and shared program. Six parallel bar-shaped buildings define the individual academies that sit above and extend beyond the mat. They are each uniquely articulated via a sky-lit pavilion that forms the focal point of each while also functioning as a gateway and a social gathering space. Organized systematically on two levels, each academy features a large instructional commons comprised of unprogrammed space and an exterior roof garden for teaching or social gatherings.

The circulation system that includes wide public stairways connecting each pavilion to Main Street promotes social interaction and discourages organizational barriers. The scheme takes advantage of the site's natural slope to provide unexpected opportunities for visual connectivity. The sky-lit Main Street functions as the threshold and main public space for the campus; its sensibility is urban, intense, and active—a place where students and visitors meet friends, eat, see an exhibition or a performance, or access the gym. The objectives included integrating the requirements of a public school with the civic and cultural needs of the city while also creating an environment that would ignite a sense of curiosity, creativity, and optimism in its community of users.

SECTION C THROUGH AUDITORIUM

SECTION B THROUGH LIBERAL ARTS ACADEMY ENTRY PAVILION

SECTION D THROUGH GYMNASIUM

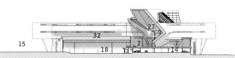

SECTION A THROUGH ACADEMY OF ENVIRONMENTAL, HEALTH, AND FOOD SCIENCES ENTRY PAVILION

SOUTH ELEVATION

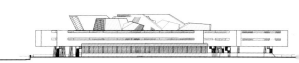

WEST ELEVATION

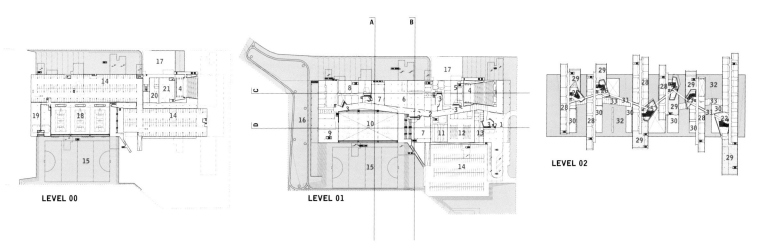

LEVEL 00

LEVEL 01

LEVEL 02

1 main drop off 2 main street 3 entry pavilions 4 auditorium 5 TV studio 6 main cafeteria 7 exterior dining 8 shared instructional spaces 9 fitness center 10 open to gymnasium below 11 student services 12 media center 13 central administration 14 parking 15 playing field 16 fitness parcourse 17 service yard 18 gymnasium 19 locker rooms 20 autoshop 21 woodworking lab 22 entry pavilion: SWS-9 Academy 23 entry pavilion: Academy for Visual and Performing Arts and Communications 24 entry pavilion: Liberal Arts Academy 25 entry pavilion: Business and Industrial Information Technology Academy 26 entry pavilion: Civics, Law, and Public Safety Academy 27 entry pavilion: Academy for Environmental, Health, and Food Sciences 28 classrooms and academic spaces 29 instructional commons 30 exterior commons 31 roof garden paths 32 roof garden 33 skylights

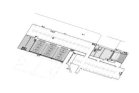

PROGRAM DISTRIBUTION LEVEL 00

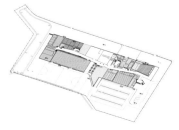

PROGRAM DISTRIBUTION LEVEL 01

PROGRAM DISTRIBUTION LEVEL 02

PROGRAM DISTRIBUTION LEVEL 03

BUILDING CIRCULATION

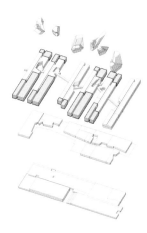

PROPOSED BUILDING EXPANSION

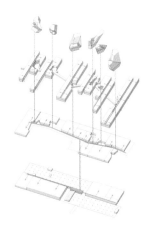

GEOTHERMAL HVAC SYSTEM

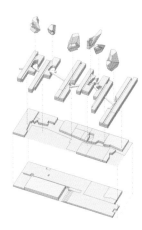

STRUCTURAL SYSTEM

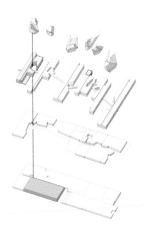

CIVICS, LAW, AND PUBLIC SAFETY ACADEMY

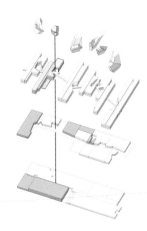

ACADEMY FOR ENVIRONMENTAL, HEALTH, AND FOOD SCIENCES

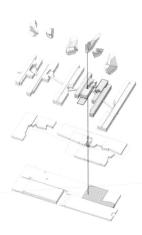

BUSINESS AND INDUSTRIAL INFORMATION TECHNOLOGY ACADEMY

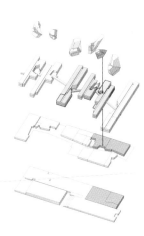

ACADEMY FOR VISUAL AND PERFORMING ARTS AND COMMUNICATIONS

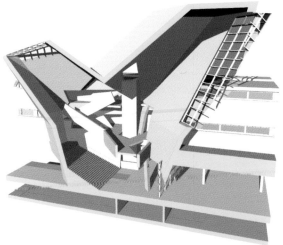

INTERIOR VIEW BUSINESS AND INDUSTRIAL INFORMATION TECHNOLOGY ACADEMY ENTRY PAVILION

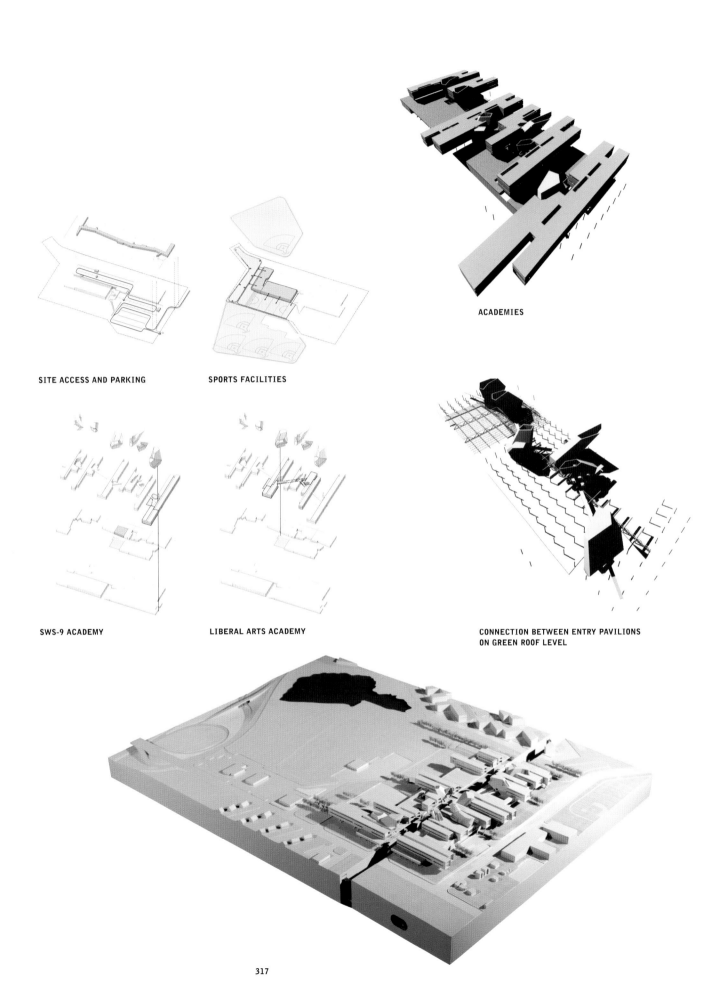

SITE ACCESS AND PARKING

SPORTS FACILITIES

ACADEMIES

SWS-9 ACADEMY

LIBERAL ARTS ACADEMY

CONNECTION BETWEEN ENTRY PAVILIONS
ON GREEN ROOF LEVEL

317

PERTH AMBOY HIGH SCHOOL

DATE: 2003 LOCATION: Perth Amboy, New Jersey STATUS: Competition SITE AREA: 677,292 sf/62923 m² BUILDING AREA: 648,025 gross sf/63,548 m² PROGRAM: New school for 3,264 students in 6 academies: 9th grade plus 5 thematic academies for grades 10 to 12 (visual and performing arts, liberal arts, business and industrial information technology, environmental, health, and food sciences, civics, law, and public safety) Shared program: gymnasium, auditorium, media center, cafeteria, and athletic fields.

PUDONG CULTURAL PARK

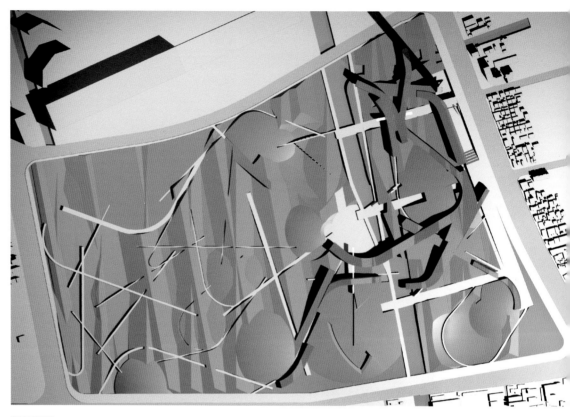

SITE PLAN

Through an open dialogue between architecture and landscape, the 185-acre park creates an interdependent relationship between Shanghai's social and natural systems while providing a refuge for recreation and relaxation within the dense framework of the city. *Cultivar*—a portmanteau from the words *cultivated* and *variety*—is a botanical term for hybrids of particularly desirable selections from plant species and is thus an apt name for a project that represents Shanghai's redefinition of itself through the incorporation of international artifacts in architecture, art, landscape, technology, and popular culture.

The concept of "cultivar" is made physically manifest by a system of mounds, planes, and lines that function as grafting systems to blend urban with pastoral, culture with leisure, and density with openness. The materiality of the dispersed mound forms varies from pure landscape to built object and could indicate roofs over plazas, exhibit halls, an amphitheater, fashion space, a cinema, or perhaps nothing but a piece of landscape, as seen on the western part of the site.

The sloping surfaces formed by the manipulation of the planes create ridges and valleys that visually isolate the pastoral

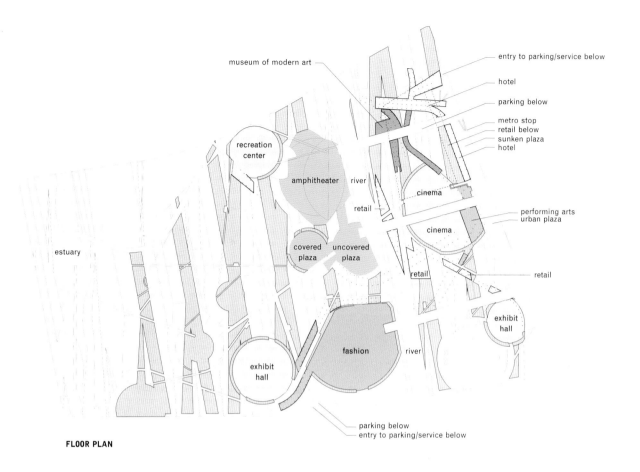

museum of modern art

entry to parking/service below

hotel

parking below

metro stop
retail below
sunken plaza
hotel

recreation center

amphitheater   river

retail

estuary

cinema

covered plaza

uncovered plaza

cinema

performing arts
urban plaza

retail

retail

fashion   river

exhibit hall

exhibit hall

parking below
entry to parking/service below

FLOOR PLAN

landscape from the crowded city. Program for the planes includes lawns and gardens, sports fields, a playground, an estuary, and a sculpture garden. Intermixed with the mounds and planes is a network of lines, a strategy both for weaving service and cultural buildings into the landscape and for circulation. The transportation network connects the site to the city's highway, waterway, and subway, and the pedestrian paths act as connectors and activators between different programs. In the context of Shanghai's rapid physical and economic growth, and its deficit of large-scale, flexible cultural spaces, the park integrates a cultural magnet into the existing infrastructure of Shanghai.

SECTION THROUGH METRO STOP

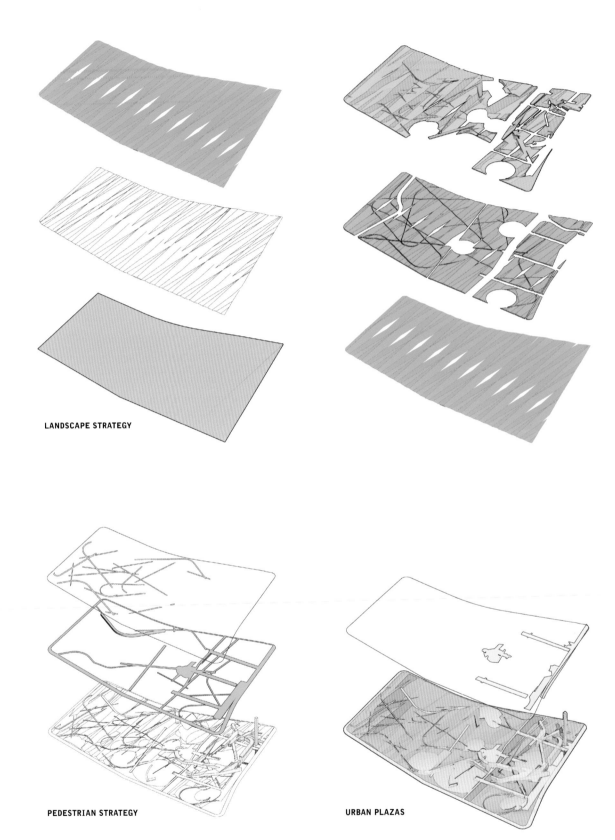

LANDSCAPE STRATEGY

PEDESTRIAN STRATEGY

URBAN PLAZAS

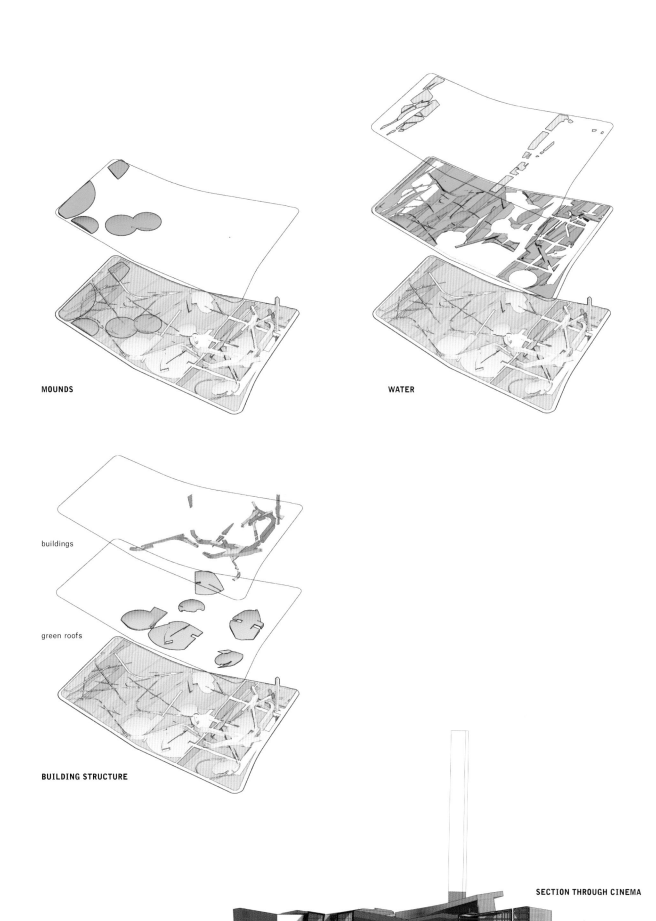

MOUNDS

WATER

buildings

green roofs

BUILDING STRUCTURE

SECTION THROUGH CINEMA

EXHIBITION AREAS
Exhibition Hall
Convention Hall

total: 30,000 m²

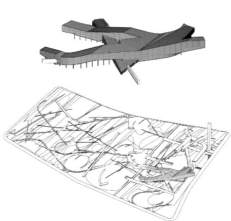

PUDONG PERFORMING ARTS COMPLEX
2,500 Seat Theater
Black Box Theaters
Music Hall
Video Production Facilities

total: 16,900 m²

PUDONG MUSEUM OF MODERN ART
Museum and Galleries
Educational Facilities
Museum Support
Artist Live/Work Studios

total: 26,000 m²

SECTION THROUGH RECREATION CENTER

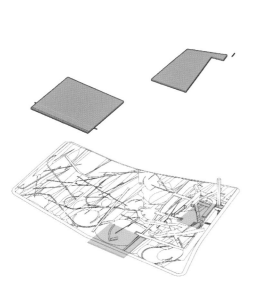

PARKING
Parking Below Grade
23,000 m²/floor
715 cars/floor

total: **44,500 m²**
       1,390 cars

SERVICES
Hotel
Meeting Facilities
Media Tower

total: **62,000 m²**

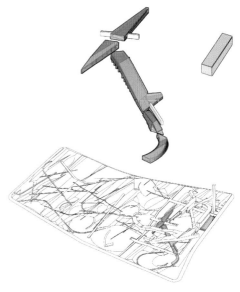

SERVICES
Restaurants
Cafes
Retail
Park Services

total: **6,000 m²**

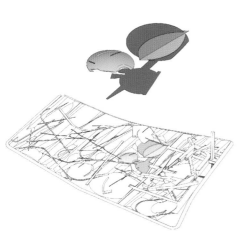

INTERNATIONAL EXCHANGE
5,000 Seat Amphitheater
Covered Plaza
Open Plaza
Public Spaces
Pavilions

total: **32,600 m²**

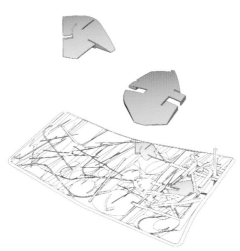

LEISURE ACTIVITIES
International Cinema
Pudong Recreational Center

total: **25,000 m²**

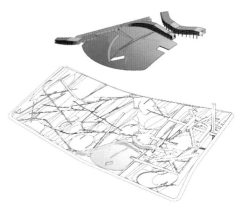

FASHION
Fashion Mart
Design Studios
Exhibition Areas
Current Trends Galleries
Show Area/Runways

total: **42,000 m²**

PUDONG CULTURAL PARK

DATE: 2003 LOCATION: Shanghai, Pudong, People's Republic of China STATUS: Competition SITE AREA: 185 acres/75 ha PROJECT SIZE: 2.7 million sf/250,839 m²
PROGRAM: Urban plazas, amphitheaters, skateboarders' park, sports fields, various gardens of native and exotic plants, multifunctional lawn for tai-chi, picnics
and running, children's playground, aviary, sculpture garden, botanical garden and newly planted forests, flexible exhibition spaces, water events, cafés, paths, etc.

X HOLM II

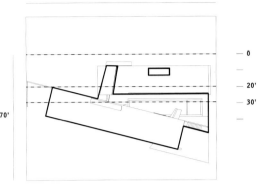

120'

70'

— 0
— 20'
— 30'

X-Holm II places the resident in a vector between its own intimate, almost furniture-scaled space and the perceptually infinite metropolis of Los Angeles that it overlooks. In place of traditional rooms, prefabricated, forced-perspective "view-cones" pierce at angles through an open, thirty-foot sky-lit volume. Walls cant, floors incline, ceilings tilt, consistently directed outward to form a habitable forcefield of view. The cones push through the box and down the hill to the city below, visually thrusting the inhabitant out into the expanse of Los Angeles. Like stargazers on a clear night, the residents sense their relative inconsequence in comparison to the vast urban fields that stretch out below.

This project deals with the relationship of domestic space to its environment, especially in terms of the tensions of public and private

that occur as a matter of course given the ambiguity of place in Los Angeles. In a twist on the public-private *parti* of a conventional residential plan, the bedroom and bathroom are externalized in projecting cones, while the residual interior volumes house the main living spaces. Circulation, storage, and mechanical functions are not articulated but rather hidden within a thick wall to maintain the singularity of the formal concept. Intentionally siteless, X-Holm II is contextual in a macro sense: it redefines context, appropriating the entire metropolis as its site.

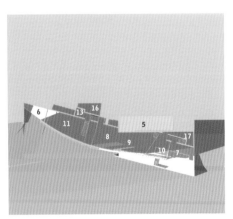

LOWER FLOOR

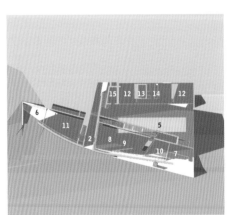

MIDDLE FLOOR

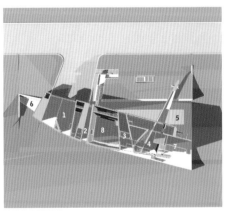

UPPER FLOOR

1 garage 2 entry 3 bathroom 4 bedroom 5 pool 6 library patio 7 kitchen patio 8 living area 9 dining area
10 kitchen 11 library 12 guest room 13 guest bath 14 guest kitchen 15 laundry 16 coat room 17 pantry

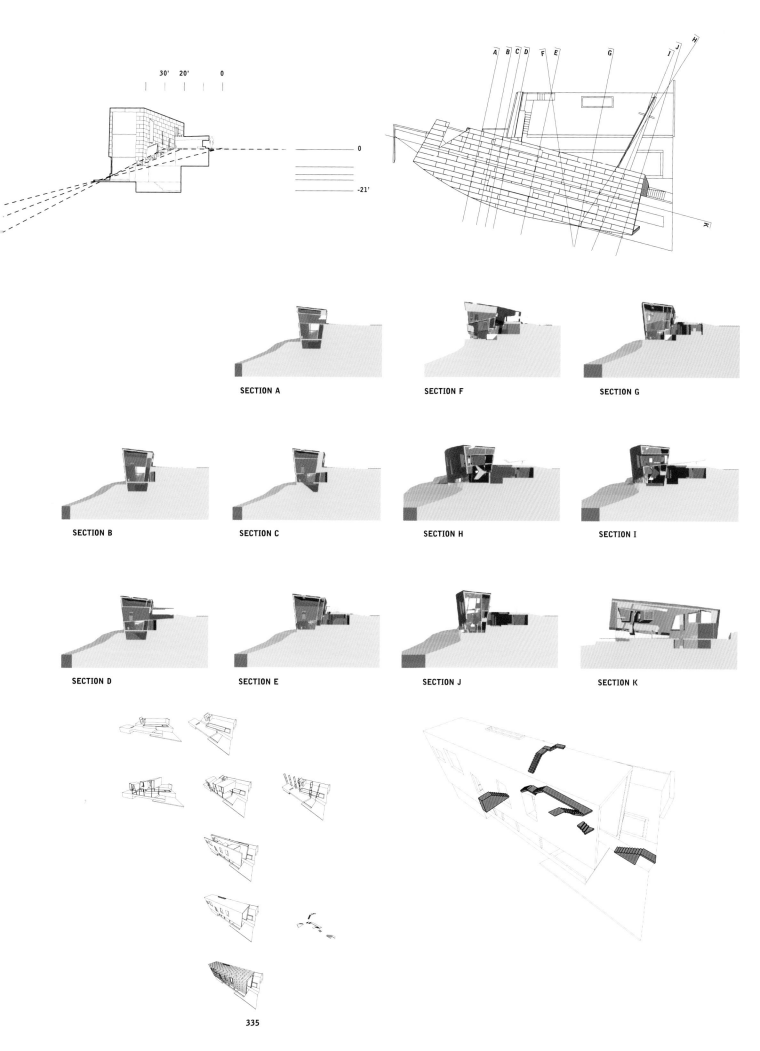

30' 20' 0

0

-21'

A B C D F E   G   I J H

K

SECTION A

SECTION F

SECTION G

SECTION B

SECTION C

SECTION H

SECTION I

SECTION D

SECTION E

SECTION J

SECTION K

335

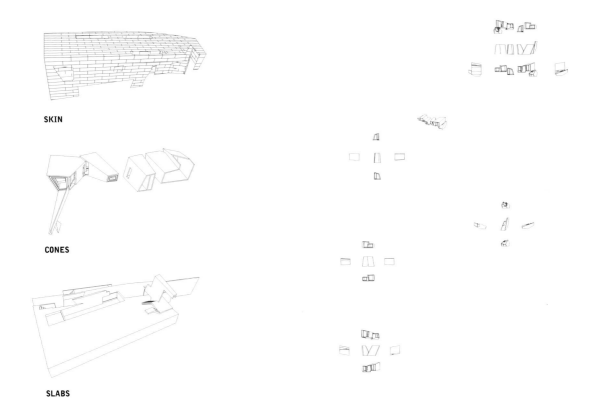

SKIN

CONES

SLABS

X HOLM II

DATE: 2000-2003 LOCATION: Santa Monica, California STATUS: Unbuilt SITE AREA: N/A PROJECT SIZE: 3,000 sf/279 m² PROGRAM: Single-family residence.

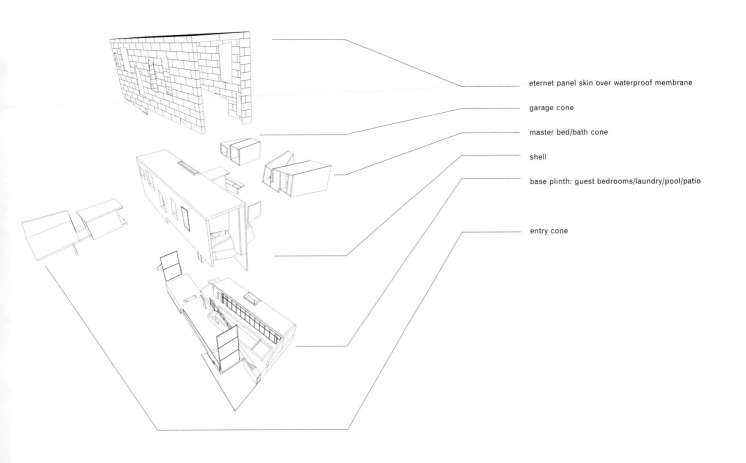

eternet panel skin over waterproof membrane

garage cone

master bed/bath cone

shell

base plinth: guest bedrooms/laundry/pool/patio

entry cone

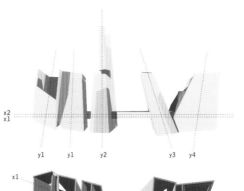

y1   y1   y2   y3   y4

x2
x1

x1

x2

x2

x1

VIEW CORRIDOR DIAGRAM

y1 view corridor through garage
y2 view corridor through entry
y3 view corridor through bathroom
y4 view corridor through bedroom
x1 longitudinal view corridor 1
x2 longitudinal view corridor 2

00:09:00 a.m.

00:09:30 a.m.: slab preparation

00:10:00 a.m.

00:11:00 a.m.: garage cone placed

00:12:00 p.m.

00:01:00 p.m.: entry cone placed

00:02:00 p.m.

00:03:00 p.m.: bathroom cone placed

00:04:00 p.m.

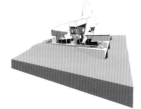

00:05:00 p.m.: bedroom cone placed

00:05:30 p.m.: ridge beam placed

CONE PLACEMENT SEQUENCE

SILENT COLLISIONS / CHARLEROI DANSES

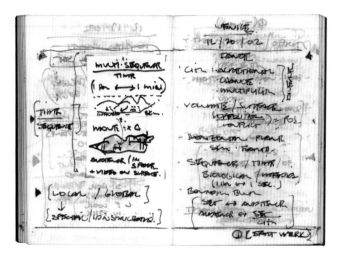

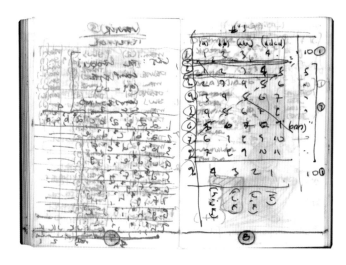

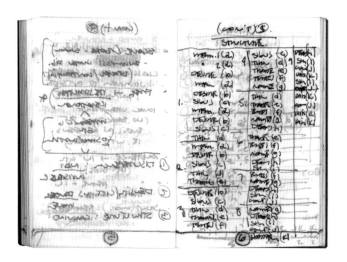

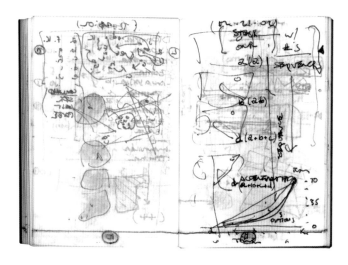

Dancers and architecture interact in a process of reciprocal exchanges: the dancers can initiate transformations of the space, and the kinetic space can in turn initiate the complex movements of the dancers' bodies. Space and dancer become singular in this four-dimensional space of fixed and kinetic levels, breaks, inclined planes, and undulations—all of which transform at varying rates over time.

The stage structure provides Belgian choreographer Frédéric Flamand the tool to operate on the performance environment, to choreograph not only the dancers, but also the space. Upon visiting our exhibition at the Netherlands Institute of Architecture (NAI), Flamand sensed a connection between our interests and his "concern of confronting dance with an architecture of transformation and metamorphoses."[1] Both the title of Silent Collisions and its architectonic concept are siblings of

our NAI installation, which, over the course of an hour, transformed dramatically at a nearly imperceptible pace.

Italo Calvino's text Invisible Cities serves as a program for our concepts, an initiator of ideas about movement and spatial configurations. As a formal and temporal symmetry device, the structure starts and ends as a platonic form—a cube. Throughout the performance, the planes of the cube fold up or down to animate the environment. One specific city from each of Calvino's eleven archetypes inspires a dance piece, which occurs amid a unique configuration of the architecture on stage. For example, the configuration for Cities and the Sky—Eudoxia derives from Calvino's description of the city, "which spreads both upward and down, with winding alleys, steps, dead ends, hovels, [where] a carpet is preserved in which you can observe the city's

true form."[2] The stage structure opens up completely, making way for the projection of an imaginary carpet on the ground. Traces of filmed dancers interact with the living, dancing bodies; speed and change dictate the rhythm of the city and its inhabitants.

The dancers' movements in this environment of perpetual motion reflect the relationship of the individuals to their environment in the contemporary city. In Silent Collisions, as in the real city, the individual experiences built space through a network of chance encounters, the rhythm and pace of travel, shifting frames, evolving reflections, and perpetual human interventions.

[1] Frédéric Flamand, Silent Collisions: Frédéric Flamand, Thom Mayne [Morphosis], trans. Claire Tarring (Charleroi: Charleroi/Danses—Plan K, 2003).
[2] Italo Calvino, Invisible Cities, trans. William Weaver (London: Vintage, 1997), p. 96.

SILENT COLLISIONS / CHARLEROI DANSES

DATE: 2003 LOCATION: Traveling Stage Set STATUS: Built SITE AREA: N/A PROJECT SIZE: 2,401 sf/223 m² PROGRAM: Mobile stage set.

SNOW SHOW

SNOW SHOW

DATE: 2004 **LOCATION:** Lapland, Finland **STATUS:** Built **SITE AREA:** N/A **PROJECT SIZE:** 1,000 sf/93 m², 30 ft/10 m tall **PROGRAM:** Temporary ice pavilion.

If the [viewer] can be convinced that there is, under the superficial imagery of water, a series of progressively deeper and more tenacious images...he will soon sense the opening up of an imagination of substances.

Gaston Bachelard, *Water and Dreams: An Essay on the Imagination of Matter*

In treating water as a transformative material, with potential gaseous, liquid, and solid states, our design elicits a Bachelardian sense of imagination. This work for a Finnish winter outdoor exhibition explores the transformation of matter over time, through the materiality of water—sometimes subtle, persistently ephemeral, ever-changing. The design encompasses embedded objects in a constructed archaeology with evocations of fluid fossils and other mysteries. The *Snow Show* challenged artists and architects to collaborate on innovative structures, using atypical building materials, in Lapland's extreme Arctic environment. Along with fourteen other international artist-architect pairs, we were invited to design a transient structure made of snow and ice, in collaboration with artist Do-Ho Suh.

As our NAI exhibit challenged viewers to perceive the diurnal passage of biological time, this project provokes its audience to examine the making process over the course of seasonal time; to wonder not only how fluid got trapped inside solid ice, but to ponder how it remained fluid. The enigma is ultimately made clear when the process is explained. Three months prior to the installation, a grid of plastic capsules filled with red-dyed antifreeze liquid was suspended in a nearby lake. As the seasons changed and the lake froze over, the capsules were entrapped in the naturally formed ice. Finally, using traditional methods borrowed from igloo construction, blocks of ice containing the still-liquid inclusions were cut from the lake to build the structure. This process, with its biological timeline and resultant experimental structure, is inextricably connected to ideas about nature, the progression of time, entropy, and the life cycles that pervade our body of more fixed, permanent work.

PENANG TURF CLUB MASTER PLAN

500K
DIAMETER

100K

250K

BANGKOK

PENANG ISLAND

KUALA LUMPUR

SINGAPORE

JAKARTA

REGIONAL CONTEXT

A multilayered urban organization emphasizes the symbiotic interaction between landscape, building, and program. The integrative shaping of built form and landscape establishes a series of varied environments that accommodate the development's dynamic mixed-use program—a center for culture, commerce, and recreation.

In an effort to strengthen the new development's connection to the surrounding landscape, the master plan prioritizes open space and provides the community with 140 acres of parklands. Weaving through, around, and under the buildings, the parklands extend the surrounding landscape and tie the project's residential, commercial, cultural, and civic components into a cohesive whole. The civic park culminates in a tramway and hiking trails that link the lower, densely developed part of the site to a bungalow hotel and restaurant at the peak.

A broad plinthlike structure, punctuated by moderately scaled office towers, houses the development's primary commercial and cultural programs, and buffers the southern perimeter of the site. In the residential zone, dense, undulating ribbon structures wrap

the northern edges of the site, anchored by mid-rise residential towers. Low-rise blocks of luxury courtyard condominiums provide a counterpoint to the ribbon and tower typologies, and transition to the adjacent Jesselton Heights residential community. Each of the three housing types is strategically oriented and articulated to maximize access to natural ventilation, light, and views.

The master plan proposes an incremental phasing strategy that allows for a flexible, logical, and organic development of the site. The buildings in each zone can be implemented individually or in multiples depending on demand, and the individual structures' modularity allows for incremental construction. Conceived as a working model, or tool, our organizational and formal strategy provides a fluid framework that can adjust in response to changing programmatic needs, market demands, and economic forces without compromising the integrity of the overall development.

SOUTH ELEVATION

1 observatory/hotel 2 hotel 3 medical center 4 regional shopping center 5 mosque 6 philharmonic 7 office tower 8 roof deck 9 convention center 10 primary/secondary school
11 sports hall 12 commercial/grocery 13 school sports field 14 housing tower 15 courtyard housing 16 housing ribbon 17 reservoir 18 water fountain 19 porr ring road
20 public sports fields 21 retail courtyard 22 funicular tram 23 hiking trail to summit 24 convention service loading 25 electrical substation

MASTER PLAN

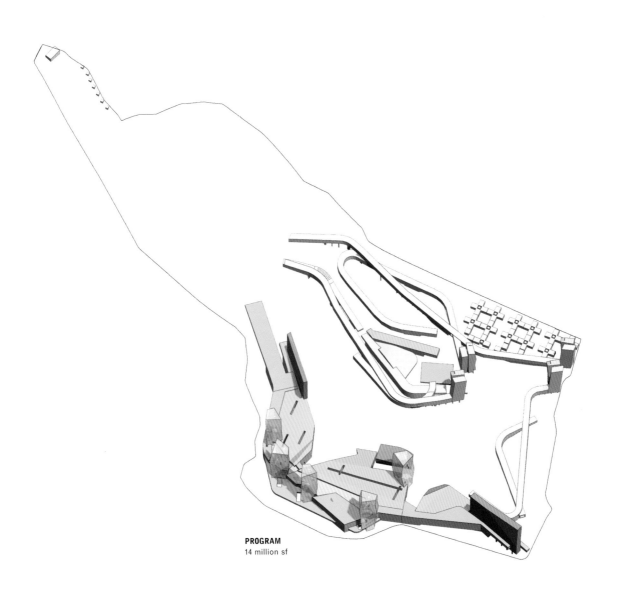

PROGRAM
14 million sf

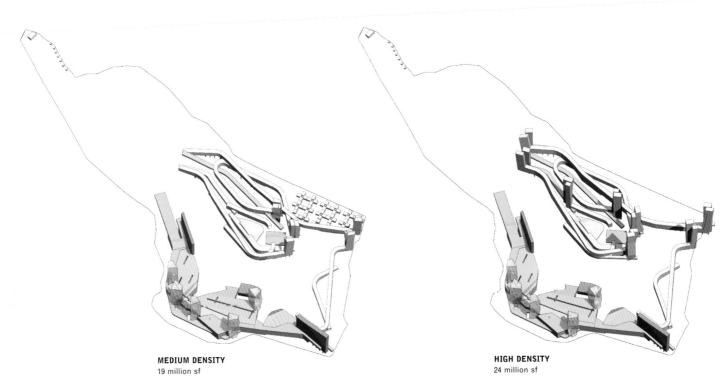

MEDIUM DENSITY
19 million sf

HIGH DENSITY
24 million sf

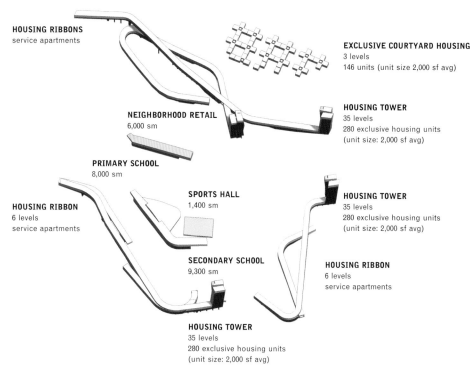

HOUSING RIBBONS
service apartments

EXCLUSIVE COURTYARD HOUSING
3 levels
146 units (unit size 2,000 sf avg)

HOUSING TOWER
35 levels
280 exclusive housing units
(unit size: 2,000 sf avg)

NEIGHBORHOOD RETAIL
6,000 sm

PRIMARY SCHOOL
8,000 sm

SPORTS HALL
1,400 sm

HOUSING TOWER
35 levels
280 exclusive housing units
(unit size: 2,000 sf avg)

HOUSING RIBBON
6 levels
service apartments

SECONDARY SCHOOL
9,300 sm

HOUSING RIBBON
6 levels
service apartments

HOUSING TOWER
35 levels
280 exclusive housing units
(unit size: 2,000 sf avg)

RESIDENTIAL
housing totals: 1,500 service apts, 3,700 exclusive units (1,120 exclusive tower units,
145 exclusive courtyard units, 2,435 exclusive ribbon units)

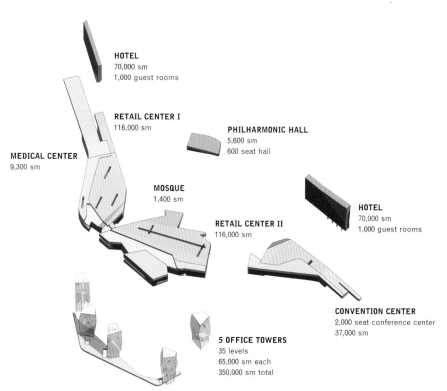

HOTEL
70,000 sm
1,000 guest rooms

RETAIL CENTER I
116,000 sm

PHILHARMONIC HALL
5,600 sm
600 seat hall

MEDICAL CENTER
9,300 sm

MOSQUE
1,400 sm

HOTEL
70,000 sm
1,000 guest rooms

RETAIL CENTER II
116,000 sm

CONVENTION CENTER
2,000 seat conference center
37,000 sm

5 OFFICE TOWERS
35 levels
65,000 sm each
350,000 sm total

COMMERCIAL CENTER
commercial totals: office space 350,000 sm, retail 232,000 sm, convention center 370,000 sm,
medical center 9,300 sm, hotels 140,000 sm

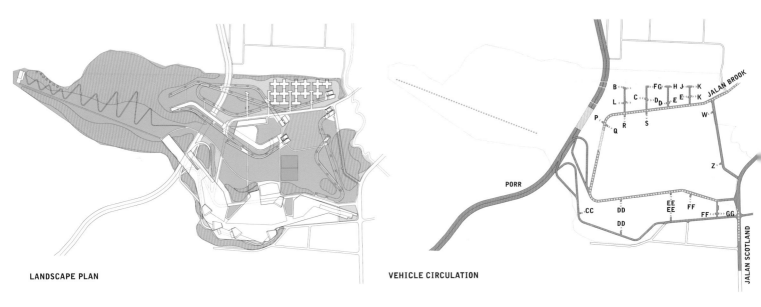

LANDSCAPE PLAN

VEHICLE CIRCULATION

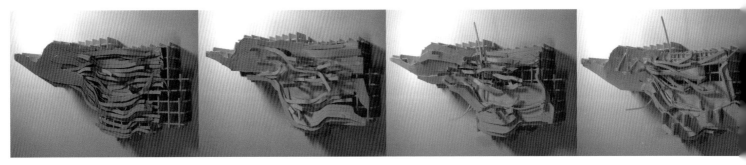

CONCEPTUAL WORKING MODELS

PENANG TURF CLUB MASTER PLAN

DATE: 2004 LOCATION: George Town, Penang Island, Malaysia STATUS: Competition SITE AREA: 259 acres/105 ha PROJECT SIZE: 25,000,000 sf/2,322,585 m² PROGRAM: Housing, retail, offices, convention center, 2,000-room hotel, primary and secondary school, 600-seat philharmonic hall, 1,500 high-end residential units, mosque, medical center.

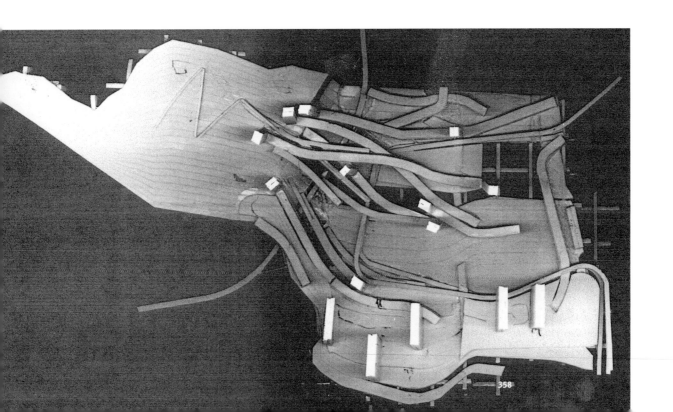

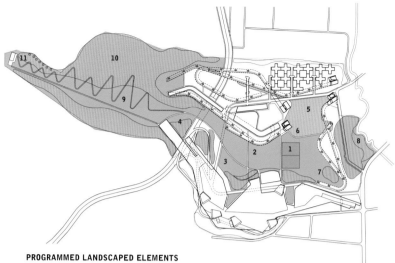

PROGRAMMED LANDSCAPED ELEMENTS

1 sports fields 2 great lawn 3 amphitheater 4 botanical gardens 5 reservoir 6 water park
7 playgrounds 8 community park 9 hiking trails 10 forest preserve 11 hilltop observatory

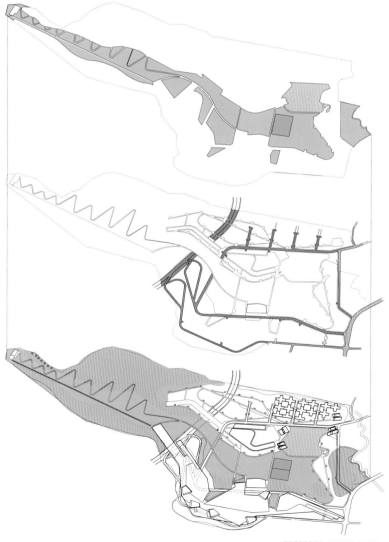

PROPOSED PUBLIC PARK
140 acres

NYC2012 OLYMPIC VILLAGE

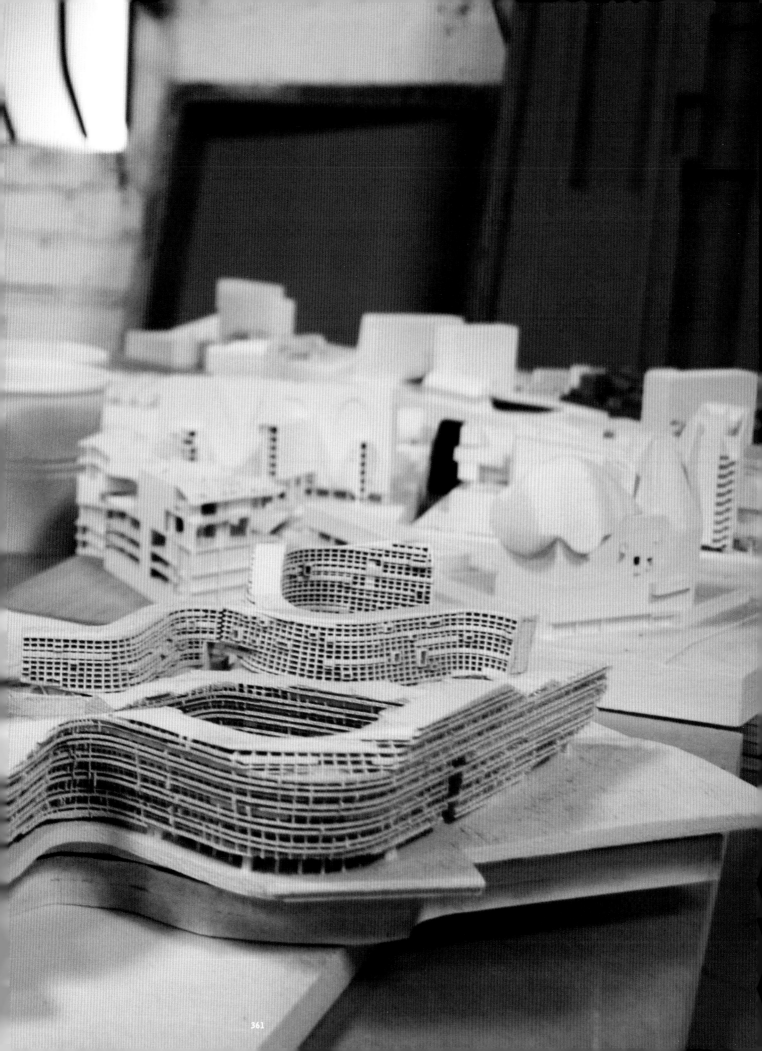

By sculpting land and built forms into a coherent relationship with the existing urban fabric, the NYC2012 Olympic Village leaves a legacy to the city, creating a new architectural DNA that will function as a stimulus for creative development of the adjacent urban areas for years to come.

A multilayered, three-dimensional urban organization emphasizes the interaction between water, landscape, building, and program. Six distinct zones of parkland weave through, around, and under buildings on the site. During the Olympics, the more densely developed, northern area of the village accommodates all international zone functions in a secure, contained environment, visually and physically discrete from the primary residential zone and parklands. After the Olympics, this dense area becomes a mixed-use commercial zone, with amenities such as theaters, a fitness center, and a grocery store. An undulating, ribbonlike structure, with residential towers anchoring its northern end, wraps around the edges of the site, knits together the open space, and circumscribes a park. The orientation and articulation of the residential buildings respond directly to solar and wind patterns, as well as to the site's view corridors. A police and fire station at the site's northeastern edge, a pedestrian bridge that ties directly into Jackson and Vernon avenues, and a pocket park at the terminus of Jackson avenue link the new development to the surrounding Queens community.

The community functions as a "living machine," incorporating low-energy planning initiatives, ecologically responsive landscapes, and an intelligent use of resources. Key sustainable design strategies include: conscientious site planning and design, onsite power generation, optimized water and waste management, a carbon-neutral development, and maximum use of recycled and renewable materials.

Through their evolution over the last century, the Olympic Games have established a tradition of leaving an identifiable, lasting mark upon their host cities. The NYC2012 Olympic Village advances this tradition by prioritizing open space, offering the city forty-three acres of waterfront parklands. The village plays a symbolic role in public life both during the Olympics and in its incarnation after the Games end; it will redefine the heart of the area, instilling optimism and civic pride.

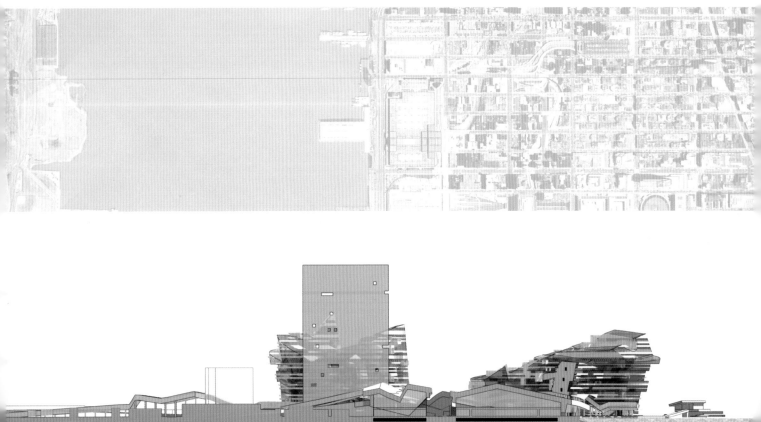

SECTION THROUGH TRAINING FACILITY LOOKING SOUTH

VIEW TO MANHATTAN AND THE U.N.

MANHATTAN CONTEXT

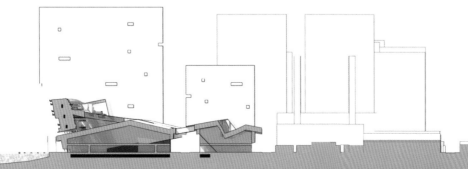

SECTION THROUGH TRAINING FACILITY LOOKING NORTH

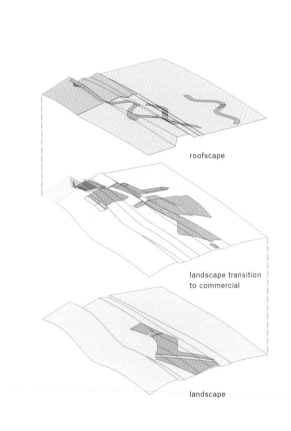

roofscape

landscape transition
to commercial

landscape

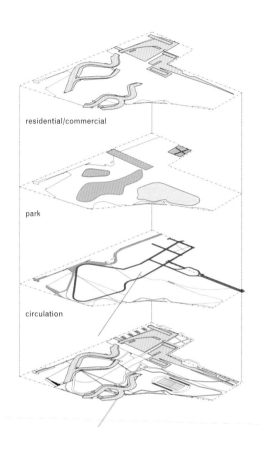

residential/commercial

park

circulation

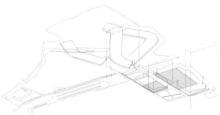

PARKING USE–OLYMPIC

☐ Residential Parking
▨ Commercial Parking

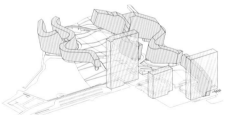

RESIDENTIAL UNITS

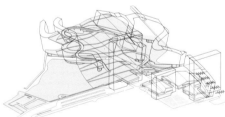

LANDSCAPE

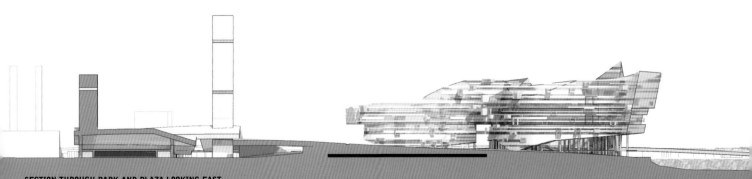

SECTION THROUGH PARK AND PLAZA LOOKING EAST

COMMERCIAL

SECTION THROUGH PARK AND PLAZA LOOKING WEST

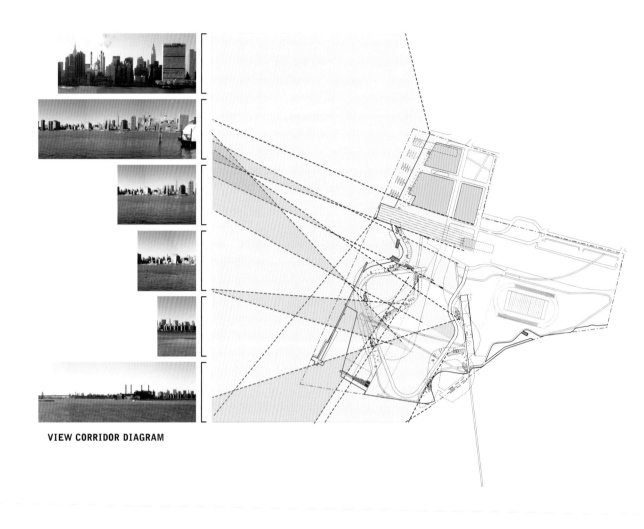

VIEW CORRIDOR DIAGRAM

WETLANDS   ACTIVE PARK   MARINA   ESPLANADE   BEACH

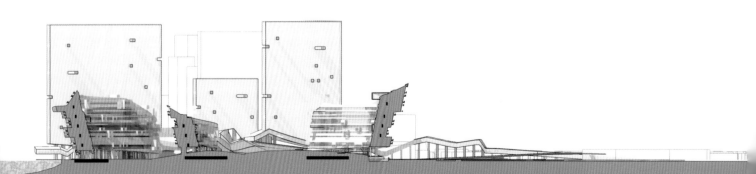

SECTION THROUGH PARK AND RIBBONS LOOKING NORTH

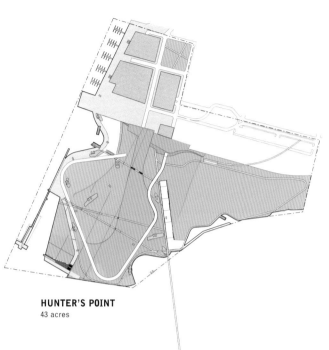

HUNTER'S POINT
43 acres

BATTERY PARK
23 acres

RIVERBANK PARK
28 acres

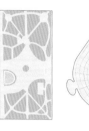

**WASHINGTON
SQUARE PARK**
10 acres

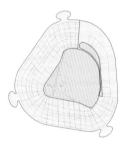

YANKEE STADIUM
4 acres

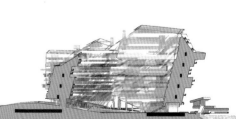

SECTION THROUGH PARK AND RIBBONS LOOKING SOUTH

367

NYC2012 OLYMPIC VILLAGE

DATE: 2004 LOCATION: Hunter's Point, Queens, New York STATUS: Competition SITE AREA: 61 acres/7.5 ha PROJECT SIZE: 6.1-million sf/566,711 m² PROGRAM: 6.1 million sf/566,711 m²
urban planning project including 5.1 million sf/473,807 m² of residential space (4,500 units), 43 acres/17.40 ha of parklands, a marina, cinemas, retail, restaurants, recreation
facilities, office, fire and police station, and parking.

SCIENCE CENTER SCHOOL

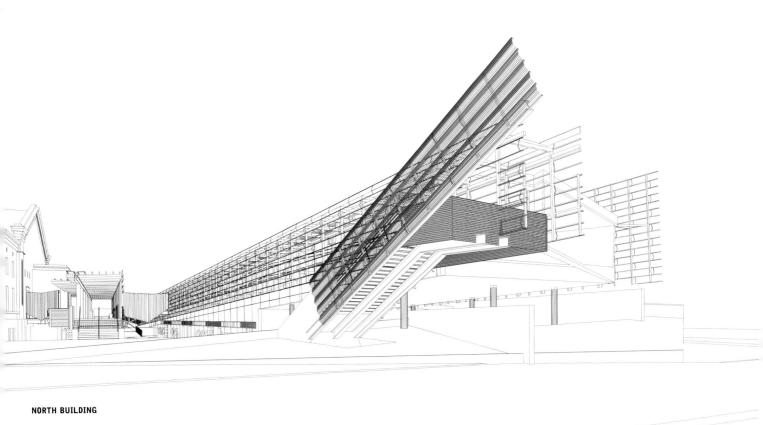

NORTH BUILDING

The program is slipped between layers of lifted landscape to dissolve the boundaries between the building systems and the ground and to prioritize views of the historically significant Armory building and the existing landscape of the Rose Garden. The hybrid campus of primary education and scholastic research serves as a gateway to the greater University of Southern California/Exposition Park area and establishes a community foothold in the heart of South Los Angeles.

The Armory's main hall, converted into a flexible, open two-story atrium and dominated by a large interior bamboo garden, is the heart of the Science Center School. Libraries, labs, meeting rooms, and classrooms flank the atrium's perimeter and are provided access to the new north school building via a pair

of bridges that lead across an outdoor garden lunchroom. The interior bamboo garden, pierced midway up by skywalks and punctuated with meeting spaces, is meant to bring a piece of nature into this somewhat blighted inner-city environment. It is possible, once the bamboo is fully grown, to find a space of respite among the plants or to use areas carved into the midst of the planted space as an experiential teaching opportunity.

The new north building burrows into sculpted earthworks along Exposition Boulevard; its landscaped roof is perceptually an extension of the garden. Classrooms are grouped in clusters of four that share a common room, to provide an open and flexible teaching environment. In response to the Exposition Park master plan and to highlight the historic

Armory, this "nonbuilding" nestles into excavated land below grade, its program essentially tucked and embedded into the park. The structure emerges quietly from the adjacent Rose Garden—a welcoming and protective environment for children that has forgone the traditionally overt sense of enclosure of most public schools. From the vantage point of the Rose Garden, the roof appears as ground plane, whereas from the heavily trafficked Exposition Boulevard the building appears autonomous and active. The project engages the site and the community and is perceived as both an intervention and a connection between the disparate adjacent conditions.

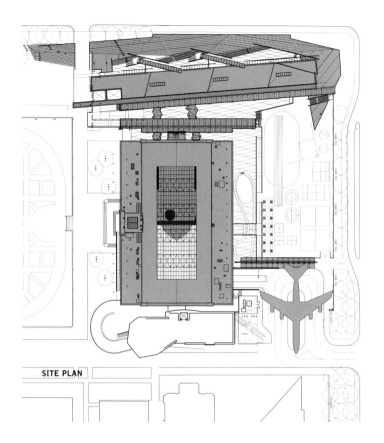

SITE PLAN

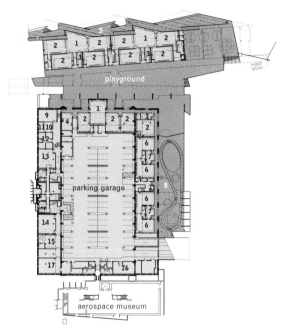

GROUND FLOOR

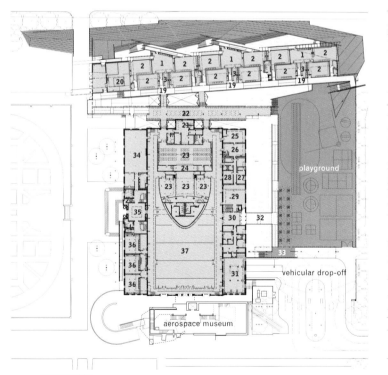

FIRST FLOOR

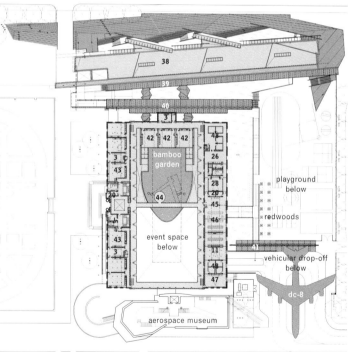

SECOND FLOOR

1 common rooms 2 classrooms 3 teachers' prep room 4 materials distribution 5 courtyard 6 kindergarten classroom 7 kindergarten prep room 8 kindergarten playground
9 sound stage 10 master control room 11 computer lab 12 editing suites 13 multimedia lab 14 student workroom 15 shop 16 archival storage 17 maintenance shop 18 passage
to aerospace museum 19 rampway 20 mechanical room 21 kitchen 22 lunch garden 23 multipurpose room 24 stage 25 faculty workroom 26 faculty lounge 27 principal's office
28 conference room 29 reception/gallery 30 lobby 31 student library 32 entry bridge 33 entry gate and canopy 34 muses room 35 main lobby 36 lab classroom 37 plaza/event
space 38 landscaped roof 39 canopy 40 lunch garden canopy 41 entry canopy 42 specialized lab 43 physics/chemistry lab 44 garden classroom 45 multimedia library 46 stacks
and front desk 47 reading room 48 offices

377

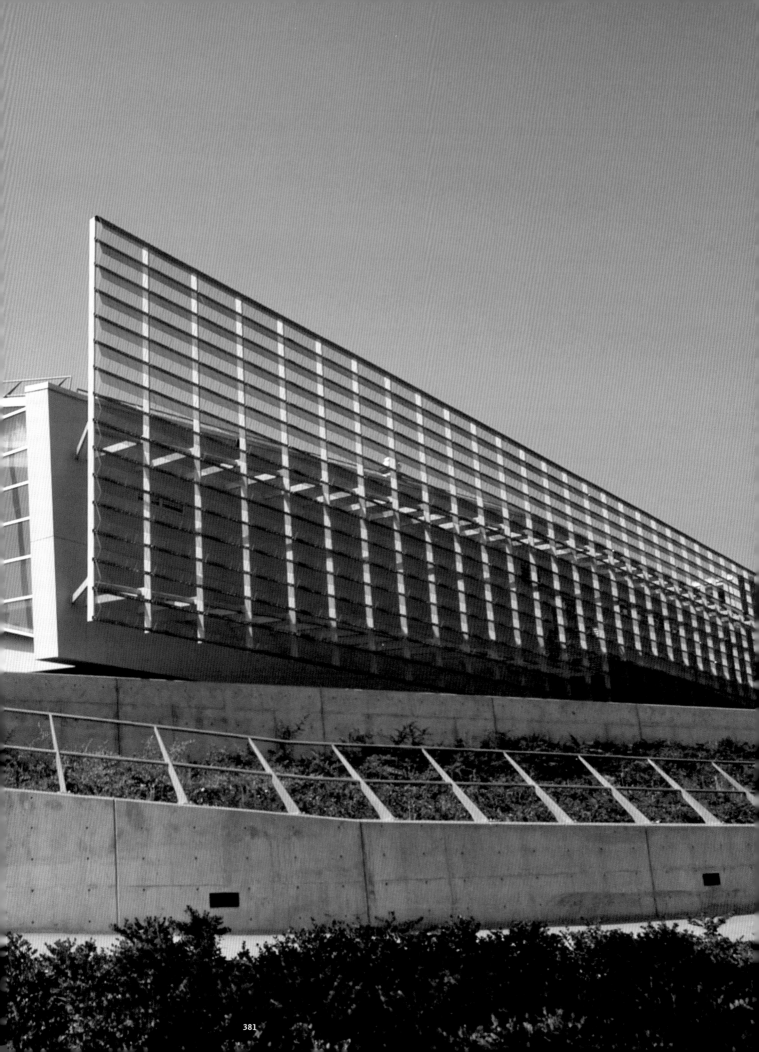

SCIENCE CENTER SCHOOL

DATE: 1992-2004 LOCATION: Los Angeles, California STATUS: Built SITE AREA: 7 acres/2.84 ha PROJECT SIZE: 196,000 gross sf/18,209 m², including parking PROGRAM: Creation of a building for a novel, hybrid institution, which combines a public elementary school (K–5) and teacher training program with the resources of a major museum, the California Science Center.

CALTRANS DISTRICT 7 HEADQUARTERS

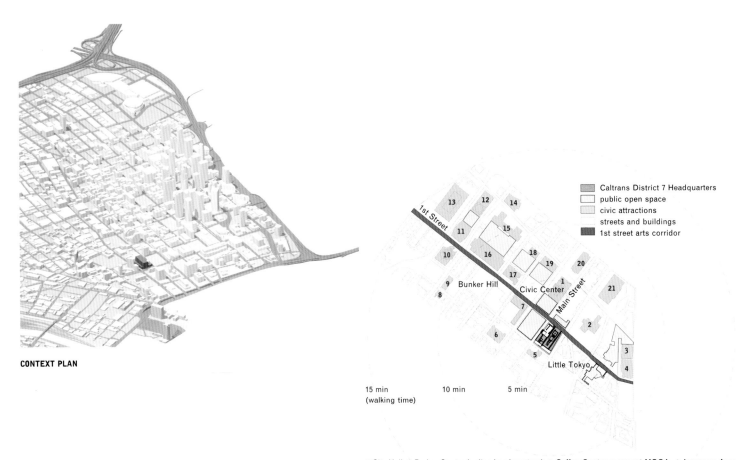

CONTEXT PLAN

Caltrans District 7 Headquarters
public open space
civic attractions
streets and buildings
1st street arts corridor

15 min   10 min   5 min
(walking time)

1 City Hall 2 Parker Center (police headquarters) 3 Geffen Contemporary at MOCA 4 Japanese Americ
National Museum 5 Saint Vibiana Cathedral 6 Ronald Reagan State Office Building 7 Los Angeles Time
8 MOCA 9 Coburn School of Performing Arts 10 Walt Disney Concert Hall 11 Dorothy Chandler Pavili
12 Mark Taper Forum 13 Department of Water and Power 14 Cathedral of Our Lady of the Angels
15 Kenneth Hahn Hall of Administration 16 Stanley Mosk L.A. County Courthouse 17 Law Library
18 Hall of Records 19 Criminal Courthouse 20 U.S. Courthouse 21 Federal Building

SITE PLAN

While its material language and structural elements allude to freeway infrastructure, the kinetic architecture of the Caltrans building facade borrows its characteristic animation directly from the car. The outer layer of the double facade delaminates from the body of the building—functioning like the car body to protect and shield its inhabitants via a constantly shifting mechanical skin of perforated aluminum panels that alternately open or close depending on the sun's angle and intensity. Appearing to be windowless and opaque at midday, the building transforms in appearance over time until it reaches near complete transparency at dusk—the fundamental reading of the building is in terms of transformation.

Research done for the San Francisco Federal Building project led to resolutions that challenge normative office culture, improve office worker comfort, and increase environmental efficiency. Floor plans were made deliberately nonhierarchical, with open, light-exposed workspaces prioritized for all workers regardless of rank. All window shades on exterior windows are manually operable to ensure that employees have a sense of control over their own work environments with respect to the amount of light and air that they deem optimum. Elevators operate on a skip-stop basis, opening onto centrally located stairwell lobbies—interim gathering places—on every third floor. This "skip-stop" scheme intensifies circulation and encourages productive social exchange.

The organizational strategy was informed by an optimistic assessment of the vibrancy that will occur as the nearby urban environment develops further. The main lobby is relocated to the exterior, as a large plaza for office workers, visitors, and the general public.

Amenities, including an exhibition gallery and cafeteria, adjoin the outdoor lobby at ground level to draw users from pedestrian and vehicular traffic. The entire budget for public art was invested in one installation that, designed in collaboration with artist Keith Sonnier, integrates inseparably with the architecture. Horizontal bands of red neon and blue argon light tubes cycle through light pattern sequences, mimicking the ribbons of headlights on California's freeways. The large cantilevered light bar connects the structure to First Street, and the forty-foot, forward-canted super-graphic "100" marks the South Main Street entrance. This layered sign, with its nod to Chandleresque LA's Hollywood sign, denotes the building as an urban landmark.

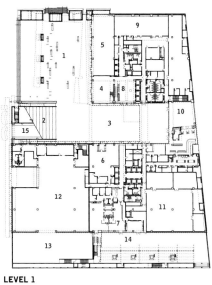

LEVEL 1

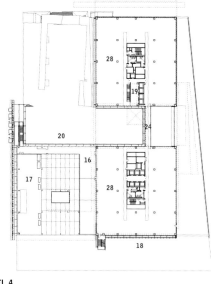

LEVEL 4

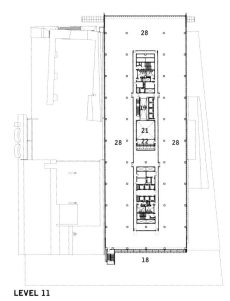

LEVEL 11

LEVEL 14

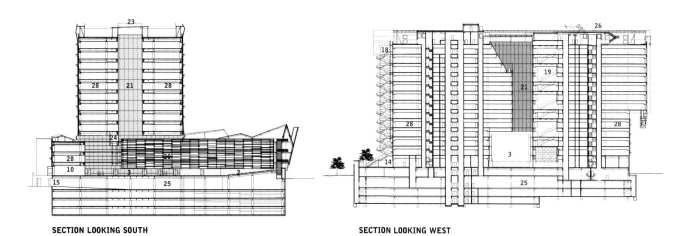

SECTION LOOKING SOUTH

SECTION LOOKING WEST

1 public plaza 2 amphitheater 3 urban lobby 4 exhibition gallery 5 retail 6 public services 7 daycare 8 entrance lobby 9 conference center 10 cafeteria 11 storage
12 autoshop 13 autoshop yard 14 daycare playground 15 parking entrance 16 roof terrace 17 mechanical area 18 solar panel wall 19 skip stop lobby 20 public art
installation 21 light well 22 exterior terrace 23 light well canopy 24 4th floor bridge 25 below grade parking garage 26 heliport 27 light bar 28 open office

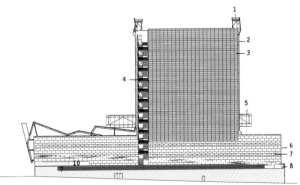

SOUTH ELEVATION

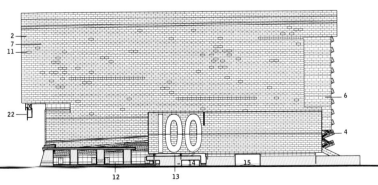

WEST ELEVATION

1 maintenance catwalks 2 perforated aluminum panels 3 solar panels 4 emergency egress stair 5 light bar 6 fiber cement panels 7 operable aluminum panels
8 glass at exterior daycare space 9 louvers 10 autoshop door 11 preformed aluminum panels 12 public plaza 13 urban lobby 14 parking entry 15 autoshop entry/exit
16 structural glazing 17 glass display case 18 public art installation 19 cafeteria 20 parking entry/exit 21 loading dock 22 light bar 23 operable perforated panels

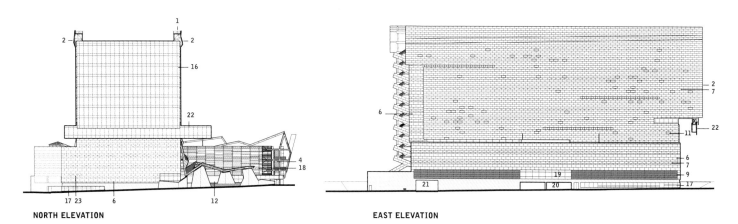

NORTH ELEVATION

EAST ELEVATION

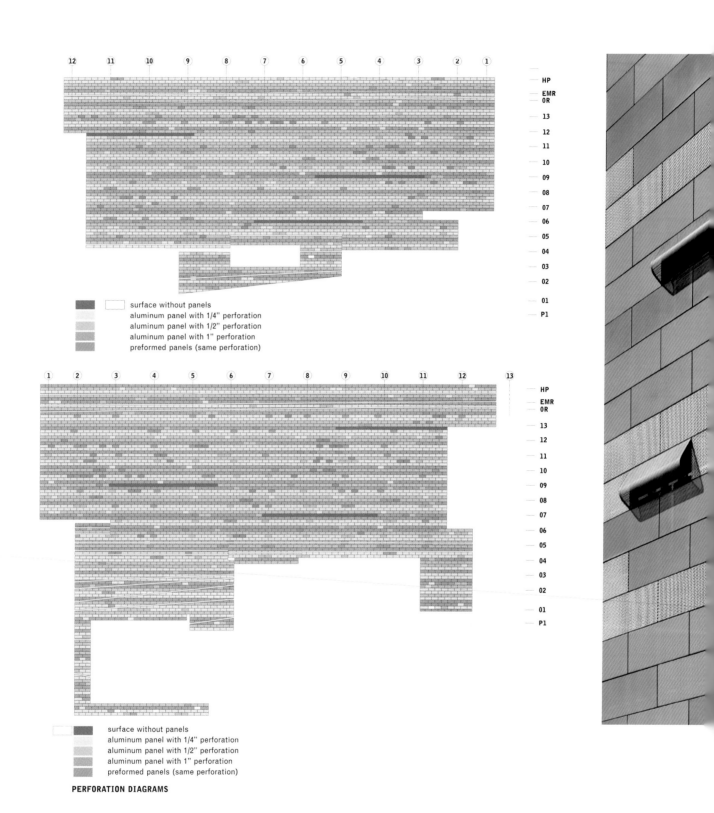

surface without panels
aluminum panel with 1/4" perforation
aluminum panel with 1/2" perforation
aluminum panel with 1" perforation
preformed panels (same perforation)

surface without panels
aluminum panel with 1/4" perforation
aluminum panel with 1/2" perforation
aluminum panel with 1" perforation
preformed panels (same perforation)

PERFORATION DIAGRAMS

CALTRANS DISTRICT 7 HEADQUARTERS

DATE: 2001-2004 LOCATION: Los Angeles, California STATUS: Built SITE AREA: 176,656 sf/16 m² PROJECT SIZE: 1.2 million gross sf/108,697 gross m²: 750,000 gsf/69,677 m² office building, 420,000 gsf/39,019 m² underground parking garage PROGRAM: main lobby (1,300 sf/121 m²), exhibition space (1,300 sf/121 m²), retail (5,000 sf/465 m²), cafeteria (5,000 sf/465 m²), warehouse (14,000 sf/1,301 m²), auto-shop (17,000 sf/1,579 m²), day-care center (4,500 sf/418 m²), conference center (6,500 sf/604 m²), wellness center (1,200 sf/112 m²), public plaza (28,000 sf/2,601 m²), outdoor lobby (10,000 sf/929 m²), day-care play area (9,000 sf/836 m²), wellness center terrace (5,000 sf/465 m²), auto-shop yard (6,000 sf/557 m²).

COOPER UNION ACADEMIC BUILDING

SITE PLAN

The new academic facility is conceived as a stacked vertical piazza, contained within a semitransparent envelope that articulates the classroom and laboratory spaces. The vertical campus is organized around a central atrium that rises to the full height of the building. This connective volume, spanned by sky bridges, opens up view corridors across Third Avenue to the Foundation Building.

The interior space configuration encourages interconnection among the school's engineering, art, and architecture departments. All institutional amenities—including meeting rooms, social space, seminar rooms, wireless hubs, restrooms, and phones—are located in the fourth- and seventh-story sky lobbies that surround the atrium. The skip-stop elevator system makes trips exclusively to the fourth and seventh floors, drawing occupants to use, and congregate on, the grand stair; in practice, 50 percent of people will use the stairs as their sole means of circulation. These key social spaces for students, faculty, and visitors become the places where education informally takes place.

The building's physical and visual permeability helps integrate the college into its neighborhood. At street level, the transparent facade invites the neighborhood to observe and to take part in the intensity of activity contained within. Many of the public functions (including retail space and a lobby exhibition gallery) are located at ground level, and a second gallery and a two-hundred-seat auditorium are easily accessible from the street.

The open, accessible building is exemplary as sustainable, energy-efficient architecture. A steel-and-glass skin improves the building's performance through control of daylight, energy use, and selective natural ventilation. The double skin system allows for heightened performance and dynamic composition on several levels: the operable panels create a continually moving pattern, provide surface variety on the facade, reduce the influx of heat radiation during the summer, and give users control over their interior environment and views to the outside.

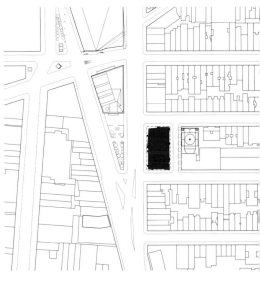

CONTEXT PLAN

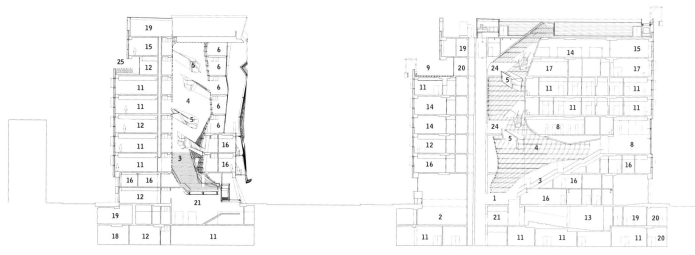

SECTION A THROUGH ATRIUM LOOKING SOUTH

SECTION B THROUGH GRAND STAIR LOOKING EAST

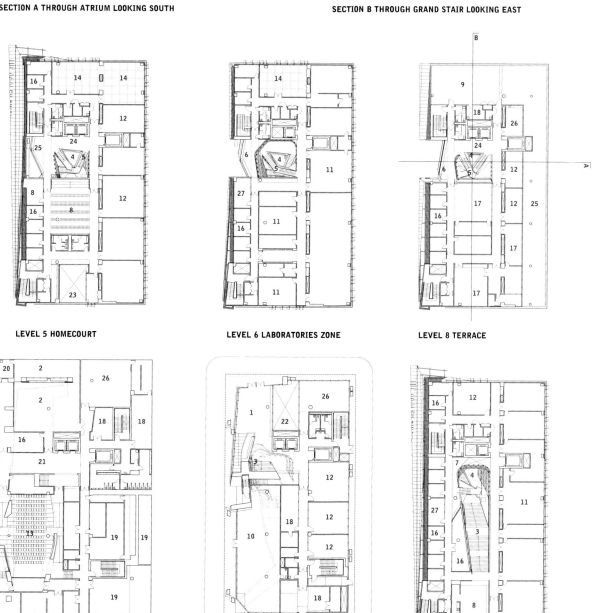

LEVEL 5 HOMECOURT

LEVEL 6 LABORATORIES ZONE

LEVEL 8 TERRACE

LEVEL 00 AUDITORIUM

LEVEL 1 ENTRY

LEVEL 4 GRAND STAIRS

1 lobby 2 gallery 3 grand stairs 4 atrium 5 skip-stop stair 6 sky bridge and lounge 7 lounge 8 student activities spaces 9 roof terrace 10 retail
11 lab zone 12 general classrooms 13 auditorium 14 individual student workspaces 15 art studios 16 offices 17 computer center 18 central services
19 mechanical 20 storage 21 foyer 22 open to gallery below 23 open to below 24 skip-stop lobby 25 green roof 26 multipurpose room 27 study lounge

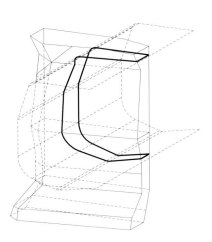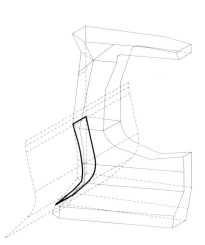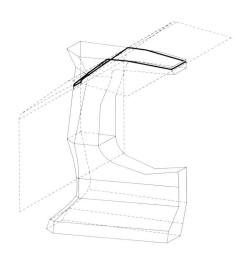

ATRIUM GEOMETRY

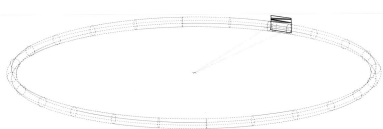

WEST FACADE GEOMETRY

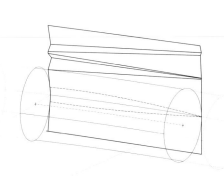

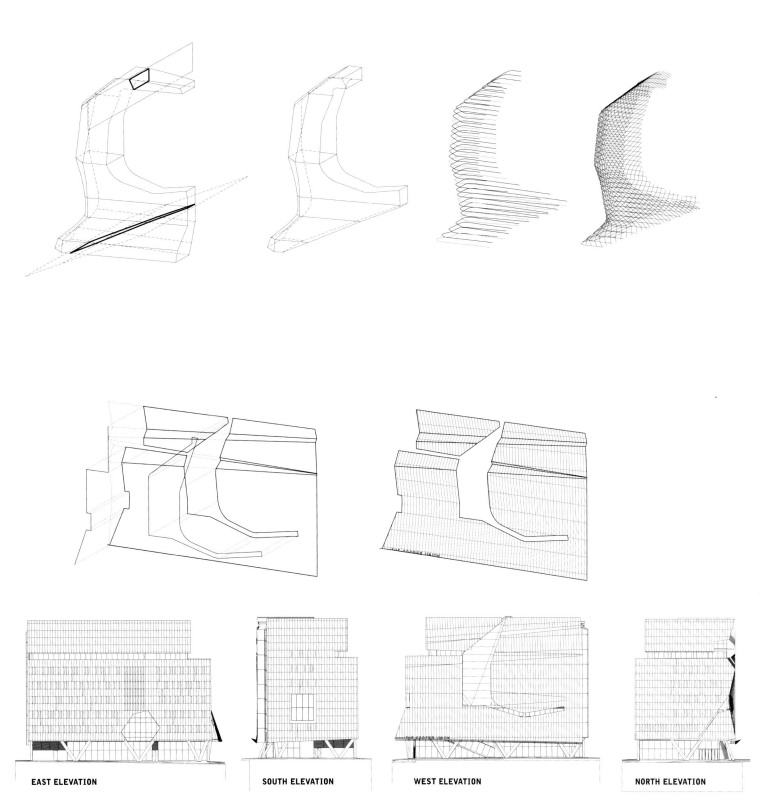

EAST ELEVATION　　　**SOUTH ELEVATION**　　　**WEST ELEVATION**　　　**NORTH ELEVATION**

ATRIUM SKIN

413

COOPER UNION ACADEMIC BUILDING

DATE: 2004-2008 LOCATION: New York, New York STATUS: In Process SITE AREA: 18,000 sf/1,672 m² PROJECT SIZE: 200,000 gross sf/18,580 gross m² PROGRAM: Public amenities including an exhibition gallery, 200-seat auditorium, lounge and multi-purpose space, shell retail space along Third Avenue, 17,000 sf/1,579 m² of classrooms (approximate), 40,000 sf/3,716 m² of laboratories (approximate), 12,000 sf/1,115 m² of individual student work and activity spaces (approximate), 15,000 sf/1,394 m² of administrative and faculty offices (approximate), centralized computer center.

SHR PERCEPTUAL MANAGEMENT
Scottsdale, Arizona 1997–1998 CLIENT: SHR Perceptual Management, Barry Sheperd, Will Rodgers

PRINCIPAL: Thom Mayne
PROJECT ARCHITECT: Patrick J. Tighe

PROJECT TEAM:
Saffet Kaya Bekirogru
Ung Joo Scott Lee
David Plotkin
David Rindlaub

CONTRACTOR: Hardison/Downey
STRUCTURAL ENGINEER: Caruso Turley Scott, Inc.
ELECTRICAL ENGINEER: SW Engineering, Inc.
MECHANICAL ENGINEER: MP Designs
STEEL FABRICATION: Tom Farrage/Co.

101 PEDESTRIAN BRIDGE
Los Angeles, California 1998 CLIENT: Metropolitan Transportation Authority, Los Angeles

PRINCIPAL: Thom Mayne
PROJECT MANAGER: Kim Groves
PROJECT DESIGNER: Eui-Sung Yi

PROJECT TEAM:
David Grant
Ung Joo Scott Lee
Robyn Sambo
Eul-Ho Suh
William Duncanson (AIJK)
PROJECT ASSISTANTS:
Jerome Daksciewiz
Marcos de Andres
Devon McConkey
Bettina Stich
Petar Vrcibradic

PARTNER: AIJK Architecture and City Design: John Kaliski
STRUCTURAL ENGINEER: Ove Arup & Partners
COLLABORATIVE ARTIST: Jenny Holzer
CIVIL ENGINEER: Ove Arup & Partners

PALENQUE AT CENTRO JVC
Zapopan, Jalisco, Mexico 1998–2007 CLIENT: Omnitrition de Mexico S.A. de C.V.

PRINCIPAL: Thom Mayne
PROJECT MANAGER: Daynard Tullis
PROJECT ARCHITECTS:
Patrick Tighe
David Rindlaub

PROJECT TEAM:
Simon Demeuse
Andreas Froesch
Maria Guest
Ung Joo Scott Lee
Eric Nulman
Jean Oei
PROJECT ASSISTANTS:
Marcos de Andres
Ben Damron
Patricia Schneider
John Skillern

CONSULTING ARCHITECT: Estudio Esteban Cervantes
PRINCIPAL: Esteban Cervantes
STRUCTURAL/MECHANICAL/ELECTRICAL ENGINEERING:
Ove Arup & Partners/Colinas De Buen S.A. de C.V
LIGHTING: Joe Kaplan Architectural Lighting and Moody Ravitz Hollingsworth
Lighting Design, Inc.
ACOUSTICS: Arup Acoustics
COST ESTIMATOR: AD TEC Gerencia De Construccion S.A. de C.V.
CODE CONSULTANT: Systech Group, Inc.

INTERNATIONAL ELEMENTARY SCHOOL
Long Beach, California 1997–1999 CLIENT: Long Beach Unified School District

PRINCIPAL: Thom Mayne
PROJECT MANAGER: Kim Groves
PROJECT DESIGNER: Silvia Kuhle

PROJECT TEAM:
David Plotkin
Robyn Sambo
Stephen Slaughter
Brandon Welling
PROJECT ASSISTANTS:
Rob Edmonds
Michael O'Dryan

EXECUTIVE ARCHITECT: Thomas Blurock Architects
PRINCIPAL: Tom Blurock
PROJECT ARCHITECT: Jim Moore
PROJECT MANAGER: Barbara Helton
PROJECT TEAM: Jose Valentin
STRUCTURAL/MECHANICAL/ELECTRICAL ENGINEERING: Ove Arup & Partners, California
Andrew Tompson, *Structural Engineer*; Catherine Wells, *Structural Engineer*
Bronagh Walsh, *Mechanical Engineer*; Alistair McGregor, *Mechanical Engineer*
Fiona Cousins, *Mechanical Engineer*; Peter Balint, *Electrical Engineer*
Vahik Davoudi, *Electrical Engineer*
CIVIL ENGINEER: Adnreasen Engineering
LANDSCAPE ARCHITECT: Fong & Associates
KITCHEN CONSULTANTS: Dewco Food Facility Consultants
COST ESTIMATOR: Adamson Associates: Nick Butcher
CONSTRUCTION MANAGER: Pinner Construction

LUTÈCE
Las Vegas, Nevada 1998–1999 CLIENT: Ark Restaurants Corp.

PRINCIPAL: Thom Mayne
PROJECT MANAGER: Kim Groves
PROJECT DESIGNER: Brandon Welling

PROJECT TEAM:
Henriette Bier
Josh Coggeshall
Jerome Daksiewicz
Ben Damron
Manish Desai
Paola Giaconia
Martin Josst
Ung Joo Scott Lee
Devin McConley
Petar Vrcibradic

STRUCTURAL ENGINEERS: Joseph Perazelli, P.E. (tenant improvement) and Martin & Peltyn (base building)
CONTRACTOR: Image Construction
ELECTRICAL ENGINEER: MSA Engineering, Inc.
MECHANICAL ENGINEER: AE Associates, Inc.
LIGHTING: Patrick Quigley + Associates
COLLABORATIVE ARTIST: Do-Ho Suh, *sculptor*
KITCHEN DESIGN CONSULTANT: Vincent Longarbardi/Bob Finkelstein Associates,
CODE CONSULTANT: Rolf Jensen Associates (egress) & Pentacore (ada/general)

TSUNAMI
Las Vegas, Nevada 1998–1999 CLIENT: Ark Restaurants Corp.

PRINCIPAL: Thom Mayne
PROJECT MANAGER: Kim Groves
PROJECT DESIGNER: David Rindlaub

PROJECT TEAM:
Simon Businger
Josh Coggeshall
Jerome Daksiewicz
Manish Desai
Martin Josst
Ung Joo Scott Lee
David McConley

CONTRACTOR: Price Woods General Contractor
STRUCTURAL ENGINEER: Martin & Peltyn
ELECTRICAL ENGINEER: MSA Engineering, Inc.
MECHANICAL ENGINEER: Ae Associates, Inc.
LIGHTING CONSULTANT: Patrick Quigley + Associates
COLLABORATIVE ARTIST: Rebeca Mendez, *Graphic Designer*
OTHER CONSULTANT: BDI Supergrafx, large format printing
KITCHEN DESIGNER: Vincent Longarbardi with Bob Finkelstein Associates
CODE CONSULTANT: Rolf Jensen & Associates (egress) and Pentacore (ada/general)

SILENT COLLISIONS / NAI EXHIBIT
Rotterdam, Netherlands 1999 CLIENT: Netherlands Institute of Architecture CURATOR: Kristin Feireiss

PRINCIPAL: Thom Mayne
PROJECT DESIGNER: Warren Techentin

PROJECT TEAM: Marta Male

CONSTRUCTION: Brandwacht & Meijer
GRAPHIC DESIGN: Ad van der Kouwe (Manifesta)

AZALEA SPRINGS WINERY
Napa Valley, California 1999 CLIENTS: Norman and Norah Stone

PRINCIPAL: Thom Mayne
PROJECT MANAGER: Daynard Tullis
PROJECT DESIGNER: Eui-Sung Yi

PROJECT TEAM:
Josh Coggeshall
Ramon Gomez Larios
John Skillern
Selwyn Ting
PROJECT ASSISTANTS:
Caroline Barat
Joseph Chang
Delphine Clemenson
Marcos De Andres

PROJECT CREDITS

NEW CITY PARK

New York, New York **1999** CLIENT: Canadian Centre for Architecture, Montreal, Canada

PRINCIPAL: Thom Mayne
PROJECT ARCHITECTS:
Marta Male
George Yu

PROJECT TEAM:
Simon Demeuse
Shigehiro Kashiwagi
Rose Mendez
Katsuhiro Ozawa
PROJECT ASSISTANTS:
Paul Anderson
Henriette Bier
Paola Giaconia
Steve Hegedis
Israel Kandarian
Ung Joo Scott Lee
Marisa Levin
Maia Johnson
Janet Pangman
Patrick Tighe
Petar Vrcibradic
Erin Wendell
Eric Wood

PLANNING/URBAN DESIGN CONSULTANT: Richard Weinstein
TRAFFIC CONSULTANT: Arup: Greg Hodkinson
COST ESTIMATOR (IMPLEMENTATION/FEASIBILITY): Don Elliot

GRAZ KUNSTHAUS

Graz, Austria **1999–2000** CLIENT: City of Graz

PRINCIPAL: Thom Mayne
PROJECT DESIGNER: Eui-Sung Yi

PROJECT TEAM:
Marcos De Andres
Martin Krammer
Ung Joo Scott Lee
Petar Vrcibradic

UNIVERSITY OF CINCINNATI STUDENT RECREATION CENTER

Cincinnati, Ohio **1999–2005** CLIENT: University of Cincinnati

PRINCIPAL: Thom Mayne
PROJECT MANAGER: Kim Groves
PROJECT ARCHITECT: Kristina Loock
PROJECT DESIGNER: Ben Damron

PROJECT TEAM:
Henriette Bier
Ted Kane
Silvia Kuhle
Eric Nulman
Martin Summers
Brandon Welling
PROJECT ASSISTANTS:
Jason Anthony
Crister Cantrell
Delphine Clemenson
Simon Demeuse
Manish Dessai
Hanjo Gellink
Lisa Hseih
Dwoyne Keith
Patricia Schneider
Scott Severson
Paxton Sheldahl
John Skillern
Christian Taubert
Natalia Traverso Caruana
Petar Vrcibradic
Chris Warren
Eui-Sung Yi

EXECUTIVE ARCHITECT: KZF Design
PROJECT ARCHITECT: Don Cornett, *Vice President*
PROJECT TEAM: Bill Wilson, *Vice President*; Dale Beeler, *Project Manager*
GENERAL CONTRACTOR: Turner Construction Company
CONSTRUCTION MANAGER: Messer Jacobs: Kevin English
STRUCTURAL CONCEPTS: Ove Arup & Partners: Bruce Gibbons
MECHANICAL CONCEPTS: IBE Consulting Engineering: Alan Locke
STRUCTURAL: THP Ltd.: Shayne Manning
MEP: Heapy Engineering: Rod Rusnak
SITE UTILITIES: M-Engineering
SPORTS AND RECREATION SPECIALISTS: Moody/Nolan Ltd., Inc.: Mark Bodien
FOOD SERVICE: Thomas Ricca Associates: Chape Whitman
AQUATICS CONSULTANT: Councilman/Hunsaker: Joe Hunsaker
LIGHTING CONSULTANT: Horton Lees Brogden: Teal Brogden
ACOUSTICAL CONSULTANT: Martin Newsom Associates: Michael Brown
GRAPHIC DESIGN: Rebeca Mendez
INFORMATION TECHNOLOGY: Affiliated Engineering, Inc.
COST ESTIMATORS: Davis Langdon Adamson: Nick Butcher,
Hanscomb, Inc.: Chris Harris

WAYNE L. MORSE UNITED STATES COURTHOUSE

Eugene, Oregon **1999–2006** **CLIENT:** GSA Northwest Region 10

PRINCIPAL: Thom Mayne
PROJECT MANAGER: Kim Groves
PROJECT ARCHITECT: Maria Guest
PROJECT DESIGNERS:
Ben Damron
Patrick Tighe
Eui-Sung Yi

PROJECT TEAM:
Caroline Barat
Linda Chung
Ung Joo Scott Lee
Rolando Mendoza
John Skillern
PROJECT ASSISTANTS:
Alasdair Dixon
Haseb Faqirzada
Dwoyne Keith
Laura McAlpine
Gerardo Mingo
Sohith Perera
Nadine Quirmbach
Michaela Schippl
Natalia Traverso Caruana

EXECUTIVE ARCHITECT: DLR Group
PRINCIPALS: Kent Larson, Bill Buursma, Jon Pettit
PROJECT ARCHITECT: Jason Wandersee
STRUCTURAL ENGINEER: KPFF: Gaafar Gaafar, *Principal*
MECHANICAL ENGINEERS: IBE Consulting Engineers
Alan Locke, *Principal;* + Glumac International: Steve Straus, *President*
ELECTRICAL ENGINEER: DLR Group: Steve Hubbs, *Electrical Engineer*
LANDSCAPE ARCHITECT: Richard Haag Associates, Inc.: Richard Haag, *Principal*
CIVIL ENGINEER: KPFF: Matt Dolan, *Associate*
LIGHTING CONSULTANT: Horton Lees Brogden
Teal Brogden, *Principal;* Heather Libonati, *Project Manager*
ACOUSTICAL CONSULTANT: McKay Conant Brook
Robert Schmidt, *Senior Consultant*
COLLABORATIVE ARTISTS: Matthew Ritchie, Cris Bruch, Kris Timkin, Sean Healy
BLAST CONSULTANT: Hinman Consulting Engineering
Eve Hinman, *Principal;* Joyce Engebretsen, *Engineer*
LOW VOLTAGE: Alta Consulting Services: Cy Humphries, *Principal*
VERTICAL CIRCULATION: Lerch, Bates of North America: Steve Mikkelsen
SIGNAGE/GRAPHICS: Mayer Reed: Michael Reed, *Principal;* Debbie Shaw
COST ESTIMATOR: Davis Langdon Adamson: Nick Butcher
CODE CONSULTANT: Tuazon Engineering: Eric Tuazon
GENERAL CONTRACTOR: J.E. Dunn
Fred Shipman, *President;* Gail Wikstrom, *Vice President Construction;*
Alan Halleck, *Project Manager*

TIME CAPSULE

Central Park, New York **2000** **CLIENT:** New York Times Magazine

PRINCIPAL: Thom Mayne
PROJECT TEAM: Marta Male

DIAMOND RANCH HIGH SCHOOL

Pomona, California **1996–2000** **CLIENT:** Pomona Unified School District

PRINCIPAL: Thom Mayne
PROJECT ARCHITECT: John Enright
PROJECT DESIGNER: Silvia Kuhle

PROJECT TEAM:
Cameron Crockett
David Grant
Fabian Kremkus
Janice Shimizu
Patrick J. Tighe
Sarah Allan
PROJECT ASSISTANTS:
Kaspar Baumeister
Jay Behr
John Bencher
Mark Briggs
Frank Brodbeck
Takashi Ehira
Magdalena Glen
Ivar Gudmunson
George Hemandez
Martin Krammer
Ming Lee
Francisco Mouzo
Christopher Payne
Kinga Racon
Robyn Sambo
Andreas Schaller
Bennett Shen
Mark Sich
Craig Shimahara
Tadao Shimizu
Steve Slaughter
Brandon Welling
Eui-Sung Yi

JOINT VENTURE: Morphosis/Thomas Blurock Architects
Tom Blurock, *Principal*
PROJECT ARCHITECT: Tom Moore
PROJECT TEAM:
Mark Briggs
Kevin Fleming
Nadar Glassemlou
Chris Samuelian
Kristina Steeves
Jose Valentin
Wendell Vaughn
Lis Zuloaga
PROJECT ASSISTANTS:
Gregory Ashton
Colleen Bathgate
Mike Blazaek
Vince Coffeen
Karen MacIntyre
Kathy Sun
Brady Titus
Robert Trucios
STRUCTURAL/MECHANICAL/ELECTRICAL ENGINEER:
Ove Arup & Partners
Bruce Gibbons, *Structural Engineer;* John Gautrey, *Mechanical Engineer;*
Gregory Morrison, *Electrical Engineer;* Anait Manjikian, *Plumbing Engineer;*
CIVIL ENGINEER: Andreasen Engineering
LANDSCAPE ARCHITECT: Fong & Associates
KITCHEN CONSULTANTS: K.I.A.
COST ESTIMATOR: Adamson Associates
CONSTRUCTION MANAGER: Bernards Brothers

UNIVERSITY OF TORONTO GRADUATE STUDENT HOUSING
Toronto, Ontario, Canada 1998–2000 CLIENT: University of Toronto

PRINCIPAL: Thom Mayne
PROJECT ARCHITECT: Kim Groves

PROJECT TEAM:
Bernard Jin
Rob Knight
Stephen Slaughter
Brandon Welling
PROJECT ASSISTANTS:
Felix Cheng
Ben Damron
Dave Grant
Ryan Harper
Joseph Jones
Fabian Kremkus
Silvia Kuhle
Ung Joo Scott Lee
Ulrike Nemeth
David Plotkin
Tarek Qaddumi
Ivan Redi
David Rindlaub
Robyn Sambo
Jose Valeros
Sandrine Wellens
Oliver Winkler

JOINT VENTURE: Morphosis/Stephen Teeple Architects, Inc.
Stephen Teeple, *Principal*
PROJECT MANAGER: Chris Radigan
PROJECT TEAM: Bernard Jin, Rob Knight
PROJECT ASSISTANTS:
Tom Arban
Tania Bortolotto
Marc Downing
Joseph Jones
Grazyna Krezel
Jeff Lotto
Madeleine Moore
Kael Opie
Matt Smith
Adolfo Spaleta
STRUCTURAL ENGINEER: Yolles Partnership, Inc.
MECHANICAL ENGINEER: Keen Engineering
ELECTRICAL ENGINEER: Carincini Bart Rogers
LANDSCAPE ARCHITECT: Janet Rosenberg & Associates
CONTRACTOR: Axor Construction Canada, Inc.

SAN FRANCISCO FEDERAL OFFICE BUILDING
San Francisco, California 2000–2006 CLIENT: GSA Region 9

PRINCIPAL: Thom Mayne
PROJECT MANAGER: Tim Christ
PROJECT ARCHITECT: Brandon Welling

PROJECT TEAM:
Linda Chung
Simon Demeuse
Marty Doscher
Rolando Mendoza
Eui-Sung Yi
PROJECT ASSISTANTS:
Caroline Barat
Gerald Bodziak
Crister Cantrell
Delphine Clemenson
Todd Curley
Alasdair Dixon
Haseb Faqirzada
Chris Fenton
Arthur de Ganay
Dwoyne Keith
Sohith Perera
Kristine Solberg
Natalia Traverso Caruana

EXECUTIVE ARCHITECT: Smith Group, San Francisco
PROJECT MANAGER: Carl Christiansen
PROJECT ARCHITECT: Jon Gherga
PROJECT ASSISTANT: Belinda Wong
STRUCTURAL, MECHANICAL, ELECTRICAL, AND PLUMBING ENGINEER:
Ove Arup and Partners
PROJECT MANAGER: Bruce Gibbons
STRUCTURAL ENGINEER: Steve Ratchye
MECHANICAL ENGINEER: Erin McConahey
NATURAL VENTILATION MODELING: Lawrence Berkeley National Laboratory
LANDSCAPE ARCHITECT: Richard Haag Associates, Inc., with J.J.R.
CIVIL ENGINEER: Brian Kangas Foulk
GEOTECHNICAL: Geomatrix
LIGHTING CONSULTANT: Horton Lees Brogden Lighting Design, Inc.
SIGNAGE: Kate Keating Associates
COST ESTIMATOR: Davis Langdon Adamson
CURTAIN WALL: Curtain Wall Design & Consulting, Inc.
BLAST CONSULTANT: Hinman Consulting Engineers
CODE: Rolf Jensen & Associates
ACOUSTICS: Thorburn Associates
VERTICAL TRANSPORTATION: Hesselberg, Keessee & Associates, Inc.
COLLABORATIVE ARTISTS: James Turrell, Ed Ruscha, Rupert Garcia, Hung Liu, Raymond Saunders, William Wiley
GENERAL CONTRACTOR: Dick-Morganti Joint Venture
CONSTRUCTION MANAGER: Hunt Construction Group

IFP WEST FILM CENTER

Culver City, California **2001** CLIENT: Independent Film Project/West

PRINCIPAL: Thom Mayne
PROJECT MANAGER: Silvia Kuhle
PROJECT DESIGNER: John Skillern

CHILDREN'S MUSEUM OF LOS ANGELES

Los Angeles, California **2001** CLIENT: Children's Museum of Los Angeles

PRINCIPAL: Thom Mayne
PROJECT MANAGER: Silvia Kuhle

PROJECT TEAM:
Mario Cipresso
Malina Palasthira
Axel Prichard-Schmitzberger
Chris Warren
PROJECT ASSISTANT:
Eui-Sung Yi

STRUCTURAL ENGINEER: John A. Martin & Associates: Chuck Whitaker, *Principal*
MECHANICAL ENGINEER: IBE Consulting Engineers
Alan Locke and John Gautrey, *Principals*
ELECTRICAL ENGINEER: Gotama Building Engineers, Inc.: Cecilia Gotama, *Principal*
CIVIL ENGINEER: Delon Hampton & Associates
LIGHTING CONSULTANT: Horton Lees Brogden: Teal Brogden, *Principal*
COST ESTIMATOR: Davis Langdon Adamson: Nick Butcher, *Principal*

LOS ANGELES COUNTY MUSEUM OF ART

Los Angeles, California **2001** CLIENT: Los Angeles County Museum of Art

PRINCIPAL: Thom Mayne
PROJECT MANAGER: Kim Groves
PROJECT ARCHITECT: Kristina Loock
PROJECT DESIGNERS:
John Skillern
Martin Summers

PROJECT TEAM: Ed Hatcher
Georgina Huljich
Laura McAlpine
Axel Schmitzberger
2003 FIBERGLASS AND RESIN MODEL TEAM:
Reinhard Schmoelzer, *Manager*
Graham Ferrier
Nadine Quirmbach
Joachim Reiter
Kurt West
MODEL METAL FABRICATOR:
Tom Farrage
PROJECT ASSISTANTS:
Caroline Barat
Mauricio Gomez
Dwoyne Keith
Maia Johnson
Alexandra Loew
Eghard Woeste

STRUCTURAL ENGINEER: John A. Martin & Associates
MECHANICAL ENGINEER: IBE Consulting Engineers
LIGHTING CONSULTANT: Horton Lees Brogden Lighting Design
ANIMATION: Dave Grant

CORNELL SCHOOL OF ARCHITECTURE

Ithaca, New York **2001** CLIENT: Cornell University

PRINCIPAL: Thom Mayne

PROJECT TEAM:
Gerald Bodziak
Crister Cantrell
Mario Cipresso
Edgar Hatcher
Dwoyne Keith
Scott Severson
Eghard Woeste

RENSSELAER ELECTRONIC MEDIA AND PERFORMING ARTS CENTER
Troy, New York **2001** CLIENT: Rensselaer Polytechnic Institute

PRINCIPAL: Thom Mayne
PROJECT DESIGNERS:
Ed Hatcher
Chris Warren

PROJECT TEAM:
Caroline Barat
Hanjo Gellink
Carlos Gomez
Dwoyne Keith
Anna Moca
Scott Severson
Eghard Woeste
Eui-Sung Yi
2003 FIBERGLASS AND RESIN MODEL TEAM:
Reinhard Schmoelzer, *Manager*
Graham Ferrier
Nadine Quirmbach
Joachim Reiter
Michaela Schippl
Kurt West
METAL FABRICATOR (MODEL):
Tom Farrage
PROJECT ASSISTANT:
Martin Summers

STRUCTURAL ENGINEER: Arup: Bruce Gibbons, *Principal*
MECHANICAL ENGINEER: Arup: John Gautrey
COST ESTIMATOR: Davis Langdon Adamson: Nick Butcher, *Principal*

BMW EVENT AND DELIVERY CENTER
Munich, Germany **2001** CLIENT: BMW

PRINCIPAL: Thom Mayne
PROJECT MANAGER: Tim Christ
PROJECT DESIGNER: John Skillern

PROJECT TEAM:
Caroline Barat
Henriette Bier
Gerald Bodziak
Linda Chung
Simon Demeuse
Carlos Gomez
Anna Moca
Eric Nulman
Eghard Woeste

NOAA SATELLITE OPERATION FACILITY

Suitland, Maryland **2001–2005** CLIENT: General Services Administration

PRINCIPAL, MORPHOSIS: Thom Mayne
PROJECT MANAGER: Paul Gonzales
PROJECT ARCHITECT: David Rindlaub
PROJECT DESIGNER: Jean Oei

PROJECT TEAM:
Edgar Hatcher
Salvador Hidalgo
Ted Kane
Maia Johnson
Chris Warren
PROJECT ASSISTANTS:
Caroline Barat
Alasdair Dixon
Haseb Faqirzada
Carlos Gomez
Dwoyne Keith
Laura McAlpine
Gerardo Mingo
Michaela Schippl
Natalia Traverso Caruana
Nadine Quirmbach

JOINT VENTURE: Morphosis/Einhorn Yaffee Prescott
TEAM AND MEP ENGINEERS: Einhorn Yaffee Prescott
Ed Kohlberg, *Partner*
PRINCIPALS IN CHARGE: Bill Lavine, Doug Gehley
PROJECT MANAGER: Randy Wong
MECHANICAL ENGINEERS: Lew Brode, Brian Carroll
ELECTRICAL ENGINEER: Eb Najadafar
PLUMBING ENGINEERS: Keith Shelton, Rolando Jaco
FIRE PROTECTION ENGINEER: Brian McGraw
SPACE PLANNING: Ken Roos, Jennifer Whitenight
CONSTRUCTION ADMINISTRATION: Doug Gehley, Eileen McNelis
CONSULTING STRUCTURAL ENGINEERS (CONCEPT DESIGN):
Ove Arup & Partners: Bruce Gibbons
CONSULTING STRUCTURAL ENGINEERS: Cagley and Associates
Jim Cagley, Frank Malits, Dave Smith
CONSULTING MECHANICAL ENGINEER: IBE Consulting Engineers, Inc.
Alan Locke, John Gautrey
CONSULTING MISSION CRITICAL ELECTRICAL ENGINEERS:
EYP Mission Critical Facilities: Geoff Cope
CONSULTING CIVIL ENGINEERS: A. Morton Thomas & Associates, Inc.:
Alex Berley
CONSULTING LANDSCAPE ARCHITECTS: EDAW: Walt Cole, Jon Pearson
COST ESTIMATORS: Davis Langdon Adamson: Nick Butcher, Sam Kelbrick
ARCHITECTURAL LIGHTING DESIGN: Horton Lees Brogden:
Teal Brogden, Heather Libonati, Emily Koonce
SPECIFICATION WRITER: CMS Consultants: Tommy Meija
FOOD SERVICE CONSULTANT: Cinni Little: Jeffrey Gardner
VERTICAL TRANSPORTATION: Vertran Enterprises: Andrew Guest
AUDIO/VISUAL AND ACOUSTICS: Shen Milsom & Wilke, Inc.
Gregory Moquin (A/V), Ben Houghton (acoustics)
SECURITY CONSULTANT: Jaycor: Doug Cameron
GENERAL CONTRACTOR: P.J. Dick
CONSTRUCTION MANAGER: 3DI

HYPO ALPE-ADRIA-CENTER

Klagenfurt, Austria **1996–2002** CLIENT: Karntner Landes-und-Hypothekenbank

PRINCIPAL: Thom Mayne
PROJECT MANAGERS:
John Enright, *phase 1 and 2*
Silvia Kuhle, *phase 3*

PROJECT TEAM:
David Grant
Martin Krammer
Fabian Kremkus
Ung Joo Scott Lee
David Plotkin
David Rindlaub
Robyn Sambo
Stephen Slaughter
Brandon Welling
Eui-Sung Yi
PROJECT ASSISTANTS:
Michael Folwell
Eugene Lee
Tomas Lenzen
Julianna Morais
Ulrike Nemeth
Brian Parish
Ivan Redi
Janice Shimizu
Bart Tucker
Ingo Waegner
Marion Wicher
Oliver Winkler

STRUCTURAL ENGINEER: Dipl. Ing. Klaus Gelbmann
MECHANICAL ENGINEER: Ing. Sorz Ingenieurburo GmbH
ELECTRICAL ENGINEER: August Gregoritsch Ingenieurburo f. Elektroplanungen
GENERAL COORDINATION: Zolestin Thomas Stich
BAUPHYSIC: Gerhard Tomberger
SPECIFICATIONS: Dipl. Ing. Reinhold Svetina
CONTRACTORS: Steiner Bau
Stahlbau Pichler GmbH SRL
Ing. Klaus Gruber GmbH
Arge Starmann-Sauritschnig
Eder Blechbau
Mossler GmbH
WKS Isoliergesellschaft GmbH
AllMetall
Wrulich
Elin Ebg
Pfrimer & Mosslacher

AIR FORCE MEMORIAL
Arlington National Cemetery, Arlington, Virginia **2002** **CLIENT:** United States Air Force

PRINCIPAL: Thom Mayne
PROJECT DESIGNERS:
Ed Hatcher
Chris Warren

PROJECT ASSISTANTS:
Deirdre Loftus
Eric Nulman

STRUCTURAL ENGINEER: Arup: Bruce Gibbons, *Principal*
COST ESTIMATOR: Davis Langdon Adamson: Nick Butcher, *Principal*

WORLD TRADE CENTER
New York, New York **2002** **CLIENT:** New York Magazine

PRINCIPAL: Thom Mayne
PROJECT MANAGER:
Brian O'Laughlin (*Tower Only*)
PROJECT DESIGNER: Chandler Ahrens

PROJECT TEAM: TOWER:
Bertrand Genoist
Laura McAlpine
Eliot Mitchell
Vahid Musah
Reinhard Schmoelzer
PLANNING:
Ed Hatcher
Martin Summers

MADRID HOUSING
Madrid, Spain **2002–2006** **CLIENT:** Empresa Municipal De La Viviende—City of Madrid

PRINCIPAL, MORPHOSIS: Thom Mayne
PROJECT MANAGER: Paul Gonzales
PROJECT ARCHITECT: Pavel Getov

PROJECT TEAM:
Simon Demeuese
Ed Hatcher
Chris Warren
PROJECT ASSISTANTS:
Eui Yeob Jeong
Joachim Reiter
Kurt West

JOINT VENTURE: Morphosis/B+DU Estudio de Arquitectura
ASSOCIATE ARCHITECT: B+DU Estudio de Arquitectura
Begoña Diaz-Urgorri, *Principal*
Leon Benacerraf, *Principal*
PROJECT MANAGER: Alicia Berenguer
PROJECT TEAM: Agustin Sanchez, Rocio Olano, Monica Hernandez
PROJECT ASSISTANTS: Sergio Calvo, Delfin Alvarez
SURVEYOR: Borja Herrero, Gerardo Berrocal
LANDSCAPING: Ana Luengo
STRUCTURE ENGINEER: Carlos Pintor, Roberto Vargas
ENGINEER: Rafael Urculo

EUROPEAN CENTRAL BANK
Frankfurt, Germany **2003** **CLIENT:** European Central Bank

PRINCIPAL: Thom Mayne
PROJECT MANAGER: Kim Groves

PROJECT TEAM:
Graham Ferrier
Ed Hatcher
Jean Oei
Nadine Quirmbach
PROJECT ASSISTANTS:
Natalia Traverso Caruana
MODEL TEAM:
Reinhard Schmoelzer, *Manager*
Luis Luz
Masako Saito
Go-Woon Seo

STRUCTURAL ENGINEER: Arup: Bruce Gibbons, Chuan Do
MECHANICAL ENGINEER: IBE Consulting Engineers: Alan Locke, John Gautrey

PERTH AMBOY HIGH SCHOOL
Perth Amboy, New Jersey **2003** CLIENT: Perth Amboy Unified School District

PRINCIPAL: Thom Mayne
PROJECT MANAGER: Silvia Kuhle
PROJECT DESIGNERS:
Ed Hatcher
Jean Oei

PROJECT TEAM:
Chandler Ahrens
Ted Kane
Kristina Loock
Anthony Mrkic
Natalia Traverso Caruana
Chris Warren
PROJECT ASSISTANTS: MODEL TEAM:
Reinhard Schmoelzer, *Manager*
Josh Barendon
Graham Ferrier
Elliot Mitchell
Masako Saito
Go-Woon Seo

ASSOCIATE ARCHITECT: Gruzen Samton LLP: Geoffrey Doban, *Managing Partner*
CIVIL ENGINEER: Yu & Associates
STRUCTURAL ENGINEER: Gilsanz Murray Steficek
MECHANICAL ENGINEER: IBE Consulting Engineers
ELECTRICAL ENGINEER: IBE Consulting Engineers
COST CONSULTANT: Davis Langdon Adamson

PUDONG CULTURAL PARK
Shanghai, Pudong, People's Republic of China **2003** CLIENT: Development and Planning Bureau of Pudong New Area

PRINCIPAL: Thom Mayne
PROJECT MANAGER: Paul Gonzales
PROJECT DESIGNERS:
Chandler Ahrens
Chris Warren

PROJECT TEAM: Rolando Mendoza
PROJECT ASSISTANTS: MODEL TEAM:
Reinhard Schmoelzer, *Manager*
Luis Luz
Masako Saito
Go-Woon Seo
Myung Suh

JOINT VENTURE: Morphosis/SWA Group
LANDSCAPE ARCHITECT/MASTER PLANNING PARTNER: SWA Group
Gerdo Aquino, *Principal*
PROJECT TEAM:
Ying Yu Hung
Kuiu-Chi Ma
Akiko Ono
Kathy Sun

X HOLM II
Santa Monica, California **2003** CLIENT: Private Residential Client

PRINCIPAL: Thom Mayne

PROJECT TEAM:
Graham Ferrier
Ed Hatcher
Jean Oei

METAL MODEL FABRICATION: Tom Farrage/Co.

SILENT COLLISIONS/CHARLEROI DANSES
Traveling Stage Set **2003** CLIENT: Frédéric Flamand/Charleroi Danses

PRINCIPAL: Thom Mayne

PROJECT TEAM:
Nadine Quirmbach
John Skillern
PROJECT ASSISTANTS:
Graham Ferrier
Joachim Reiter
Reinhard Schmoelzer

SNOW SHOW
Lapland, Finland **2004** CURATOR: Lance Fung

PRINCIPAL: Thom Mayne
PROJECT DESIGNER: Nadine Quirmbach

COLLABORATIVE ARTIST: Do-Ho Suh

PENANG TURF CLUB MASTER PLAN

George Town, Penang Island, Malaysia 2004 CLIENT: Equine Capital Berhad (the Sponsor) on behalf of Abad Naluri Sdn. Bhd.

PRINCIPAL: Thom Mayne
PROJECT MANAGER: Tim Christ
PROJECT DESIGNERS:
Mario Cipresso
Ted Kane

PROJECT ASSISTANTS: MODEL TEAM:
Reinhard Schmoelzer, *Manager*
Charles Austin
Eui Yeob Jeong
Shannon Loew

ASSOCIATE ARCHITECT: ATSA Architects
Azim Aziz, *Principal*
PROJECT TEAM: Zulqaifar Hamidin
TRANSPORTATION CONSULTANT: Symonds Travers Morgan (M) SDN.BHD

NYC2012 OLYMPIC VILLAGE

Hunter's Point, Queens, New York 2004 CLIENT: NYC2012

PRINCIPAL: Thom Mayne
PROJECT MANAGER: Paul Gonzales
PROJECT DESIGNERS:
Ben Damron
Graham Ferrier
Ed Hatcher
Marty Summers
Nadine Quirmbach
Chris Warren

PROJECT TEAM:
Anne Marie Burke
Natalia Traverso Caruana
MODEL TEAM:
Reinhard Schmoelzer, *Manager*
Luis Luz
Masako Saito
Go-Woon Seo

LANDSCAPE ARCHITECT: Hargreaves Associates
George Hargreaves, *Principal*; Brennan Cox, *Project Architect*
ASSOCIATE ARCHITECT: Gruzen Samton, LLP: Jordan Gruzen, *Principal*
MECHANICAL/ELECTRICAL ENGINEER: IBE Consulting Engineers
John Gautrey, *Principal*; Peter Simmonds, *Project Engineer*
TRANSPORTATION: Arup: Greg Hodkinson, *Principal*
PLANNING: Richard Weinstein

SCIENCE CENTER SCHOOL

Los Angeles, California 1992–2004 CLIENTS: Los Angeles Unified School District, California Science Center

PRINCIPAL: Thom Mayne
PROJECT MANAGERS:
Paul Gonzales
Daynard Tullis
PROJECT ARCHITECTS:
Mario Cipresso
Selwyn Ting
PROJECT DESIGNERS:
Kristina Loock
Jean Oei
Eui-Sung Yi

PROJECT TEAM:
Henriette Bar
Tim Christ
Josh Coggeshell
Jerome Daksiewicz
Ben Damron
Simon Demeuse
John Enright
Dave Grant
Martin Josst
Fabian Kremkus
Silvia Kuhle
Ung Joo Scott Lee
Devin McConley
Eric Nulman
Tarek Qaddumi
Ivan Redi
David Rindlaub
Josh Sherman
Patrick Tighe
Sandrine Wellens
Brandon Welling
Jose Valeros
Petar Vrcibradic

GENERAL CONTRACTOR: Bernards Brothers, Jeff Bernards
STRUCTURAL ENGINEER: Englekirk and Sabol Consulting Engineers
Bill Wallace, Pete Hatalsky
MEP: Donn C. Gilmore Associates: Mike Gilmore, Rob Grant
SPECIFICATIONS: CMS Consultants
HARDWARE CONSULTANT: Brownell Associates: Mike Brownell
CIVIL ENGINEER: Cali Land: Kevin Lai
KITCHEN: Dewco
LANDSCAPE ARCHITECT: Katherine Spitz Associates: Katherine Spitz
COST ESTIMATOR: Davis Langdon Adamson: Rick Lloyd
EXPOSITION PARK: Zimmer Gunsul Frasca
MASTER PLANNING: Brian Glover
HISTORIC PRESERVATION: Kaplan Chen Kaplan: David Kaplan

CALTRANS DISTRICT 7 HEADQUARTERS

Los Angeles, California 2001–2004 CLIENT/OWNER: State of California, Department of General Services

DESIGN/BUILD TEAM: Main & First Design/Build Associates, Inc.
DESIGN AND EXECUTIVE ARCHITECT: Morphosis GENERAL CONTRACTOR: The Clark Construction Group, Inc. DEVELOPER: Urban Partners

PRINCIPAL: Thom Mayne
PROJECT MANAGER: Silvia Kuhle
PROJECT ARCHITECT: Pavel Getov
JOB CAPTAIN: Anthony Mrkic

PROJECT TEAM:
Chandler Ahrens
Irena Bedenikovic
Tim Christ
Mario Cipresso
Simon Demeuse
Marty Doscher
Ed Hatcher
Salvador Hidalgo
Georgina Huljich
Olivia Jukic
Ted Kane
Dwoyne Keith
Kristina Loock
Axel Schmitzberger
Martin Summers
Eui-Sung Yi
PROJECT ASSISTANTS:
Ben Damron
Paul Gonzales
Jean Oei
Nadine Quirmbach
Natalia Traverso Caruana
Daynard Tullis
Chris Warren

CLARK CONSTRUCTION: Richard Heim, *President*
John Williams, *Senior Vice President;* Marc Kersey, *Project Executive*
URBAN PARTNERS: Dan Rosenfeld, *Partner*
Laura Benson, *Project Manager*
CONSULTING ARCHITECT (INTERIORS AND PARKING): Gruen Associates
Debra Gerod, *Partner*
STRUCTURAL ENGINEER: John A. Martin Associates, Inc.
Chuck Whitaker, *Principal;* Barry Schindler, *Project Manager*
MEP/FIRE SAFETY/ TELECOM ENGINEER: Ove Arup & Partners Ltd.
ACOUSTICS: Schaffer Acoustics, Inc.
GRAPHICS: Follis Design
SUSTAINABLE DESIGN: KMI Associates
SPECIFICATIONS: Technical Resources Consultants, Inc.
HARDWARE CONSULTANT: Ingersoll-Rand Company
VERTICAL TRANSPORTATION: Edgett Williams Consulting Group, Inc.
AUDIO/VISUAL: Menlo Scientific Acoustics, Inc.
CIVIL ENGINEER: Fuscoe Engineering, Inc.
CODE: Rolf Jensen and Associates, Inc.
FOOD SERVICES: Laschober and Sovich, Inc.
TRAFFIC/PARKING: Meyer Mohaddes Associates
SPACE PLANNING: AI
LANDSCAPE ARCHITECT: Campbell and Campbell
LIGHTING DESIGNER: Horton Lees Brogden Lighting Design, Inc.
GEOTECHNICAL: Leighton and Associates
FACADE CONTRACTORS: Model Glass and Raymond
MECHANICAL CONTRACTOR: Scott Co. of California
ELECTRICAL CONTRACTOR: Dynalectric
PHOTOVOLTAIC CONTRACTOR: Atlantis
SECURITY: ASSI Security

COOPER UNION ACADEMIC BUILDING

New York, New York 2004–2008 CLIENT: The Cooper Union for the Advancement of Science and Art

PRINCIPAL: Thom Mayne
PROJECT MANAGER: Silvia Kuhle
PROJECT ARCHITECT: Pavel Getov
PROJECT DESIGNERS:
Chandler Ahrens
Jean Oei
JOB CAPTAIN: Salvador Hidalgo

PROJECT TEAM:
Irena Bedenikovic
Debbie Lin
Kristina Loock
Go-Woon Seo
Natalia Traverso Caruana
PROJECT ASSISTANTS:
Ben Damron
Marty Doscher
Graham Ferrier
MODEL TEAM:
Reinhard Schmoelzer
Charles Austin
Eui Yeob Jeong
Shannon Loew

ASSOCIATE ARCHITECT: Gruzen Samton LLP
Peter Samton, *Principal;* Tim Schmiderer, *Project Manager;*
Susan Drew, *Project Manager;* Robert Stack, *Project Manager*
PROJECT TEAM: Cathy Daskalakis, Alfreda Radzicki, Sari Mass, Mani Muttreja
CONTRACTOR: F.J. Sciame Construction Co. Inc.
Frank Sciame, *President,* Robert Da Ros, *Project Manager,*
Steven Colletta, *Estimator,* Lily Chu, *Assistant Project Manager*
STRUCTURAL ENGINEER: John A. Martin Associates, Inc.
Chuck Whitaker, *Principal;* Kurt Clandening, *Project Manager*
Goldstein Associates PLLC, Keith Loo, *Principal*
MEP: IBE Consulting Engineers: Alan Locke, *Principal;* John Gautrey, *Principal;*
Peter Simmonds, *Project Manager,* Syska Hennessy Group: Mark Yakren, *Principal*
IT/AV/SECURITY: Syska Hennessy Group: Peter Rancan, *Project Manager*
IT: Barnes Wentworth: Herb Hauser, *Principal;* Kathleen Kotarsky, *Project Manager*
LABORATORY CONSULTANT: Steve Rosenstein Associates
Steve Rosenstein, *Principal;* T.H. Chang, *Principal;* John Janoz, *Project Manager*
GRAPHICS: Pentagram Design Inc.: Abbott Miller, *Principal*
SUSTAINABLE DESIGN/LEED: Davis Langdon: Lisa Fay Matthiessen, *Associate*
COST CONSULTANT: Davis Langdon: Ethan Burrows, *Associate Principal*
SPECIFICATIONS: Gruzen Samton LLP: Stefanie H. Romanowski
HARDWARE CONSULTANT: Rich Hausler: Rich Hausler, *Principal*
ACOUSTICS: Martin Newson Associates: Michael Brown, *Principal*
VERTICAL TRANSPORTATION: Van Deusen & Associates: Rick Sayah, *Associate*
EXPEDITOR: Berzak Schoen Consultants, LTD: Irene Berzak, *Principal*
CODE: Arup Fire: Nathan Wittasek, *Project Manager*
LIGHTING DESIGNER: Horton Lees Brogden Lighting Design, Inc.:
Teal Brogden, *Principal;* Stephen Lees, *Principal;* Justin Horvath, *Project Manager*

ACKNOWLEDGMENTS:

I must begin by thanking the authors of the written pieces in this book—Peter Cook, Steven Holl, Jeff Kipnis, Sylvia Lavin, Lars Lerup, Eric Moss, Wolf Prix, Michael Sorkin, Anthony Vidler, and Lebbeus Woods—for their astute, often very personal perspectives on my work; they've each allowed me to look at my own work with new insight.

Though the essays refer to me personally, their sentiments really extend to the entire Morphosis team, and I thank all members of the studio for their commitment and energy. As I discuss in the introduction to this book, our work is a result of a collective engagement, and our studio continues to actively redefine the nature of the collective practice.

This book could never have materialized without Lorraine Wild, who was responsible for the graphic design of the three previous Morphosis monographs published by Rizzoli, along with Emily Morishita, both of whom sustained the design process through their collaboration and patience.

I would like to thank Anne Marie Burke, without whose Herculean management and coordination efforts the book would never have come together. Thanks to Mario Cipresso, Graham Ferrier, and Chris Warren, and to Simone Lueck and Christopher Smith for the hours they each spent organizing and culling project materials. I would like to thank Penny Herscovitch for editing and rewriting the project texts; and finally, a special thanks to my wife, advisor-on-all-things-important-and-interesting, and companion, Blythe Alison Mayne, for her valuable contribution to the writing and criticism of the manuscript.

—Thom Mayne

BOOK DESIGN:
Morphosis/Green Dragon Office, Los Angeles
Thom Mayne, Lorraine Wild, and Emily Morishita

PROJECT MANAGEMENT:
Anne Marie Burke

WRITING:
Penny Herscovitch
Blythe Alison Mayne

BOOK ORGANIZATION:
Simone Lueck
Christopher Curtis Smith

PROJECT COORDINATION:
Mario Cipresso
Graham Ferrier
Chris Warren

PROJECT ASSISTANTS:
Soohyun Chang
Leonore Daum
Patrick Dunn-Baker
Amy Kwok
Natalia Traverso Caruana
Shana Yates

COVER ART:
Natalia Traverso Caruana

PHOTOGRAPHY CREDITS:
Tom Arban 164-165, 168-169, 170, 171, 174-175; Farshid Assassi 38-39, 44, 45, 46, 47, 84, 85, 86, 87, 88-89, 90-91, 96, 97; Michael Awad ARCH/PHOTO 172; Tom Bonner 68-69, 72, 74 (bottom), 77, 78, 79; Henry Cabala 76; John Carpenter 400 (top left and right); Jeffrey Debany 350, 351; Steve Evans 173, 176-177; Pavel Getov 2-3, 4-5, 376, 377, 378, 382-383, 388; Roland Halbe, 384-385, 389, 391, 392, 394-395, 396-397, 398, 399, 402-403; Salvador Hidalgo 395; Timothy Hursley 152-153, 158-159, 162-163; Courtesy Hypo Bank 266; Gary Leonard 380-381; Simone Lueck and Emily Morishita 48-49, 108-109, 196-197, 206-207, 246-247, 338-339, 360-361, 372-373, 404-405, 418-431; Simone Lueck and John Carpenter 379; Pinky Mix 267 (right); Ferdinand Neumuller 261; Pino Pipitone 342, 343, 344, 345, 346-347; Ernst Peter Prokop 256-257, 260, 262-263, 268, 267 (top), 270-271; Christian Richters 267 (left); The Snow Show Winter Art Education Project of University of Lapland/SnowNow Media Channel/ Jouko Väärälä 348-349; Martin Summers 400 (bottom), 401; Brandon Welling 74 (top), 75, 80-81, 138-139, 160, 161, 216-217; Kim Zwarts 98-99, 102, 103, 264, 265, 269.

MORPHOSIS HAND MODELS:
Sean Anderson 404-405; Soohyun Chang 108-109; Dom Cheng 372-373; Patrick Dunn-Baker 108-109; Caroline Durat 228-229 (right); Dwoyne Keith 228-229 (left); Amy Kwok 422-423; Shannon Loew 352-353; Claudia Lugo 48-49, 338-339 (right); Thom Mayne 300-301; Scott Mitchell 196-197; Emily Morishita 206-207, 246-247, 338-339 (left), 360-361; Reinhard Schmoelzer 138-139; Go-Woon Seo 322-323; Chris Warren 228-229 (center); Brandon Welling 178-179.